W9-BNH-310

FILM ESSAYS
and a Lecture
by Sergei Eisenstein

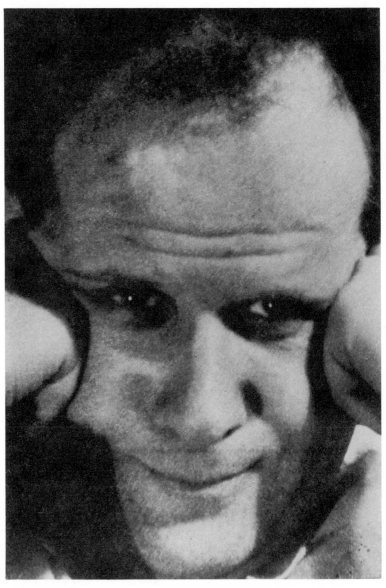

Sergei Eisenstein in 1934.
Photograph by Jay Leyda

FILM ESSAYS

AND A LECTURE

by

SERGEI EISENSTEIN

edited by
JAY LEYDA

Foreword by Grigori Kozintsev

Princeton University Press
Princeton, New Jersey

LCC: 81-47283
ISBN: 0-691-03970-4
ISBN: 0-691-00334-3 pbk.

THIS COLLECTION OF TRANSLATIONS
IS DEDICATED TO
PERA ATASHEVA

First Princeton Paperback printing, 1982

Dobson Books edition, 1968;
Praeger Publishers, Inc. edition, 1970

Published by arrangement with Praeger Publishers, Inc.

Printed in the United States of America by Princeton University
Press, Princeton, New Jersey

CONTENTS

PREFACE

Before I left Moscow in 1936 Eisenstein prepared a list of the publications in journals and newspapers that he would like drawn upon if some miracle made it possible to publish a collection of his essays in the United States. His first book did not appear here until 1942; that miracle was made by a war, a cable from him, and a publisher who admired his films. The four connected essays that made up *The Film Sense* had appeared in print after his compilation of the selected list, but it was to that list I turned when both author and publisher urged a second and third collection. Between these two volumes several events affected this plan: Eisenstein died early in 1948 before the publication of *Film Form*, then a Cold War turned a Soviet author into such a publishing risk that I turned over the contents of the third volume to a London publisher. In the meantime, a Soviet volume of Eisenstein's writings appeared in Russian, English, and French, and I enlarged the third volume to include writings that had not been officially approved in the posthumous estimation of Eisenstein as a Soviet filmmaker.

Film Essays is the third and last of my collections of Eisenstein translations. Last, because when it was first prepared (in 1964, four years before it was published in England and, later, in the United States), I was hopeful that an English translation would soon appear of the immense Soviet project then beginning to publish all of Eisenstein's writings, including the several texts that he had prepared in 1947 for eventual publication, found in his archive by his widow, Pera Atasheva.

Now that we have reached 1981 I am still hopeful, though the writings are far from fully available, either in Russian or English. The six volumes that Atasheva planned in 1964 appeared in due course and continued to appear after her death in 1965. The Eisenstein Committee headed by Sergei Yutkevich supervised the last volumes and proposed six more volumes for publication; close examination of the archive continues to disclose texts and documents of obvious value.

At the time of his death, his reputation there was at its lowest (the repairs on the shelved *Ivan II* had not been completed,

1

and all that had been filmed and edited of *Ivan III* was destroyed). The remaining years of his widow's life were devoted to re-establishing a recognition of his place in Soviet history. The first six volumes of his writings occupied the chief place in her rehabilitation program. Their contents are indicated in the extended "Published Writings," an appendix to this edition of *Film Essays*. Two large texts were only partially represented in the *Selected Works*, to make the fact of their existence known.

I was glad to see that most of the troublesome essays, hastily included in this third volume of translations, also made their way into the increasingly liberal contents of the first six volumes.*

After the sixth volume appeared in 1971, six more volumes (without exhausting the archive!) were contracted for publication, but there has been a delay in their approval. Awaiting paper and print are the full texts sampled in the first set; a volume on "Method" that was written alongside his large work "On Direction"; a volume of unrealized films and projects to exceed (in quantity) the realized scripts of Volume VI; a journal of theater ideas kept during the civil war tour of the "Front-Line Theater"; a collection of his correspondence; and the full text of his memoirs to replace the incomplete text hastily prepared as the opening Volume I of the *Selected Works*. Before this second set of six volumes appears, the writings of other artists of the first generation of Soviet filmmakers must become available. The works of Dovzhenko and Pudovkin have already been added to Eisenstein's, and the volumes of Kozintsev are ready for the printer; the writings of Romm and Kuleshov are in preparation.

---

* The "personal statement" written in 1926 for a Berlin newspaper was not among the autobiographies gathered as an introduction to Volume I, though it can be found in an appendix to that volume (after Eisenstein's death, lists of his published writings gently omitted works that he published in a foreign language). Still missing: the generalized essay written for Joseph Freeman's *Voices of October*. "A Close-Up View" closed *Iskusstvo Kino* to further contributions from him during his lifetime (but it was reprinted in Volume V). I did not expect "Perspectives" to appear in the *Selected Works*, as it had caused the death of the journal where it first appeared: I was wrong—it can be found in Volume II, leading the theoretical writings. I hope this key essay will some day attract the attention of a translator more able to cope with its difficulties.

Since 1971, while awaiting an official signal for the next volumes, the Eisenstein Committee has wisely published some of the most basic texts in other formats (periodicals, annuals, etc.). We now have in print Eisenstein's notes for *Capital* and *The Glass House*, as well as the whole scenario of the 1932 project for a satirical comedy, *MMM*. (See ''Published Writings.'')

Of the films prepared by Eisenstein outside the Soviet Union we have the two Hollywood scripts, *Sutter's Gold* and *An American Tragedy*, written in collaboration with Grigori Alexandrov and Ivor Montagu, published in Montagu's *With Eisenstein in Hollywood* (1969). (His Hollywood proposal of *The Glass House* is incorporated into the notes published in 1979.) Most of the correspondence and documents relating to the unrealized Mexican film is published in *The Making and Unmaking of* Que Viva Mexico! (1970).

When foreign admirers of Eisenstein's films and principles heard of the Soviet publication project, they felt certain that translations would soon be in their hands. The speed and care with which most of the new materials appeared in French and German were envied by readers and students in the United Kingdom and America who are still waiting for an Anglo-American edition. Instead, we hear of conflicting texts and variant translations in circulation through publishers on both sides of the Atlantic.

For those who wish to trace Eisenstein's theoretical aims from their beginnings to his end, the wait will be longer. That is, if they feel dependent on new English translations. One may not freely publish translations of newly available Russian texts without negotiating recent copyright laws.

A suggestion: You can prepare yourself for the large new texts by reading older English translations of the great amount that Eisenstein published in his lifetime, including pieces taken from books in progress. For example, the two important essays on structure (Nos. 187 and 200 in ''Published Writings'') were extracted by their author from his unfinished work, *Nature Is Not Indifferent* (now in Volume III). With the exception of the incomplete *Montage*, English translations of most of the materials in Volume II can be traced through ''Published Writings.''

3

The memoirs of Volume I present particular problems—and rewards. I've explained the haste with which Atasheva rushed it into print. There was also haste—*not* Atasheva's—in removing sections too "offensive" in 1964 for a Soviet autobiography. In composing his memoirs (at first intended as a "comic autobiography" to while away hospital hours) Eisenstein did not worry about his future editors. There was no attempt at a continuing chronology; he preferred Joycean clusters of associations, often touching several decades within a page. Rude memories (of his parents, among others) are mixed with light-hearted and more publishable ones. The great whom he respected find themselves among the great whom he recognized as arrogant or empty. That, to paraphrase a remark in his essay on Orozco, is not the way to write "acceptable" memoirs. Moreover, he was fully aware that he would not be present to offer apologies when these clusters would see print. This removed the main inhibitions. It is not surprising that Anglo-American publishers are being offered two texts of Volume I—the earlier "official" one, and the new fuller life; this contradiction, too, may delay a published English translation.

There will always be more Eisenstein writings to wait for, in Russian and, later, in English. Let us use them whenever they come.

J. L.

ILLUSTRATIONS

Foreword

by

GRIGORI KOZINTSEV

An Eisenstein is born but once in a century. Human nature reaches a zenith of spiritual development. An instrument of astonishing responsiveness is formed, unique and never to be duplicated: a genius has been added to mankind. If that man is an artist, his imaginative world leaves a mark on the real world of his time and conquers time itself: some part of his epoch will live on in his art. He does not function as a mirror: the quality of his image of the epoch stirs more than a reflecting surface. The art of Eisenstein was inseparable from his temperament, and his taste. Temperament and taste could be observed in everything about him—in the nature of his creative work, in the appearance of his rooms, in his way of speaking. Wherever he lived, you could walk in and know at once who lived there. All bore the imprint of this occupant. From the door-sill, heaps of books; doubled rows of them on the shelves; on tables, chairs, anywhere: philosophy, painting, psychology, theory of humour, history of photography, dictionaries of slang and argot, circus, caricature . . . even to name their subjects would consume too much space here. Erudition and imagination combined to produce inventions of fun all around the room. He treated objects like pieces of a joke: a strange bas-relief on the wall turned out to be a globe of the earth sawn in half set in a magnificent renaissance frame; a silver candelabrum served as a necktie-hanger. A corner of one book-shelf was filled with a gallery of astonishing faces, autographed—from the inventor of the safety razor, Gillette, to Yvette Guilbert. On top of the wardrobe personages from the Chinese theatre gestured among wooden Russian angels. In

7

the place of honour—a rubber glove inscribed to him by Harpo Marx (who had employed it in a "number" as an udder). Any room of his reminded one of a theatre warehouse, inundated with objects from some recent carnival. No resemblance to a collector of precious antiques. No ordinary order, no hint of recognizable unity. His juxtapositions had a single governing power: contrasts. And over it all he thumbed his nose at aesthetics.

But books were his passion. His library was in ceaseless motion, here books were allowed no rest: the volumes of a work were rarely in the right order; you could see bookmarks (made of anything that was handy!) sticking out everywhere, margins were thick with annotations, even sketches, many lines were marked and underlined, often with coloured pencils. Everything in the room was sucked into this whirlpool. But the appearance of the room often changed. And all this apparatus of treatises, reproductions, curiosities—from research into primitive thought to a nineteenth-century rebus—was treated like some sort of clay: the sculptor remoulds it, converts it all into pliable material for his next work. Without comprehending this fusion and flexibility its nourishment of Eisenstein's art can be either under-estimated or over-estimated.

When Eisenstein entered films he decided: It's time to plan the miracle of art. If only we apply more strength, we'll find the philosopher's stone, and straightway *any* material can be changed to gold. And this pure gold—composition to shake the souls of people—would have nothing in common with what we knew as artistic cinema. A new art would be shaped somewhere where the sciences must intersect all those monumental forms of art—the fresco, the symphony, the tragic rituals of ancient theatre—there, where the structure of pathos lived and waited to be used.

In order to understand the art of Eisenstein, one must find the unfinished research in his films, and find in his research—the films he never made. Perhaps of all that he achieved *Potemkin* was the only completed work, and that because there was no time to spare, no time to reconsider the problems.

*　　　*　　　*

Nowadays there is little respect for aesthetic manifestoes: who in art today attaches any value to words? But our generation felt differently about this. Without having accomplished very much, people would immediately launch theoretical structures, and attract disciples. All young film directors were to this degree also "researchers". No limits to their production plans, but the projects rarely found room in the actual films they made. Such research usually came to an end in montage-lists, diaries, stenographic records of feelings. Substance consisted not so much in analysis as in prospects. It is not easy to read such old pages. Even their language belongs to other times.

Eisenstein's first essays had an individuality peculiar to him. One was struck by an oddness of juxtaposition: the wildest artistic ideas with an academically impassive tone, and scientific phraseology:

> The basic materials of the theatre arise from the spectator himself—and from our guidance of the spectator into the desired direction (or desired mood), which is the main task of every functional theatre (agitational, poster, health education, etc.). The weapons for this purpose are to be found in all the left-over apparatus of theatre (the "chatter" of Ostuzhev no more than the pink tights of the prima-donna, a roll on the kettledrums as much as Romeo's soliloquy, the cricket on the hearth no less than the cannon fired over the heads of the audience). For all, in their individual ways, bring us to a single ideal— from their individual laws to their common quality of an *attraction*.

This was written in 1923, and we fought academicism with lowly genres (circus and vaudeville, for instance), shocking juxtapositions and a cult of tricks—how this smells of the past! Note, however, that young people then did not resort to scientific terminology, they neither sought nor used a calm voice. And no one had yet referred to the pink tights of the prima-donna as an "ideal" or "weapon". Eisenstein seems to have made use of LEF theories: functionalism, directness, social demand. But the term "attraction" itself, with its brisk circus associations and objective (Ostrovsky adapted to the music-hall) had little in common with constructivism. The same issue of LEF that published Eisenstein's essay included a photograph, LEF in practice: two armchairs arranged in a bed. No, the "ideal" of Sergei Mikhailovich was the sum of other elements.

To understand the essays of Eisenstein one can recall his definition of a scenario. Meyerhold's pupil saw a scenario in the same way that his teacher saw a play. Only one author—the director. Mise-en-scène and gesture are the real language of the production (a literary scenario is merely a departure point for associations), and the film is made with movement and montage. The scenario—in Eisenstein's definition (at the end of the '20s)—sets down the emotional perception of an event; the director interprets it in images.

In many ways the essays of Sergei Mikhailovich bear the same relation to his films that his ideal scenario bore to his ideal film. His thoughts or, more exactly, his feelings, usually outran the reality of film. And he would feverishly hurry to fix on paper the countless clusters of associations: his concept would be embodied in something new, not yet realised in art.

He wanted to express the scene of the separator in *Old and New* with a structure built entirely on pathos. Explaining why the leading role in this scene was not taken by the farmers (their shy behaviour gives them a secondary role), but by "pure cinema", revealing the inner pathos of the event through montage, the director made this retreat:

Imagine a scene of Moses smiting a rock in the desert with his rod, causing a stream of water to burst forth, and thousands who are dying of thirst throw themselves towards it,
or the frenzied dance of the godless around the golden calf,
or the Shakhsei-Vakhsei with its frenzied hundreds throwing themselves on the sabres of the fanatics,
or even the zeal of the flagellants,
—then you could reverse the picture of the crowd in my

scene, absorbing into the pathetic structure the ecstasy of their action!*

(Notice that modest "even"—and one finds the word "frenzied" rather often in his essays.)

It would be meaningless now to dispute old concepts of the scenario, to explain to a great artist that he should have directed our attention to the people in the scene, etc., etc. His world now leaves us nothing to quarrel with. And we don't know the cinema he might have achieved. Too often, and through no fault of his own, his films were not finished and his researches were cut short.

* From the chapter on "Pathos" in an unfinished book (written in 1946–47), published in Vol. III (1964) of Eisenstein's selected works.

A Personal Statement

written for a Berlin newspaper, 1926

I am twenty-eight years old. Before 1918 I was a student for three years. At first I wanted to become an engineer and architect. During the civil war I was a sapper in the Soviet Army. While doing that work I spent any free time in studying questions of art and theatre: in particular theatre history and theory. In 1921 I entered the Proletcult organization as a theatre designer. The Proletcult Theatre busily sought new art forms that would correspond to the ideology of the new Russian state structure. Our troupe was composed of young workers who wished to create genuine art; they brought to this aim a quite new kind of temperament and a new viewpoint on the world and on art. At that time their artistic ideas and demands fully concurred with mine, though I, belonging to another class, had arrived at their deductions only through a process of speculation. The next years were a fierce struggle. In 1922 I became director of the First Moscow Workers' Theatre and completely broke with the views of the Proletcult administration. The Proletcult staff adhered to Lunacharsky's position: to maintain old traditions and to compromise on the question of pre-revolutionary artistic efficiency. I was one of the most unbending supporters of LEF (Left Front), where we wanted *the new*, meaning works that would correspond to the new social conditions of art. We had on our side at that time all the young people and innovators, including the futurists Meyerhold and Mayakovsky; in the most rigid opposition to us were the traditionalist Stanislavsky* and the opportunist Tairov.

* I have always been amused when the German press identified my anonymous actors, my "simple people", as artists of the Moscow Art Theatre, my "deadly enemy"!

13

In 1922–23 I staged three dramas at the Workers' Theatre: in principle their staging was a mathematical calculation of the elements of affect, which at that time I called "actions". In the first production, *The Sage*, I tried to dissect cubistically a classical play into separately affective "attractions". The action took place in a circus. In the second production, *Do You Hear, Moscow?*, I used fundamentally technical means in trying to realize theatrical illusions with mathematical calculations. This was the first success of the new theatrical affects. The third production, *Gas Masks*, was staged in a gas factory, during working hours. The machines worked and the "actors" worked; for the first time this represented the success of an absolutely *real*, highly objective art.

Such an understanding of theatre led in a straight path to cinema; only the most inexorable objectivity could be the sphere of cinema. My first film was begun in 1924; it was produced with members of Proletcult and was entitled *Strike*. The film had no story in the generally accepted sense: there were the progressive stages of a strike, there was a "montage of attractions". According to my artistic principle, we did not depend on intuitive creativeness but on a rational construction of affective elements; each affect must be subjected previously to a thorough analysis and calculation: this is the most important thing. Whether there are individual elements of affect within the story (in the generally accepted sense of the term) or whether they are strung along the "story carcass", as in my *Potemkin*, I cannot perceive any substantial distinction here. I myself am neither sentimental, nor bloodthirsty, nor at heart lyrical, as I have been occasionally in Germany accused of being. Yet all these elements are, of course, familiar to me, and I am quite aware that temptation is all that is needed to combine these with whatever is at hand to arouse the required reaction and to achieve the greatest tension. I am sure that this is a purely mathematical matter and that "sincerely creative genius" has no place here. No more readiness of wit is needed here than in the design of the most utilitarian building of reinforced concrete.

As for my view on cinema in general, I must confess that

14

I understand it as bias and only bias. In my opinion, without a clear presentation of the "why" one cannot begin work on a film. It is impossible to create without acknowledging on what latent feelings and passions you wish to speculate—excuse the expression, I know that it is not "nice", but it is professionally and by definition exact. We goad the passions of the spectators, but we also employ a safety valve, a lightning-rod, and this is—bias. To ignore bias and to waste energy I consider the greatest crime of our generation. For me and in itself bias is a great artistic potential, though it need not always be as political, as consciously political, as in *Potemkin*. When it is completely absent, when the film is regarded as a simple time-killer, as a sedative or hypnotic, then such an absence of bias can be interpreted as quite biased in the maintaining of tranquillity and keeping the audience satisfied with conditions as they are. Just as if the cinema "community", similar to the church community, had to train the good, the well-balanced, the stripped-away wishes of the citizens. Isn't this the philosophy of the American "happy ending"?

It has been alleged against me that the German adaptation of *Potemkin* weakens the power of its political tension, makes it too pathetic. But, after all, aren't we people with temperament, with passions? Is it possible for us to be unaware of duties or aims? The success of the film in Berlin and in post-war Europe, sinking in the twilight of a shaky *status quo*, must have been heard as a summons to whatever of dignified humanity that has survived. For this, isn't pathos justified? The bias of this film demands that one lifts one's head and feels oneself a person—a human, becoming human.

Battleship Potemkin was made for the twentieth anniversary of the 1905 Revolution, and had to be ready by December 1925: three months for production—even in Germany this might be considered a record production schedule. Two-and-a-half weeks were left to me for the montage of the film, for the editing of 15,000 metres of film.

Even if all roads lead to Rome—even if all genuine works of art come, in the long run, to the same intellectual level—I must emphasize that neither Stanislavsky and the

Art Theatre, nor Proletcult, for that matter, can create anything at present. I have not worked in Proletcult for a long time. I have completely moved into cinema, while the Proletcult people stay in the thèatre. It's my opinion that an artist must make his choice between theatre and cinema; he cannot be "possessed" by both at the same time if he wants to really create.

There are no actors in *Battleship Potemkin*,* there are only real people in this film and the director's task was to find the right people; instead of looking for creative revelations of talent, he sought the correct physical appearances. Such a filming method is possible in Russia, where each and every matter is a government matter. The slogan of "All for one—one for all!" is more than a sub-title on the screen. If we are making a naval film, the whole fleet is at our service; if a battle film, the whole Red Army; when we make an agricultural subject, various Commissariats give us assistance. The point is that we film not just for ourselves, nor just for you, not for this or that person, but for all.

I am positive that the cinema collaboration of Germany and Russia could have great results. The fusion of German technical potentialities and Russian creative fire could produce something extraordinary. But for me personally to work in Germany is extremely doubtful. I could not forsake my native soil, which gives me the strength to create. Perhaps I can make myself understood more easily by reminding you of the myth of Antaeus rather than giving a Marxist explanation of the links between artistic creation and the social economic base. Furthermore, there is in the German film industry a tendency to follow stereotypes and to aim at profits that could create for me quite impossible working conditions. There have been, of course, German films that one must respect, but now I can see that a *Faust* or a *Metropolis* had to fight its way through distracting triviali-

* It was only at the time of *Potemkin*'s introduction to European and American screens that E. insisted on this half-truth, though a justification for it may be that the functions of the several actor-assistants were not, strictly, *acting* functions. It was probably the fabricated publicity story that *Potemkin* was acted by "members of the Moscow Art Theatre" that made him swing to this extreme statement.—J. L.

ties; pornography on the one hand and sentimentality on the other. German films are not audacious. We Russians either break our necks or win the day, and more often than not we win.

And so, for the present, I'll stay at home. I am at the moment making a film on the economic struggle in the countryside, an intense struggle for a new agricultural policy.

The appealingly brash tone of this statement (written during a brief visit to Berlin at the time of Potemkin's *triumph there) is characteristic of Eisenstein's youthful writings. He knew that his revolutionary ideals for the theatre and cinema would excite opposition, and he made each of his public declarations as challenging as a performance. His earliest manifesto, "Montage of Attractions", appeared in 1923, just before his theatre work led him to apply the same method of "a montage of attractions" to films. Two years later another important declaration grew from his first film,* Strike.

The Method of Making Workers' Films

There is one *method* for making *any* film: montage of attractions. To know what this is and why, see the book, *Cinema Today*,[1] where, rather dishevelled and illegible, my approach to the construction of film works is described.

Our class approach introduces:

1. A *specific purpose for the work*—a socially useful emotional and psychological affect on the audience; this to be composed of a chain of suitably directed stimulants. This *socially useful affect* I call the *content of the work*.

17

It is thus possible, for example, to define the *content* of a production. *Do You Hear, Moscow?*: the maximum tension of aggressive reflexes in social protest. *Strike*: an accumulation of reflexes without intervals (satisfaction), that is, a focusing of reflexes on struggle (and a lifting of potential class tone).

2. A *choice of the stimulants*. In two directions. In making a correct appraisal of the class inevitability of their nature, certain stimulants are capable of evoking a certain reaction (affect) only among spectators of a certain class. For a more precise affect the audience must be even more unified, if possible along professional lines: any director of "living newspaper" performances in clubs knows how different audiences, say metal workers or textile workers, react completely differently and at different places to the same work.

Such class "inevitability" in matters of action can be easily illustrated by the amusing failure of one attraction that was strongly affected by the circumstances of one audience: I refer to the slaughter-house sequence in *Strike*. Its concentratedly associative affect of bloodiness among certain strata of the public is well known. The Crimean censor even cut it, along with—the latrine scene. (That certain sharp affects are inadmissible was indicated by an American after seeing *Strike*: he declared that this scene would surely have to be removed before the film was sent abroad.) It was the same kind of simple reason that prevented the usual "bloody" affect of the slaughter-house sequence from shocking certain worker-audiences: among these workers the blood of oxen is first of all associated with the by-product factories near the slaughter-house! And for peasants who are accustomed to the slaughter of cattle this affect would also be cancelled out.

The other direction in the choice of stimulants appears to be the class accessibility of this or that stimulant.

Negative examples: the variety of sexual attractions that are fundamental to the majority of bourgeois works placed on the market; methods that lead one away from concrete reality, such as the sort of expressionism used in *Caligari*; or the sweet middle-class poison of Mary Pickford, the exploited and systematically trained stimulation of all middle-class inclinations, even in our healthy and advanced audiences.

The bourgeois cinema is no less aware than we are of class taboos. In New York City's censorship regulations[2] we find a list of thematic attractions undesirable for film use: "relations between labour and capital" appears alongside "sexual perversion", "excessive brutality", "physical deformity"...

The study of stimulants and their montage for a particular purpose provides us with exhaustive materials on the question of *form*. As I understand it, content is the *summary of all that is subjected to the series of shocks* to which in a particular order the audience is to be exposed. (Or more crudely: so much per cent of material to fix the attention, so much to rouse bitterness, etc.). But this material must be organized in accordance with a principle that leads to the desired effect.

Form is the *realization of these intentions* in a particular material, as precisely those stimulants which are able to summon this indispensable per cent are created and assembled—in the concrete expression of the factual side of the work.

One should, moreover, keep in mind the "attractions of the moment", that is, those reactions that flame forth temporarily in connection with certain courses or events of social life.

In contrast to these there are a series of "eternal" attraction phenomena and methods.

Some of these have a class usefulness. For example, a healthy and integrated audience always reacts to an epic of class struggle.

Equal with these are the "neutrally" affective attractions, such as death-defying stunts, *double entendres*, and the like.

To use these independently leads to *l'art pour l'art* so as to reveal their counter-revolutionary essence.

As with the attraction moments, one ought to remember that neutral or accidental attractions cannot, ideologically, be taken for granted, but should be used only as a method of exciting those unconditioned reflexes that are necessary

19

to us not in themselves but in the training of socially useful conditioned reflexes that we wish to combine with certain objectives of our social aims.

When this manifesto appeared in Kino, *on 11 August 1925, the Eisenstein group had put aside the planned sequels to* Strike *and were shooting a film to celebrate the twentieth anniversary of the 1905 Revolution. Out of the broad scope of* The Year 1905 *came the concentrated drama of* Battleship Potemkin, *the first world-wide triumph of the Soviet cinema.*

The subject to follow Potemkin *was not an easy choice. There was a plan for* First Cavalry Army, *with the help of Isaac Babel, and a plan for* Zhunguo, *a Chinese epic with a script by Sergei Tretiakov; the group finally went to work on a dramatization of the new agricultural policy. This film,* The General Line *(eventually released as* Old and New*), was interrupted in 1927 to make* October, *to celebrate the tenth anniversary of the October Revolution.*

In 1928, during the final cutting of October *and before returning to the revised agricultural film, Eisenstein enjoyed an interval of writing and teaching. Joseph Freeman invited him to contribute a cinema chapter to a volume on Soviet arts that was published two years later in the United States as* Voices of October. *Following is the article as it appeared there, with a few passages restored from Eisenstein's manuscript.*

Soviet Cinema

In a militant and active culture, the subject of this book, bookkeeping and statistics cannot occupy the central place. In this matter one must be intolerant, implacable, fundamental. Nor is this a question yet to be shelved in archives.

We must be prepared daily for quarrels, mistakes, corrections and fresh mistakes.

I shall use the section of the book that has been allotted to me for an analysis, according to my principles, of that section of Soviet culture where I have worked for seven out of its ten years of existence (three years in the theatre and four years in the cinema).

Thus you have before you, not a mere report, but a militant programme.

Imagine a cinema which is not dominated by the dollar; a cinema industry where one man's pocket is not filled at other people's expense; which is not for the pockets of two or three people, but for the heads and hearts of 150 million people. Every motion picture affects heads and hearts, but as a rule motion pictures are not produced especially for heads and hearts. Most motion pictures are turned out for the benefit of two or three pockets; only incidentally do they affect the heads and hearts of millions.

Suddenly a new system arises. A cinema is created, based not on private profit but on popular needs. Such a cinema may be hard to imagine; it may even be considered impossible; but one has merely to study the Soviet cinema, and one will see that it is not only possible, but has already been achieved.

To achieve such a cinema, however, certain prerequisites are necessary. Commercial competition must be eliminated. Big pockets must not devour little pockets; big fish must not be swallowed up by still bigger fish. The simplest way to arrive at such a state of affairs would be to destroy the big fish and deprive the bigger fish of their food, and to unite the little fish in innumerable shoals with common interests.

In 1917, something like that took place in Russia. The fat individual whales were terrified by a vast collective whale composed of little fish. The fat individual whales fled through all the seas and oceans; while the herd, 150 million strong, which for centuries had been oppressed by a small body of masters, suddenly became master of itself: the immense collective master of an immense collective enterprise. Everyone protected and continues to protect his own personal interest; but the amusing part of it all is that these

21

interests need not collide with the interests of one's neighbour, for the simple reason that all these personal interests are directed towards one goal. There is no longer a mutual destruction of energy and power; instead, there is a tremendous accumulation of collective energy for the benefit of all these interests.

These interests are class interests, the interests of that young proletarian class which took power into its hands in 1917. This class is a single organism based on solidarity, collectivism and collaboration. It realizes that, if all are to be fed, there is no worse way of attaining it than by throttling one's fellow worker. Hence, this class abolished the system of throttling one's neighbour and established a system of healthy collaboration.

This class realizes that when the general interests of all are satisfied, the individual interests of each are satisfied. In the place of individual competition there has been substituted planned collective construction. This was the intention of the victorious working class, and its highest expression was achieved in social centralization and monopoly. These form part of the indestructible basis of the first Soviet state; they were attained by concentrating productive forces and implements in one organizing centre. There can be no regularity of supply without system; there can be no system without centralization and monopoly. Rationalization is unthinkable without the participation of the masses in every aspect of work and construction whose goal is the satisfaction of the interests of the working masses.

"EVERY COOK SHOULD BE ABLE TO GOVERN"

A Soviet poster, showing the figure of a woman in a red shawl, carries this phrase by the "Utopian" Lenin. This is the teaching of the leader Lenin; and every cook in the Soviet Union realizes that she must know how to govern. What is more, she does govern. As a delegate to the Congress of Soviets, the Women's Congress, the Party Congress, the trade union, she rules, improves and corrects the policies of her government. These corrections are necessary, for where can there be more errors and unexpected situations than in this new and unprecedented social structure?

In the workers' and peasants' State, which is one organism, there must be on the part of the people the most vigilant attention, control and concentration of the State's creative energies. For if there are errors and inaccuracies in one section, if a single part is defective, the whole apparatus suffers. If in one region of the country the grain harvest fails, this calamity does not enrich some speculator in a more fortunate region; the crop failure is rather a tragedy for every worker and every peasant homestead, whose interests all merge in the general interests of the state.

But the country of the Soviets is not yet a paradise; it is surrounded on every hand by more or less unfriendly neighbours. The fat whales driven away in 1917 anxiously await an opportunity to strike a blow at the new social structure. This state of affairs gives our art, like our politics, a peculiar character. Centralization and monopoly determine the organizational method of the cinema in the Soviet Union, and the dictatorship of the proletariat determines the militant and "aggressive" character which differentiates our culture generally from other cultures, but more especially our cinema from the cinema of other countries.

Lenin said: "The cinema is the most important of all the arts." We firmly believe this. The innovations of our cinema in form, organization, and technique have been possible only as a result of our social innovations, as a result of our social order and the new modes of thought it has stimulated. In art innovations are not produced at will; they are dictated by new social forms. The apprehension of the social order is the high goal towards which artists proceed slowly and mathematically, attaining it only after great effort. An art corresponding to the social order develops according to the laws of natural selection; an art which is unsuited to the social order in which it seeks to function suffers greatly; on the other hand, a social system which is unsuited to our highest conception of art should be swept away.

Nowhere except in the Soviet Union does the cinema benefit by a unification of three forms of centralization. These are: the centralization of economic production, the centralization of ideology, and the centralization of method.

As in other countries, the Soviet cinema is one of our leading industries, and organizationally it is conducted like other branches of our socialized industry. Both the production and the sale of Soviet motion pictures have been centralized. At present, for example, Sovkino controls all foreign sales through its representatives in those countries which have trade relations with the Soviet Union, as well as all business connected with the purchase of motion picture equipment and machinery. It also controls the entire purchase and sale of foreign films in the Soviet Union. It controls 60 per cent of the domestic market in the Soviet Union, monopolizing the entire production and sale of Soviet films with the exception of the autonomous republics, such as the Ukrainian and Georgian films. Sovkino also controls a large number of motion picture theatres throughout the Soviet Union and handles 25 per cent of the sales to those theatres which it does not control. The cinema organizations of the autonomous republics, while acting independently and exercising a monopoly within their own national boundaries, have close business relations with Sovkino. It is to be hoped that in the future there will be a still further concentration of the cinema industry, which will unify the various cinema organizations into one state monopoly. Such a unification will make the cinema one of the strongest of Soviet industries, and will eventually lead to a change in economic control. At present the cinema is under the control of educational and political institutions; when completely unified, its economic administration should logically be handed over to the Supreme Economic Council.

Centralization of production is the first stage towards a highly unified cinema. At present we are also developing the second stage: the centralization of ideology. We are convinced that the cinema is intended not for mere entertainment, but for general cultural and social aims. These aims should be pursued without any element of private interest or private gain. The cinema is partly an industrial undertaking, and partly an art. The commercial and economic aspects of this art must be completely subordinated to the social and cultural tasks set by the Revolution of 1917. The plan for completely unifying the industrial side of the Soviet cinema makes it possible to establish not only the economic but primarily the ideological dictatorship of those organs established by the workers for the protection and propagation of those ideas for which they fought. The Soviet cinema aims primarily to educate the masses. It seeks to give them a general education and a political education; it conducts an extensive campaign of propaganda for the Soviet State and its ideology among the people. These aims are pursued by all the arts in the Soviet Union, guided by the agitational-propaganda section of the Central Committee of the Communist Party. The Soviet cinema, specifically, works under the direction of the People's Commissariat of Education and the Supreme Council of Political Education. With us "art" is not a mere word. We look upon it as only one of many instruments used on the battlefronts of the class struggle and the struggle for socialist construction. Art is in the same class as the metallurgical industry, for example.

In the Soviet Union art is responsive to social aims and demands. One day, for example, all attention is centred on the village; it is imperative to raise the village from the slough of ancient custom and bring it into line with the Soviet system as a whole; the peasant must learn to see the difference between private ownership and individualistic survivals on the one hand, and co-operation and collective economy on the other.

S O S !

The seismograph of the Party apparatus notes a vacillation in this section of Soviet life. At once, all social thought is directed towards it. Throughout the country the press, literature, the fine arts are mobilized to ward off danger. The slogan is: "Face the Village!" The *smichka*, the union of proletarian and poor peasant is established. Opponents of Soviet aims are ousted. The strongest propaganda guns are put in action; there begins a bombardment on behalf of socialist economy. Here the cinema plays a big role.

Again, attention may be concentrated in another direction. There has been a break with a foreign country. War seems imminent. Defend the Soviet Union! Every form of art co-operates with the country in clarifying the situation.

What shall we defend? Our achievements, our all—not the private wealth of a few individuals or financial concessions in the colonies or recently seized markets.

The Soviet cinema and theatre can hardly keep pace with the new social orders issued every day by the people carrying out tremendous social tasks. There is no time to reflect, to present the situation "objectively" through art. It is a neck and neck race between the cinema and the newspaper. For instance, the campaign for grain sowing begins. Motion pictures dealing with the most suitable kinds of grain must be rushed to various parts of the country. Motion pictures impressing the necessity for sowing selected seeds must be exhibited in the villages again and again. The peasant must be shown that crops cannot improve as a result of religious processions and prayers for rain.

The twentieth anniversary of the 1905 revolution arrives. The Soviet cinema must reproduce that stirring year. The workers must know the history of their past, when the proletariat of St Petersburg and Odessa sacrificed their lives for freedom. Or the tenth anniversary of the 1917 revolution comes. The great fighters who participated in the "ten days that shook the world" are passing away; the towns which were the centres of the Revolution of 7 November are changing. The events of those days must be accurately recorded by the cinema while there are still living eyewitnesses. Posterity must have a photographic reproduction of the great Revolution, a living textbook for the inspiration of other generations.

As for history "in general", that is a sweet idealization of bourgeois historians. The "great" and "illustrious" personages of the past ruled the fate of millions according to their limited views. They were "gods" invented out of whole cloth. It is time to reveal the truth about these paid romantic heroes. The concealed traps of official history must be exposed. We want to know the social basis of these fabulous figures, glorified by hired scholars in the interests of their class and their descendants. Ivan the Terrible as a personality in the manner of Edgar Allan Poe will hardly interest the young Soviet worker; but as the creator of the linen trade, the Czar who enriched and strengthened Russia's economic position, he becomes a more interesting figure. The story of Ivan the Terrible should go on to tell how he became absolute monarch, head of a dominant aristocratic class; it should tell of the struggle among the higher classes of society, how they became weakened. On this basis the story would be nearer reality and of more importance than a fantasy about a mephistophelian figure, a Czar who was a wild beast. The merchant-Czar, what could be more concrete! Recall our recent "first landlord", Nicholas II. In a motion picture lasting an hour and a half all the years of tinsel, falsehood and deception are dispersed.

The Soviet cinema, then, is a cultural instrument serving the cultural aims of the Soviet state. In our country the leaders of the cinema do not sit around discussing whether or not the public wants sea films; or that movie fans are crazy about costume films dealing with the eighteenth century; or that it is too soon to change the programme to a new wild west film; or that it has been a long time since there have been jungle films and they would now be a great novelty; or that *The Big Parade* continues to hold the interest of the public and there must therefore be an increased production of war movies. In the Soviet Union a discussion of proposed films is not carried on with both eyes on the box office. If it is planned to produce a photoplay dealing with the life of Soviet youth, the cinema directors talk the matter over with the Young Communist League, which is the leader of Soviet youth. The object of the film is to clarify various problems in such a way that it will arouse discussion and thought among the young people of the Soviet Union. Love films are not produced for the mere purpose of exciting the audience, but to throw some light on sexual relations, on the new moral code which has taken the place of the old.

The cinema handles other living problems in the same way. There are themes on every hand. The government is carrying on a campaign for the reduction of prices by lowering the cost of production through efficient methods. We call this "rationalization"; but we do not wish to impose rationalization by force. It must come through understand-

27

ing. The situation must be made clear; the masses must be made enthusiastic about it. A fascinating theme for a movie. Again, the local and central economic institutions are too rigid. Bureaucracy interferes with socialist construction. This weakness must be attacked either by treatment in satire or in tragedy or in both. The cinema must show how the tragedy of the small man is caused by the inflexibility of the credit apparatus. The cinema finds another theme in nepotism. Some responsible workers have an over-developed family feeling; they introduce relatives and friends into the institutions where they work. Such preferences are forbidden by Soviet law. The wife may live with her husband, but she cannot serve under him in public office. Regulations for obtaining positions are established by the trade unions and labour exchanges; and the cinema assists in impressing the evils of nepotism on millions of spectators. In this way the Soviet film is an integral part of the entire cultural apparatus of the country, which is directed towards a better life for all.

Occasionally, someone makes the mistake of trying to improve the commercial aspects of a film to the detriment of its educational aspects. Organized Soviet society meets such attempts with the most merciless criticism and the fiercest attacks. Dispute follows dispute. Conferences are held. The matter is discussed at provincial and national congresses, and finally the Communist Party institutes an official discussion on the cinema which results in definitely laying down a correct policy. We realize that every ideological or tactical institution is primarily based on organized society, and, as in the nervous system, every part affects the whole.

The internal organization of our cinema industry is like that of other Soviet industries. All workers connected with the cinema industry, in whatever capacity, belong to a trade union, to the Photo-Cinema Section of the Union of Art Workers. Every cinema unit, like every Soviet factory, has its factory committee, elected by the workers of the unit. The factory committee is the vigilant defender of the workers' rights, especially of those rights which they secured through the October revolution. The factory committee is the centre of social life in the factory. One of its jobs is to conduct regular discussions on film production. These discussions are attended by every kind of worker in the industry, and everything is considered which in any way pertains to the enterprise. Nobody is omitted, from the director to the janitor, from the costume-maker to the "star". Before such meetings of all the workers in his unit the director reports on the plan of work for the coming year. At the end of a year, the workers make a strict examination of his report and of the actual work accomplished. The manager of the laboratory reports on possible innovations. The director of the cinema is called to order for exceeding the financial estimates of a film or for the misdeeds of its hero. All the workers participate in the appraisal of a new film, each on the basis of his speciality.

I should like to see how Von Stroheim would reply to the attacks of the youngest critics on excessive expenditures for *The Wedding March*; or Griffith listening to the tailors pointing out that *America* does not sufficiently establish the economic basis of the War of Independence;[1] or Carl Laemmle explaining his balance sheet to carpenters, painters. In our country that is what every movie director must do; and under our conditions I cannot imagine a healthier or more useful system. These tailors, assistants, carpenters and painters represent those countless tailors, assistants, carpenters and painters in whose interests, and in whose interests alone, the film is made and released. Every penny wasted is the workers' penny; it is a loss which his enterprise and his factory sustains. In addition to serious criticism from the members of the factory committee, the movie director has to submit to criticism in caricature and satire in the factory's wall newspaper.

On a small scale, the factory committee reflects the structure of the cinema industry as a whole, from the chief regulating committee and the estimating department of the Commissariat of Education, which controls the ideological and economic plans of the cinema industry as a whole, to the Workers and Peasants Inspection, that strict ultimate censor which controls the ideological and economic aspects of all Soviet enterprises.

One solution we have arrived at already: the Soviet film serves the mass of people, their interests, their organizations; it is the expression of the collective strivings of various organized units. Specialists, directors, cameramen and scenario writers realize that they are the voice of this collective mass demand. Hence the Soviet film has real life; hence it expresses the true spirit of the people and the essence of the epoch. Soviet films are based on Soviet life; whether they deal with the new moral code, the workers' family or films celebrating historical events and requiring the collaboration of thousands of people, they are true to life. They must be true to life. This was impressed on me in the making of my own films, beginning with *Strike* and ranging through *Potemkin, Old and New* and *October*. The Soviet scenario writer and film producer must draw his material from living sources. If the scenario deals with family problems, they must get in touch with the Women's Section, that department of the Communist Party which specializes in work among women, which knows most about what is being done for mothers and children. If a film is to deal with historical subjects, the director gets in touch with local and central historical associations which specialize in collecting material about the Revolution, with the Association of Old Bolsheviks, with the Association of Ex-Political Prisoners, with the Communist Academy and so on. If the theme deals with village life, the director obtains invaluable material from the Commissariat of Agriculture, from the trade union of agricultural workers and similar bodies. Through these organizations, and under their leadership, the movie director obtains the co-operation of every organized body which knows anything about the theme of his film. He has at his disposal as advisers and actors those who personally participated in historical events; organisations of specialists; newspapers and magazines specializing in the subject of the film. All these collaborators in the making of the film meet and express opinions; material is collected; the most important facts about the theme of the film are placed at the director's disposal. Throughout the making of the film the director works in the closest co-operation with these organizations. This contact with the life of the Soviet Union is carried even further. The scenario is taken directly to the people. A scenario dealing with the new relations in the worker's family is discussed at factory meetings and out of their own experience the workers make extensive alterations. A scenario dealing with farm problems is submitted to agricultural experts; biologists revise scenarios where cattle-breeding is described.

This system pervades the whole Soviet cinema. We are opposed to "constructing" sets. Our system is different from Hollywood's. If we need a factory for a film, we do not have to "construct" one; we go to an actual factory; we believe that a faked factory can never reproduce the atmosphere of a real one. When we made *October*, I needed the Winter Palace in Leningrad; I preferred to transplant the production of the film to this dead palace, rather than make it in the comfortable atmosphere of a studio. The damp cellars and the rats of the real palace helped us in our work, so that on the screen we were able to reproduce with complete accuracy the milieu necessary for our film. Furthermore, in making this film three or four thousand organized workers participate in it as actors depicting the mass shooting in the streets of Petrograd in July 1917. No rehearsals were necessary; the workers know too well just how it was done. Thus the film was the product of an immense collective effort, in which thousands of experts and workers participated, and whose contributions were shaped according to the individuality of the director. This is one of our methods of work; and developing it, we are moving to the third and last centralization necessary for the cinema: the centralization of method.

translation by Joseph Freeman

Nineteen twenty nine was a critical year in the development of Eisenstein's theories as well as in his career. During the completion of the final version of the agricultural policy film, released as Old and New, *Eisenstein glimpsed a new, startling direction that the Soviet film could take—towards the filming of abstract ideas. In the hasty production of* October *there had been opportunities to test this discovery in several passages (notably in the "gods" sequence) and, despite official interference in* Old and New, *that film remains the only finished work by Eisenstein to convey what he intended by the term, "intellectual cinema". However, his statements and interviews and lectures of this year positively bubble with the excitement of his discovery, into which his ideas about sound-film were also poured.*

An important untitled manuscript, written in German, and dated "Moscow April 1929", was later published abroad in two variants: "The Principles of Film Form" and "A Dialectic Approach to Film Form". Written at the same time were two additions to Russian books on film subjects quite remote from Eisenstein's chief concerns: the more familiar of these is his afterword to N. Kaufmann's brochure on the Japanese cinema; the other is his foreword to the translation by Vladimir Nilsen (supervised by Tisse) of Der Trickfilm, *by the German cameraman, Guido Seeber.*

The New Language
of Cinema

Soviet cinema has now arrived at the most curious stage of its development.

More than this.

I believe that only now can we begin to hazard a guess concerning the ways in which a genuine Soviet cinema will be formed, i.e. a cinema which not only will be opposed to bourgeois cinema in respect of its class attributes, but will also categorically *excel* it by virtue of *its methods.* Not long ago I expressed the view that cinematography began its career by making use of popular literature (of the detective-story genre), through the system of highly sophisticated theatrical art (the system of the "star" and "vedette"), German pictorial films (from impressionism to *Caligari*), of films without any definite aim, etc.—and is now returning to that condition, which I named, to distinguish it from the first, the *second literary period.*

But if, in the first literary period, cinematography had recourse to the fabulous subjects and the dramatic and epic experience of literature, i.e. borrowed from literature the elements of construction as a whole; the second literary period, on the contrary, makes use of literature along a different line—along the line of its experience in the technology of the materials with which literature is concerned.

Here cinema is for the first time availing itself of the experience of literature for the purpose of working out *its own language, its own speech, its own vocabulary, its own imagery.* The period is ending when the most brilliant productions—from a dramaturgical point of view—were pronounced, from the point of view of genuine cinematography, in a childish lisp. As an example we might instance Chaplin's *A Woman of Paris,* perhaps the most remarkable production of the past epoch of cinematography.*

The new period of cinema attacks the question *from within*—along the line of the methodology of purely cinematographic *expressiveness.*

It is not surprising that at first the construction should be somewhat halting. The truth is that the new cinema language which is being formed is only beginning to grope its way towards a perception of that for which it is suitable and intended. The attempts to say what is unsuitable and ill-

---

* This remarkable picture, which has very striking merits, is quite incorrectly judged by us as regards the nature of its significance. According to my point of view, its significance is in no sense practical, but of a purely stimulative character. *A Woman of Paris* is for us significant in a purely abstract sense, as a stage of accomplishment possible of attainment in any domain whatsoever. In this respect its significance for the cinema is of exactly the same order as the Doric temple, a well-executed somersault, or the Brooklyn bridge.

In our country it was received as a phenomenon of practical advantage to us: in fact, as an object for imitation and even plagiarism. Examples of such an attitude are among the sad pages of our cinema history: elements of reaction and retrogression along the line of the general development of the ideology of the forms of the Soviet cinema.

adapted lead to confusion. The sphere of work of the new cinematographic possibilities seems to be the *direct screening of class-useful conceptions*, methods, tactics and practical watchwords, not having recourse for this purpose to the aid of the suspect trappings of the dramatic and psychological past. The social aim of cinematography is being essentially transposed.

The cinematography of the first period was primarily confronted with the task of straining to the utmost the aggressive emotions in a definite direction, with a direct (and, as far as possible, deafening) temperamental volley in that direction, whereas the task of cinematography at the present day is very much more complicated: its task is the deep and slow drilling in of new conceptions or the transplanting of generally accepted notions into the consciousness of the audience. Whereas in the first case we were striving for a quick emotional *discharge*, the new cinema must *include deep reflective processes*, the result of which will find expression neither immediately nor directly.

Such a task was, of course, beyond the scope of the old halting cinematography. The new cinematography, by which conceptions are conveyed, is still at its initial stage of formal construction.

And, just as examination, from the new point of view, of the first guide to cinema's infancy—literature—did immeasurably much to strengthen the actual formal ideology of the new cinema, so examination (also from the new point of view) of the technical alphabet of its possibilities, doubly popular in its youthful period, should give a great multitude of data for the new formal methods.

The technical cinema trick *yesterday*—was a playing to the gallery (trick in the true sense) or an employment of the overloaded baroque style of the letters of eloquent stage-managers (the picture postcard effects repeatedly on exhibition, or purely stylistic mannerism, for instance—meaningless dissolves in and out). *Today* it has a new significance. "The technical possibility", foolishly called a "trick", is undoubtedly just as important a factor in the construction of the new cinematography as is the new conception of filmmaking from which it is sprung.

translation by Winifred Ray

One of Eisenstein's most important essays was published shortly before the release of Old and New *and his departure in August 1929, with Alexandrov and Tisse, to study sound-film techniques abroad. "Perspectives" is his fullest formulation in the Soviet press of the "intellectual cinema" theory; it was then and since used as evidence by his critics of "decadent" or "formalist" tendencies. The severe reaction to this essay may even have contributed to the early death of the journal* Iskusstvo (Art), *sponsored by Lunacharsky, in which the essay appeared. It may be helpful for the reader of this key piece of Eisenstein's writing to keep in mind that the first subject to which he planned to apply his new theory was the filming of Marx's* Capital—*hence the emphasis here on the clarification and definition of terms. In his mind the journey abroad was as related to the wish to film* Capital *as it was to the study of sound-film in European and American studios.*

Perspectives

In the hurly-burly of crises, imagined and real,

in the chaos of discussions, serious or worthless (example: "to work with or without actors?"),

there is a need—with scissors clenched in fist—to move film culture forward, together with the need to make it immediately accessible to all.

In the jostlings and contradictions between the urgency to find forms equal in height with the post-capitalist forms of our socialist construction and the cultural capacity of the class that is creating this construction,

in the steady fundamental direction towards an immediacy of communication to masses and the understanding by millions,

we have no right to establish limits of theoretical

solutions to this problem or this basic condition alone. Parallel with this must come solutions in the daily tactical course of research on cinema form, to work out problems and general principles on how to advance our cinema's perspectives.

But if we put on one side all the clever practical approaches to the social consumer's narrowly day-to-day instruction, we must think out all the more sharply a programme for a theoretical Five-Year-Plan for the future.

And find the new functional perspectives for a genuinely Communist cinema—as distinguished from all past and present cinematography.

It is in such a context that the following considerations are offered.

*   *   *

In general it is pleasant and useful to understand Marxism. But to Mr Gorky this understanding brings more of that irreplaceable benefit of making clear how unsuitable is the role of preacher, that is, of the man who prefers to speak in the *language of logic*, rather than the role of the artist, that is, of the man who prefers to speak in the *language of images*. When Mr Gorky realizes that this is so, he will be saved . . .[1]

Thus wrote Plekhanov—fifteen years ago.

Since then Gorky has, fortunately, been "saved". Apparently he mastered Marxism.

Since those times the role of the preacher has merged with that of the artist. There has arisen the *propagandist*.

Yet the dispute continues between the language of images and the language of logic. Nor can they "come to terms" in the language of dialectics.

Indeed on the arts front the centre of attention has shifted from the Plekhanov antithesis to a quite different pair of antagonists.

Let us deal with them first so that later we can indicate the possibility of a synthesis as a way out of their initial opposition.

And so: contemporary art-understanding ranges itself

36

from pole to pole, starting from the formula: "art is the perception of life" to the formula: "art is the building of life." Such a polar opposition is, in my view, deeply mistaken: not in its functional definition of art, but in its incorrect understanding of what lies hidden behind the term, "perception".

Colliding with the definition of a concept, it would be wrong for us to disregard the method of purely linguistic analysis of its significance. Sometimes the words we pronounce are often "more clever" than we.

We are often quite irrationally reluctant to investigate a definition in the purified and contracted formula of its verbal significance, as opposed to its concept. To analyse this formula means freeing it of its extraneous "marketable" trappings of associative material: chiefly superficial associations, distorting its essence.

The dominant associations are, of course, those responding to the class that dominates in the era in which this or that term was formulated or had its maximum use. We have received all our "rational" verbal and terminological baggage from the hands of the bourgeoisie. Along with the dominant bourgeois understanding of a term come whole bundles of associations that correspond to bourgeois ideology and convenience.

Meanwhile each term, as with any phenomenon, has a "duality" of reading—I might even say, an "ideological reading". Static and dynamic. Social and individual.

The traditionalism of such an associative "encirclement", responding to the previous class hegemony, invariably baffles us.

And instead of effecting an internal verbal "class stratification", the word-concept is written, understood and used by us in its traditional form, in no way corresponding to our class-outlook.

This fact of a word's significance, analysed for the meaning of its concept, is a matter noted by Berkeley:

It cannot be deny'd that words are of excellent use, in that by their means all that stock of knowledge which has been purchas'd by the joint labours of inquisitive men in

37

all ages and nations, may be drawn into the view and made the possession of one single person.[2]

He also notes what we indicated above: the distortion of a concept's perception by applying a one-sided or incorrect use of a term:

> But at the same time it must be owned that most parts of knowledge, whose fruit is excellent, and within the reach by the abuse of words, and general ways of speech wherein they are deliver'd, that it may almost be made a question whether language, has contributed more to the hindrance or advancement of the sciences.

Berkeley's proposed escape from this situation is that of an idealist, not in making a cleansing, based on class analysis, of a term from the viewpoint of its social comprehension, but in aiming at "pure idea".

> It were, therefore, to be wish'd that every one wou'd use his utmost endeavors, to obtain a clear view of the ideas he'd consider, separating from them all that dress and incumbrance of words which so much contribute to blind the judgment and divide the attention . . . we need only draw the curtain of words, to behold the fairest tree of knowledge, whose fruit is excellent, and within the reach of our hand.

It is in a quite different way that Plekhanov approaches the similar problem of "word usage". He studies the word in an inseparable social-productive connection, restoring it for analysis from the sphere of the superstructure to the sphere of productive base and its practical connections and origins. His approach seems a convincing materialist argument, as much as the other research materials that we use. Thus basing "the inevitability of a materialist explanation of history on the most studied part of primitive society's ideology, its art" he brings in as evidence the linguistic considerations of von den Steinen:

> Von den Steinen considers that "Zeichnen" [drawing] developed from "Zeichen" [making signs], adopted with a practical aim in order to point out objects.[3]

Our habitual acceptance of words makes us reluctant to listen to them carefully, and our ignoring of this sphere of research leads to much distress and to a sea of irrational wastage of diverse polemical temperaments! For example, see how many broken bayonets lie around the question of "form and content"!

All because the dynamic, active and real act of "content" (with-keeping, as "keeping to ourselves") changed to an amorphous and static, passive understanding of content—as *capacity*.

Though it occurs to no one to speak of the "capacity" of the play, *The Rails Are Humming*, or the novel, *The Iron Flood*.

And how much inky blood has been spilt because of the persistent wish to understand *form* only as deriving from the Greek *phormos* (wicker basket) with all the consequent "organizational deductions" from that.

A wicker basket in which, quivering under the inky flood of polemics, rests that same unhappy "capacity".

Meanwhile, just turn from the Greek dictionary to a Russian dictionary of 'foreign words', where you will see that in Russian *form* is *obraz* (image). *Obraz* itself is a cross-breeding of the meanings of *obrez* (edge) and *obnaruzheniye* (disclosure)—according to Preobrazhensky's *Etymological Dictionary of the Russian Language*. Each of these points of view gives a brilliant characterization of form: from an individually static (*an und für sich*) viewpoint, as "edge"— the cutting off of a given phenomenon from attendant circumstances (for example, an un-Marxist definition of form, such as Leonid Andreyev's, which confines it *strictly* to this definition).

"Disclosure" characterizes *obraz* from another viewpoint —the socially active function of "disclosure", i.e., determining the social connection between a given phenomenon and its environment.

"Content"—an act of restraint—is a *principle of organization*, to express it in a contemporary way. The principle of organized thinking is the factual "content" of a work. This principle, the materializing combination of socio-physiological stimulants, by means of *disclosure*, appears as form.

No one assumes that the *content* of a newspaper is: news about the Kellogg Pact, a scandal at the *Gazette de France*, or such a daily incident as that of a drunken husband murdering his wife with a hammer.

When we speak of the *content* of a newspaper we mean the principle of organization and cultivation of the newspaper's *capacities*—aimed at the class-cultivation of the reader.

And in this is the production-based inseparability of combined content and form that makes an *ideology*.

Though proletarian newspapers and bourgeois newspapers may have equal factual capacities, this is what sets them poles apart in *content*.

As for the term "perception", where is our error here?

Its roots are linked to the ancient North German "Kna"* (I can) and with another word, the ancient Saxon "biknegon" (I take part)—which is forced out of existence by the one-sided contemplative *understanding* of "perception" as an abstractly contemplative function, the "pure perception of an idea", i.e., a deeply bourgeois understanding of this term.

By now it seems impossible to make any replacement in the term *perception* of the act of "perception" as an act with immediately operative consequences.

Though in reflexology it has been sufficiently determined that the process of perception is to increase the number of conditioned stimulants, conducive to the operative reflex reaction of the given subject—i.e. even in the most mechanical process is an actively operative but not passive manifestation—yet *practically*, when we get down to reasoning about perception, we tend to go even further in this perverted formula of separation from activity and labour, similar to the aim of "pure perception" that Plekhanov found expressed by Renan:

> ... Ernest Renan, in his essay on *Intellectual and Moral Reform*, called for a strong government, "which would compel the sturdy country folk to do our work for us, while we give ourselves up to reflections".[4]

* From this came directly into the German language "Können" (power) and "kennen" (to perceive).

Perceptional abstraction outside immediately active effectiveness is, for us, inadmissible. The dissociation of the perceptional process from the productive can have no place with us.

It is worth our attention that in Renan's original text this citation ends: "tandis que nous spéculons". "Spéculons" could be translated "give ourselves up to speculations". It is also noteworthy that we link such a term, inseparably, to a quite different chain of associations.

In abstract science scientific thinking is outside all links with immediate operation—"science for the sake of science", "perception for perception's sake"—attitudes that we are ready to brand as 'speculation', no matter in which branches of science they may rise.

Speculative philosophy has as little place in conditions of socialist construction as does speculation in products of prime necessity.

For us, to know is to participate.

For this we value the biblical term—"and Abraham *knew* his wife Sarah"—by no means meaning that he became acquainted with her!

Perceiving is building. The perceiving of life—indissolubly—is the construction of life—the *rebuilding* of it.

In the epoch of construction an opposition to such an understanding cannot be! Not even in the form of research dissection. The very fact of the existence of our epoch of socialist reconstruction and of our social order refutes this.

The forward movement of our epoch in art must blow up the Chinese Wall that stands between the primary antithesis of the "language of logic" and the "language of images".

We demand from the coming epoch of art a rejection of such opposition.

Qualitatively: we desire to return the differentiated and insulated concepts to the *quantitatively* correlated. We do not wish any further to oppose science and art *qualitatively*.

We want to compare them quantitatively, in order to introduce them into a *unified new view of socially-active factors*.

Is there a basis for foreseeing such a synthetic path? I say *synthetic*, for we expect this solution to be infinitely remote from any departmental formula, such as that "instructional work must not be devoid of entertainment, and entertainment must not be without didactics".

Is there a basis? In their sphere of influence what have these domains, for the moment mutually antagonistic, in common?

There is no art outside conflict. Art as a process.

As in the collision of the arrow-like flight of Gothic vaults with the inexorable law of gravity.

In the clash of the hero with the turns of fate in a tragedy.

In the functional purpose of a building with the conditions of soil and building materials.

In the conquering rhythms of verse over the dead metrics of the canons of versification.

Everywhere—struggle. A stabilization born from the clash of opposites.

The fulfilment of this increases in intensity, drawing in ever new spheres of perceptional sense-responses. Meanwhile, at the apogee, it is not altogether involved. Not units, individuals, but a collective, an audience. Moreover, this audience meanwhile does not enter into creative play. Here is the split.

Collective from collective. Split by little walls. Even in sport-play, walls attempt to divide one collective from another. Sport-play viewed as art, completely involving both spectator and creator. Into participation. Into a contemporary aspect of returning through sport to the cycle that began with the pre-tragedy play of the ancients.

There is, of course, such a "formal" correlation, in certain communities, between modern communism and primitive communism.

Nevertheless—what about *science*?

Book. Printed word. Eyes. Eyes—to brain. Bad!

Book. Word. Eyes. *Moving* from corner to corner. Better! . . .

Who hasn't crammed, pacing from corner to corner of a four-walled space, book in hand?

Who hasn't drummed rhythmically with his fist as he committed to memory, "surplus value is . . ."! i.e. who has not helped his optical stimulation by including some sort of motor rhythm in fixing an abstraction in his memory? Better. Audience. Lecturer. Of course, not some emasculated bureaucrat from Education. But one of those flaming old fanatics (fewer around now) like the late Professor Sokhotzki,* who could by the hour and with the same fire of enthusiasm, discourse on integral calculus and analyse in infinite detail how Camille Desmoulins, Danton, Gambetta or Volodarsky thundered against the enemies of the people and the revolution.

The temperament of the lecturer absorbs you completely. And all those around you. In this steely embrace the breathing of the entire electrified audience suddenly becomes rhythmic.

The audience suddenly becomes one—as at a circus, a hippodrome, or a meeting. In this arena there is a single collective impulse. A single pulsating interest.

And suddenly the mathematical abstraction has become flesh and blood.

The most difficult formula is committed to memory—in the rhythm of your breathing—

A dry integral is recalled in the feverish glow of eyes. In the mnemonics of a *collectively* experienced *perception*.

To go further. To the theory of music. A rattling one-horse carriage exhaustingly strives to climb the dusty hills in a scale of intervals—*do-re, re-mi, mi-fa, sol* . . . The piano overstrains itself. In the end strings as well as nerves are jangling . . . No, it doesn't work out. You can't turn back to the organic dissociation process that links voice and hearing. And then suddenly a chorus of all the individual "pipes". And a "miracle" takes place. Rapping out distinctly interval by interval, in *collective action*, the weak little voices are expanded, built up. It sounds—it works out—it's accomplished.

Suddenly it slips away. And a strangely measured dance moves through the room. What is this? Dionysian ecstasy? No—this is Jaques-Dalcroze who had the idea of perfecting

* In his German text for this part of the essay E. mentions that Sokhotzki was his mathematics professor at the engineering academy.—J. L.

the rhythmic memory of his students in solfeggio, by introducing a rhythmic movement of the *entire body* instead of merely clapping hands. He found that this helped to conquer the most delicate nuances of tempo.

And yet further. And the collective is torn in two. Two desks. Two opponents. Two "catapults". In the fires of dialectics, in discussion, the objective data, the values of phenomena, of facts, are tempered and forged—"from wall to wall".

The authoritarian-teleological "Thus it is so" flies to the devil. Axioms taken on faith—crash. "In the beginning was the Word . . ." But, *perhaps*, not "was"? A theorem in contradictions, requiring demonstration, includes *dialectical* conflict.

Includes a dialectic comprehension of contradictions to grasp the essence of a phenomenon. Irrefutably.

With *limited intensity*. Resolved in an internal struggle, the opposing viewpoints must comprehend elements of personal logic and temperament. A complex deepened by the experience of conditioned reflexes and the immediate flaming of unconditioned reflexes.

In the test of dialectical fires is smelted the new factor of construction. A new social reflex is wrought.

Where is the difference? Where is the abyss between tragedy and essay? Isn't the reason for both *to awaken inner conflicts and through their dialectical resolution to provide a fresh stimulus for creativity in the perceptive masses?*

Where is the difference between a perfected method of oratory and a perfected method of gaining knowledge?

The duality in the spheres of "feeling" and "reasoning" must have new limits by the new art:

To restore sensuality to science.

To restore to the intellectual process its fire and passion.

To plunge the abstract reflective process into the fervour of practical action.

To give back to emasculated theoretical *formulas* the rich exuberance of life-felt *forms*.

To give to formal *arbitrariness* the clarity of ideological *formulation*.

Those are the challenges. Those are the demands that we make on the period of art that we are now entering.
To which art will this not be too much to demand?
Wholly and only to the cinema.
Wholly and only to the *intellectual cinema.* A synthesis of the emotional, the documentary, and the absolute film.
Only an *intellectual* cinema can resolve the discord between the "language of logic" and the "language of images". Based on a language of film-dialectics.*
An *intellectual* cinema unprecedented in form and social function. A cinema with new boundaries of perception and sensuality, mastering the whole arsenal of affective stimulants—visual, aural, bio-mechanical.
But on the road to it someone will have to be sacrificed.
Someone lying across the road.
Who is this? This is the so-called "living man".
He is being asked for in literature. In theatre he is already half-abandoned at the stage door of the Moscow Art Theatre.
Now he is knocking at the door of cinema.
Comrade "Living Man"! As to literature I am not qualified to say. Nor as to theatre. But your place is not in

* For his German text E. provided at this point a new conclusion for the essay (quoted here in Christel Gang's translation for *The Left*, Autumn 1931):
Only through such a cinema, which alone is capable of uniting immediate dialectical conflicts in the development of conceptions, does it become possible to penetrate the mind of the great masses with new ideas and new perceptions. Such a cinema alone will dominate, by its form, the summit of modern industrial technique. Such a cinema alone will have a right to exist among the wonders of radio, the telescope and the theory of relativity. The old type of primitive cinema as well as the type of abstract-aloof film will disappear before the new intellectual, *concrete* film. Nor will the former be saved by its combination with the sound film. In the intellectual film sound will receive its humble necessary place among the other means of effect! The revolution of the cinema will not come from the sound-film. The revolution of the cinema will be along the lines of the intellectualization of the film.
This is the genuine contribution which Soviet art brings to the universal history of the arts. This will be the contribution of our whole epoch to art. To art, which has ceased to be art, on its way to the goal, which is Life.

cinema. In cinema you are a "right deviation". The demand for you is not on the highest level of technical means and potentialities, nor could you fulfil the duty of expressing that—for the level of industrial growth dictates ideological form. You have been dictated by what, in the field of art, corresponds to the lowest stage of industrial development. Thematically you are too plough-like for a highly industrialized form of art, such as cinema in general, and the intellectual cinema in particular. To adapt such cinema to you, or you to it, would be like using the hand of a stop-watch to gut a whitefish!

The "living man" is exhaustingly appropriate within the cultural limits and the cultural limitations of the theatre medium. And then not of theatre of the Left, but the Moscow Art Theatre in particular: The Moscow Art Theatre and its tendencies; and this is quite logical and consistent at this moment, pompously celebrating its "second youth" around these demands.

The Left theatre, owing to inadaptability, factually hasn't survived. It split up in its last stage of growth—either into the cinema or else returned to its former stage of the AKhRR* type. Between these two stages remains only Meyerhold, not as a theatre but as a master.

In the conditions of *Realpolitik* the cinema does not reject certain Moscow Art Theatre influences, but nevertheless must stubbornly hold its course in the direction of intellectual cinema as the highest possible form of cinema. To have the "living man" capture the screen would be precisely "unsuitable progress" on the way to the industrialization of film-culture.

The cinema is capable of, and consequently must achieve, a concrete sensual translation to the screen of the essential dialectics in our ideological debates. Without recourse to story, plot, or the living man.

The intellectual cinema can and must resolve the thematics of such matters as "right deviation", "left deviation", "dialectic method", "tactics of Bolshevism". Not only in characteristic "little scenes and episodes", but in the arrangement of whole *systems* and *systems of reasoning*.

* Association of Artists of Revolutionary Russia.

Specifically "Tactics of Bolshevism" and now "The October Revolution" or "The Year 1905" for example. Schemes, more primitive both in its themes—psychological and psycho-representative—and in its method of exposition "via intermediary protagonists", remain the share of less highly industrialized means of expression. And the very method and system, undoubtedly, must use concrete material, but in a totally different setting and from another point of view. Theatre and cinema of the old play-acting type.

To the share of the new cinema, the only one capable of including dialectical conflict in the promotion of understanding, falls the task of inculcating Communist ideology in the millions.

This comes as the last link in the chain of means employed in the cultural revolution, linking up everything in a single monistic system, from collective training and complex methods of instruction to the newest form of art, as it ceases to be an art and moves on to the next stage of its development.

Only with such a solution of its problems can the cinema truly deserve the designation, "the most important of the arts".

Only as such will it be distinguished fundamentally from bourgeois cinema.

Only as such will it become a part of the future epoch of Communism.

The Capital *project and the "intellectual cinema" theory went with the Eisenstein group to the United States in 1930 when the Paramount studio signed a contract with Eisenstein. But the project and the theory remained as unrealized in Hollywood as did the dozen other film projects proposed to them and by them. Just before leaving for Mexico to make a film financed by Mr and Mrs Upton Sinclair, Eisenstein attended a special meeting, on 17 September 1930, organized by the Academy of Motion Picture Arts and Sciences, to discuss new screen dimensions suggested by the wide films recently introduced. He was not satisfied that his contribution had clarified his position, so, soon after getting*

47

to Mexico, he set out his ideas in an article which he sent to Kenneth Macpherson for publication in Close Up. *Macpherson introduced the article with a portion of Eisenstein's accompanying letter.*

The Dynamic Square

It is possible that, at first glance, this article may seem too detailed or its subject not of sufficiently "profound" value, but it is my wish to point out the basic importance of this problem for every creative art director, director, and cameraman. And I appeal to them to take this problem as seriously as possible. For a shudder takes me when I think that, by not devoting enough attention to this problem, and permitting the standardization of a new screen shape without the thorough weighing of all the pros and cons of the question, we risk paralysing once more, for years and years to come, our compositional efforts in new shapes as unfortunately chosen as those from which the practical realization of the Wide Film and Wide Screen now seems to give us the opportunity of freeing ourselves.

S. M. E.

Rio Papagayo
Guerrero
Mexico

Mr Chairman, Gentlemen of the Academy,

I think this actual moment is one of the great historical moments in the pictorial development of the screen. At the moment when incorrect handling of sound is at the point of ruining the *pictorial* achievements of the screen—and we all know only too many examples where this actually has been done!—the arrival of the wide screen with its opportunities for a new screen shape throws us once more headlong into questions of purely spatial composition. And much more—it affords us the possibility of reviewing and re-analysing the whole aesthetic of pictorial composition in the cinema which for thirty years has been rendered inflexible by the inflexibility of the once and for all inflexible frame proportions of the screen.

Gee, it is a great day!

And the more tragic therefore appears the terrible enslavement of mind by traditionalization and tradition that manifests itself on this happy occasion.

The card of invitation to this meeting bears the representation of three differently proportioned horizontal rectangles: 3—4: 3 x 5: 3—6, as suggestions for the proportions of the screen for wide film projection. They also represent the limits within which revolves the creative imagination of the screen reformers and the authors of the coming era of a new frame shape.

I do not desire to be exaggeratedly symbolic, or rude, or to compare the creeping rectangles of these proposed shapes to the creeping mentality of the film reduced thereto by the weight upon it of the commercial pressure of dollars, pounds, francs, or marks according to the locality in which the cinema happens to be suffering!

But I must point out that, in proposing these proportions for discussion, we only underline the fact that for thirty years we have been content to see excluded 50 per cent of composition possibilities, in consequence of the *horizontal shape* of the frame.

By the word "excluded" I refer to all the possibilities of *vertical, upright composition*. And instead of using the opportunity afforded by the advent of wide film to break that loathsome upper part of the frame, which for thirty years—me personally for six years—has bent and bound us to a passive horizontalism, we are on the point of emphasizing this horizontalism still more.

It is my purpose to defend the cause of this 50 per cent of compositional possibilities which have been banished from the light of the screen. It is my desire to chant the hymn of the male, the strong, the virile, active, *vertical* composition!

I am not anxious to enter into the dark phallic and sexual

ancestry of the vertical shape as symbol of growth, strength, or power. It would be too easy, and possibly too offensive for many a sensitive hearer!

But I do want to point out that the movement towards a vertical perception led our savage ancestors on their way to a higher level. This vertical tendency can be traced in their biological, cultural, intellectual and industrial efforts and manifestations.

We started as worms creeping on our stomach. Then for hundreds of years we ran horizontally on our four legs. But we became something like human only from the moment when we hoisted ourselves on to our hind legs and assumed the vertical position.

Repeating the same process locally in the verticalization of our facial angle too.

I cannot, nor need I, enter in detail into an outline of the whole influence of the biological and psychological revolution and shock which followed from that paramount change of attitude. Enough if we mention man's activities. For long years man was herded in tribes on an endless expanse of fields, bound to the earth in an age-long bondage by the nature of the primitive plough. But he marked in vertical milestones each achievement of his progress to a higher level of social, cultural, or intellectual development. The upright lingam of the mystical Indian knowledge of the olden time, the obelisks of the Egyptian astrologers, Trajan's column incarnating the political power of Imperial Rome, the cross of the new spirit brought in by Christianity. The high point of medieval mystical knowledge bursting upright in the Gothic ogive arch and spire. Just as the era of exact mathematical knowledge shouts its paean to the sky with the Eiffel Tower! And introduces the huge skylines assailing the vault of amazed heaven with armies of skyscrapers and infinite rows of the smoking chimneys or trellised oilpumps of our great industries. The endless trails of wandering wagons have heaped themselves upon one another to form the tower of a Times or Chrysler building. And the camp fire, once the homely centre of the travellers' camp, has now paused to vomit its smoke from the unending heights of factory chimneys. . . .

By now, surely, you will suppose that my suggestion for the optical frame of the supreme and most synthetic of all arts—the possibilities of all of which are included in the cinema notwithstanding the fact that it doesn't use them!—is that it must be vertical.

Not at all.

For in the heart of the super-industrialized American, or the busily self-industrializing Russian, there still remains a nostalgia of infinite horizons, of fields, of plains and deserts. Individual or nation attaining the height of mechanization and yet marrying it to our peasant and farmer yesterday.

The nostalgia of "big trails", "fighting caravans", "covered wagons" and the endless breadth of "old man rivers" . . .

This nostalgia cries out for horizontal space.

And on the other hand industrial culture too sometimes brings tribute to this "despised form". She throws the interminable Brooklyn Bridge to the left of Manhattan and attempts to surpass it by Hudson Bridge to the right. She expands without end the length of the body of poor *Puffing Billy* to that of the Southern Pacific locomotives of today. She lines up endless outspread chains of human bodies (as a matter of fact—legs) in the innumerable rows of musical-hall girls, and indeed what limit is there to the other horizontal victories of the age of electricity and steel!

Just as, in contrast to her pantheistic horizontal tendencies, mother nature provides us at the edge of Death Valley or Mojave Desert with the huge 300-foot height of the General Sherman and General Grant trees, and the other giant Sequoias, created (if we may believe the geography school books of every country) to serve as tunnels for coaches or motor cars to pass through their pierced feet; just as, opposed to the infinite horizontal contredanse of the waves, at the edge of the ocean, we encounter the same element shot upright to the sky as geysers; just as the crocodile stretched out basking in the sun is flanked by upright standing giraffe in the company of the ostrich and flamingo —all three clamouring for a decent screen frame appropriate to their upright shape!

51

So neither the horizontal nor the vertical proportion of the screen *alone* is ideal for it.

Actually, as we saw, in the forms of nature as in the forms of industry, and in the mutual encounters of these forms, we have the struggle, the conflict of both tendencies.

And the screen, as a faithful mirror, not only of conflicts emotional and tragic, but equally of conflicts psychological and optically spatial, must be an appropriate battleground for the skirmishes of both these optical-by-view, but profoundly psychological-by-meaning, space tendencies of the spectator.

What is it that, by readjustment, can in equal degree be made the figure of both vertical and horizontal tendencies of a picture?

The battlefield for such a fight is easily found—*it is the square*—the rectangular space form exemplifying the quality of equal length of its dominant axes.

The one and only form equally fit by alternate suppression of right and left, or of up and down, to embrace all the multitude of expressive rectangles of the world. Or used as a whole to engrave itself by the "cosmic" imperturbability of its *squareness* in the psychology of the audience.

And this specially in a *dynamic* succession of *dimensions* from a tiny square in the centre to the all-embracing of a full sized square of the whole screen!

The "dynamic" square screen, that is to say one providing in its dimensions the opportunity of impressing, in projection, with absolute grandeur every geometrically conceivable form of the picture limit.

(Note here 1: This means that dynamism of changeable proportion of the projected picture is accomplished by masking a part of the shape of the film square—the frame.

And note here 2: This has nothing to do with the suggestion that the proportions 1:2 (3:6) give a "vertical possibility" in masking the right and the left to such an extent that the remaining area has the form of an upright standing strip. The *vertical spirit* can never thus be attained: 1st, because the occupied space comparative to the horizontal masked space will never be interpreted as something *axially opposed to it,* but always *as a part* of the latter, and

52

2nd, because, *never surpassing the height* that is bound to the horizontal dominant, it will never impress as an opposite space axis—the one of uprightness. That is why my suggestion of squareness puts the question in quite a new field, notwithstanding the fact that vari-typed masking has been used even in the dull proportions of the present standard film size, and even by myself—in the opening shot of the Odessa steps in *Potemkin*.)

No matter what the theoretic premises, only the square will afford us the real opportunity at last to give decent shots of so many things banished from the screen until today. Glimpses through winding medieval streets or huge Gothic cathedrals overwhelming them. Or these replaced by minarets if the town portrayed should happen to be oriental. Decent shots of totem poles. The Paramount building in New York, Primo Carnera, or the profound and abysmal canyons of Wall Street in all their expressiveness—shots available to the cheapest magazine—yet debarred for thirty years from the screen.

So far for my form.

And I believe profoundly in the rightness of my statement because of the synthetic approach upon which its conclusions are based. Further, the warm reception of my statement encourages me to a certainty in the theoretic soundness of my argument.

But the lying form of the screen (so appropriate to its lying spirit!) has a host of refined and sophisticated defenders. There exists even a special and peculiar literature on these questions and we should leave our case incomplete did we not pass in critical review the arguments therein contained for the form it prefers.

II

The memorandum distributed to us before this meeting (attached to this discourse as appendix[1]) and brilliantly compiled by Mr Lester Cowan, assistant secretary of the Academy) provides a brief and objective survey of all that has been written regarding the proportions of the screen. Most of these writings show a preference for the horizontal frame.

Let us examine the arguments that have brought different authors from different sides and special fields, to the same, unanimously acclaimed, —— wrong suggestion.

The principal arguments are four:

Two from the dominion of aesthetics.

One physiological.

And one commercial.

Let us demolish them in that order.

The two aesthetic arguments in favour of the horizontal shape of the screen are based on deductions deriving from traditions in the art forms of painting and stage practice. As such, they should be eliminated from discussion even without being taken into consideration, for the greatest errors invariably arise from the attempt to transplant practical results based upon the resemblance of the superficial appearances of one branch of art to those of another. (An entirely different practice is the discovery of similarity in the *methods* and *principles* of different arts corresponding to the psychological phenomena identical and basic to all art perceptions—but the present superficially exposed *analogies*, as we shall see, are far from this!)

Indeed, from the methodological similiarity of different arts it is our task to seek out the strictest differentiation in adapting and handling them according to the organic specifics typical for each. To enforce adoption of the laws organic to one art upon another is profoundly wrong. This practice has something of adultery in it. Like sleeping in another person's wife's bed ...

But in this case the arguments in themselves bring so mistaken a suggestion from their own proper dominion that it is worth while considering them to demonstrate their falsity.

1. Loyd A. Jones (No. 9 on the list) discusses the various rectangular proportions employed in artistic composition and gives the result of a statistical study of the proportions of paintings. The results of his research seem to favour a ratio of base to altitude considerably larger than 1, and probably over 1·5.

A statement startling in itself. I don't repudiate the enormous bundle of statistics that was doubtless at the disposal of Mr Jones in enabling him to make so decisive a statement.

But as I set about summoning up my pictorial recollections gathered through all the museums that I have so lately visited during my rush through Europe and America, and recalling the heaps of graphic works and compositions studied during my work, it seems to me that there are exactly as many upright standing pictures as pictures disposed in horizontal line.

And everyone will agree with me.

The statistical paradox of Mr Jones derives probably from an undue weight placed upon compositional proportions of the nineteenth century pre-impressionistic period—the worst period of painting—the "narrative" type of picture. Those second- and third-rate paintings, right off the progressive highroad of painting development, and even today far surpassing in volume the new schools of painting, abundant even in the neighbourhood of Picasso and Léger as petty-bourgeois oleographs in most concierge offices of the world!

In this "narrative" group of painting the $1 : 1 \cdot 5$ proportion is certainly predominant, but this fact is absolutely unreliable if considered from the point of view of pictorial composition. These proportions in themselves are "borrowed goods"—entirely unconnected with pictorial space organization, which is a painting problem. These proportions are barefacedly borrowed—not to say stolen!—from—the stage.

The *stage composition* each of these pictures intentionally or unintentionally reproduces, a process in itself quite logical, since the pictures of this school are occupied not with pictorial problems but with "representing scenes"—a painting purpose even formulated in *stage* terms!

I mention the nineteenth century as especially prolific in this type of picture, but I do not wish to convey the impression that other periods are entirely lacking in them! Consider, for example, Hogarth's series *Marriage à la Mode*—satirically and scenically in their "represented" anecdotes a most thrilling series of pictures . . .

It is remarkable that in another case, where the author of

the painting was, practically and professionally, at the same time a stage composer (or "art director" as we would say in Hollywood), this phenomenon has no place. I mean the case of the medieval miniature. Authors of the tiniest filigree brushwork in the world, on the leaves of gilded bibles, or *livres d'heures* (do not confound with *hors d'oeuvres*!), they were at the same time architects of the various settings of the mysteries and miracles. (Thus Fouquet and an innumerable quantity of artists whose names have been lost to posterity.) Here, where, owing to subject, we ought to have the closest reproduction of the aperture of the stage—we miss it. And find a freedom entirely void of such bounds. And why? Because at that time *the stage aperture did not exist*. The stage was then limited far off to right and left by Hell and Heaven, covered with frontally disposed parts of settings (the so-called mansions) with blue unlimited sky overshining them—as in many Passion Plays of today.

Thus we prove that the supposedly "predominant" and characteristic form of the painting by itself belongs properly to another branch of art.

And from the moment in which painting liberates itself by an impressionistic movement, turning to purely pictorial problems, it abolishes every form of aperture and establishes, as an example and an ideal, the framelessness of a Japanese impressionistic drawing. And, symbolic as it may be, it is the moment for the dawn of—photography. Which, extraordinary to remark, conserves in its later metempsychosis, the moving picture, certain (*vital* this time) traditions of this period of the maturity of one art (painting) and the infantilism of its successor (photography). Notice the relationship between Hokusai's *Hundred Views of Fuji* and so many camera shots made with so pronounced a tendency towards shooting two planes of depth—one through another (especially *Fuji seen through a cobweb* and *Fuji seen through the legs*, or Edgar Degas, whose startling series of compositions of women in the bath, *modistes* and *blanchisseuses*, is the best school in which to acquire training in ideas about space composition within the limits of a frame —and about frame composition too, which, in this series, restlessly jumps from 1:2 over 1:1 to 2:1.

This is, I think, the right point at which to quote one of Miles's (1) arguments much more closely concerned with the pictorial element here discussed than with the psychological where it was intended to be placed. For Miles, "the whole thing (the inclination towards horizontal perception) is perhaps typified in the opening through which the human eye looks; this is characteristically much wider than it is high".

Let us suppose for a moment this argument to be true in itself, and we can even provide him with a brilliant example for his statement, one even "plus royaliste que le roi".— Still it won't help him!—But, by the way, the example is the typical shape of a typical Japanese landscape woodcut. This is the only type of standardized (not occasional) composition known, compositionally not limited at the sides by the bounds of any frame, and typified in its vertical limit by a shaded narrow strip from lowest white to, at its topmost, darkest blue, rushing in this limited space through all the shades of this celestial colour.

This last phenomenon is explained as the impression of the shadow falling on the eye from the upper eyelid, caught by the supersensitive observation of the Japanese.

It might be presumed that we have here, in this configuration, the fullest pictorial testimony to the above view of Miles. But once more we must disappoint: inasmuch as the idea of a framed picture derives not from the limits of the view field of our eyes but from the fact of the usual framedness of the glimpse of nature we catch through the frame of the window or the door—or stage aperture as shown above—equally the composition of the Japanese derives from his lack of door frames, doors being replaced by the sliding panels of the walls of a typical Japanese house opening on to an infinite horizon.

But, even supposing that this shape represents the proportions of the view field, we must consider yet another remarkable phenomenon of Japanese art: the materialization on paper of the above-mentioned absence of side boundaries in the form of the horizontal *roll picture*, born only in Japan and China, and not prevalent elsewhere. I would call it *unroll picture*, because, unwound horizontally from one roll to another, it shows interminable episodes of battles, festivals, processions: for example, the pride of the Boston Museum: the many-foot-long *Burning of the Sanjo Palace*; or the immortal *Killing of the Bear in the Emperor's Garden* at the British Museum. Having created this unique type of horizontal picture out of the supposed horizontal tendency of perception, the Japanese, with their supersensitive artistic feeling, then created, illogical as it may be according to the view of Mr Miles, *the opposite form*—as a matter of purely aesthetic need for counter-balance, for Japan (with China) is also the birthplace of the *vertical roll picture*. The tallest of all vertical compositions (if we disregard the Gothic vertical window compositions). Roll pictures are also found to take the form of curiously shaped coloured woodcuts of upright composition, with the most amazing compositional disposition of faces, dresses, background elements and stage attributes.

This, I hold, shows pretty clearly that even if the diagnosis of perception as horizontal should be correct (which should by no means be regarded as proved), vertical composition also is needed as harmonic counter-balance to it.

This tendency towards harmony, and perceptive equilibrium, is of a nature quite other than a different "harmonic" and "aesthetic" argument introduced by another group of defendants of the horizontal screen.

To quote Mr Cowan's summary:

Howell and Dubray (10), Lane (7), Westerberg (11), and Dieterich (8) agree that the most desirable proportions are those approximating 1·618:1, which correspond to those of the so-called "whirling square" rectangle (also known as the "golden cut"), based on the principles of dynamic symmetry which have predominated in the arts for centuries. For simplicity the ratio 5:3 (which equals 1·667:1), or 8:5 (equalling 1·6:1) are generally advocated instead of 1·618:1. . . .

"Predominance in the arts for centuries" should in itself be a cause for the profoundest suspicion when the idea is applied to an entirely and basically new form of art, such as the youngest art, the art of cinema.

Cinema is the first and only art based entirely on dynamic

and speed phenomena, and yet *everlasting* as a cathedral or a temple; having, with the latter, the characteristics of the static arts—i.e. the possibility of intrinsic existence by itself freed from the creative effort giving it birth (the theatre, the dance, music*—the only dynamic arts before the cinema, lacked this possibility, the quality of everlastingness independent of the artistic act that created it, and by this means were characteristically distinguished from the contrasting group of static arts).

Why should a holy veneration for this mistaken "golden cut" persist if all the basic elements of this newcomer in art —the cinema—are entirely different, its premises being entirely different from those of all that has gone before?

Consider the two other denominations of the "golden cut", denominations expressive for the tendency of these proportions: the "whirling square", the principle of "dynamic symmetry".

They are the *cry* of the static hopelessly longing towards dynamism. These proportions are probably those most fitted to give the maximum tension to the eye in causing it to follow one direction and then throw itself afterwards to follow the other.

But—have we not attained, by projection of our film on the screen, a "whirling" square that exists in actuality?

And have we not discovered in the principle of the rhythmical cutting of the strip a "dynamic symmetry" that exists in actuality?

A tendency practically attained and triumphantly materialized by the *cinema as a whole*. And which therefore does not need to be advanced by the *screen shape*.

And why the hell should we drag behind us in these days of triumph the melancholy memory of the unfulfilled desire of the static rectangle striving to become dynamic?

Just as the moving picture is the tombstone of the futuristic effort of dynamism in the static painting.

There is no logical basis for preserving this mystical worship of the "golden cut". We are far enough away from

---

* The gramophone record, also a dynamic form made everlasting, has to be considered now as a part of the film.

the Greeks who, in exaggeration of their extraordinary feeling for harmonic proportion, used a proportion for their irrigation channels based upon some sacred harmonic formula, dictated by no practical consideration. (Or was that case one of war trenches? I don't remember exactly but I do remember that it was some practical enchannelling process determined by considerations purely abstract, aesthetic and unpractical.)

The imposition of these century-old proportions upon the month-young wide screen by force would be as illogical as this Greek business was. And, to finish with all this painting tradition, *if* it be desired to establish the relationship of the screen frame to *something else*, why on earth not use for comparison the intermediary between painting and the moving picture—the postcard or amateur photography?

Well, here we can insist that, at least in this field, justice be equally done to both tendencies!

By the mere fact that our pocket Kodak snaps with equal facility and accuracy either vertical or horizontal shots of our kid, pa, ma or grandma, according to whether they are lying in the sunshine on the beach, or posing hand in hand in their wedding, silver wedding or golden wedding dress!

The second aesthetic argument emerges from the domain of the theatre and musical show, and, as reproduced by Mr Cowan, runs as follows: ". . . another argument for wide film rests on the possibilities inherent in sound pictures which were lacking [were they really lacking???—S.E.] in the silent pictures of presenting entertainment more of the nature of the spoken drama of the stage." (Rayton (3)).

Preserving my usual politeness, I shall not say outright that this is the most terrific plague hanging over the talkie. I won't say it, I shall only think it, and shall confine myself to an observation with which every one must agree, viz., that the aesthetics and laws of composition of the sound film and talkie are far from being established. And to consider the present misuse of the talking screen as the basis for a suggestion that will bind us for the next thirty years to a proportion fitting that thirty months' misuse of the screen, is, to say at least, presumptuous.

Instead of approximating the cinema to the stage, the

wide screen, in my opinion, should drag the cinema still further away from it, opening up for the magic power of montage, an entirely new era of constructive possibilities.

But more of that later—as dessert.

The third distinctly formulated argument for horizontal proportion derives from the domain of physiology. It does not prevent it from being as mistaken as its predecessors. Dieterich (8) and Miles (1) have pointed out that the wider picture shows itself more accessible to the eye by virtue of the physiological properties of the latter. As Miles says,

> The eyes have one pair of muscles for moving them in the horizontal but two pairs for moving them in the vertical. Vertical movements are harder to make over a wide visual angle. As man has lived in his natural environment, he has usually been forced to perceive more objects arranged in the horizontal than in the vertical [!!!—S.E.]. This has apparently established a very deep seated habit which operates throughout his visual perception. . . .

This argument sounds very plausible. But its plausibility largely disappears the moment our research glides from the surface of the face, provided with its horizontally disposed perceptive eyes, towards . . . the neck. Here we could paraphrase exactly the same quotation in the directly opposite sense. For here the mechanism of bending and lifting the head as opposed to its turning movement from right to left provides for exactly the opposite conditions of muscular effort. The lifting and bending of the head (vertical perception) is carried out just as easily as eye movement from left to right (horizontal perception). We see that also in this case, in the purely physiological means of perception, the Wisdom of Nature has provided us with compensatory movements tending to the same all-embracing square harmony. But that is not all.

My example, as well as my counter-example, has established another phenomenon of the perceptive auditor: the phenomenon of *dynamism in perception*. In horizontal dimensions of the eyes and vertical of the head.

And this by itself overthrows another of Dieterich's (8) arguments:

> On physiological grounds that the total field covered by the vision of both eyes (for fixed head position), and also the field comfortably covered by the vision of both eyes, both approximate, a 5 × 8 rectangular form, although the actual boundaries of these fields are somewhat irregular curves . . .

For fixed head position . . . but the *unfixed* head position has just been established and that argument thereby loses its force.

(By the way, the only really insuperably bound and fixed position of the head in a movie theatre is when it is at rest . . . on one's sweetheart's shoulder. But we cannot pause for the consideration of such facts, notwithstanding that they concern at the very least 50 per cent of the audience.)

III

There remains the last argument—the economic.

The horizontally extended form corresponds most closely to the shape left for the eye by the balcony overhanging the back of the parterre, and by the series of balconies each overhanging the other. The absolute possible limit of screen height in these conditions is estimated by Sponable (2) as 23 feet to every 46 of horizontal possibilities.

If we are to remain governed by strictly economic considerations—we might well allow that by using vertical compositions we should oblige the public to move to the more expensive forward seats free of overhanging balconies. . . .

But another fact comes to our rescue—and this is the inappropriateness of the present shape and proportions of the present-day cinema theatre for *sound purposes.*

Acoustics help optics!

I have not the time to examine references in looking up the ideal proportions for a sound theatre.

I faintly recall from my dim and distant past study of architecture that, in theatre and concert buildings, the vertical cut should, for optimum acoustics, be parabolic.

What I do remember clearly is the shape and the typical proportions of two ideal buildings. One ideal for optical display:
Let us take the Roxy (New York).
And one for auditive display:
The Salle Pleyel in Paris—the peak acoustic perfection hitherto attained in a concert hall.
They are *exactly* opposed in proportions to each other. If the Salle Pleyel were to lie down upon its side it would become a Roxy. If the Roxy were to stand upright it would become a Salle Pleyel. Every proportion of the Roxy split horizontally into parterres and balconies opposes itself directly to the strictly vertical, deeply receding, corridor-like Salle Pleyel.

The sound film—the intersection of optic and auditive display, will have to synthesize, in the shape of its display hall, both tendencies with equal force.

In the days to come the sound theatre will have to be reconstructed. And its new shape—in intersecting the horizontal and vertical tendencies of "ye olden Roxy" and "ye olden Pleyel" for these new coming days conditioned by a mingling of an optic and acoustic perception—will be the one most perfectly appropriate to the dynamic square screen and its display of vertical and horizontal affective impulses.*

* The actual reconstruction and readjustment of the now existing theatres, to adapt them to new forms of screen, would cost (considered entirely independently of the artistic value consquent upon any given kind of adaption), on the estimate of the experts of the Motion Picture Academy, about $40,000,000. But mechanical genius has found a way out: by the method of first taking the picture on 65 mm. Grandeur negative; reducing it so as to confine it where desired to the limits of a 35 mm. positive (not covering the whole field provided in the smaller-sized celluloid, owing to its different proportion); and finally throwing it on to the screen by magnifying lenses, enlarging it in dimension and transforming its proportion in accordance with the facing wall of the cinema theatre. This same proceeding would equally well be used for vertical composition which, as shown by the drawing, could, by a very slight alteration of horizontal line, provide for the equally vertical, and then (when reduced) would equally not surpass the dimension of the ordinary screen. It remains to bewail the partial and very slight loss of the limits of the vertically composed pictures, and that wail only for the worst balcony and parterre seats, and even there only a very small loss.

And now, last but not least, I must emphatically challenge one more creeping tendency that has partly triumphed over the talkies and is now stretching out its unclean hands towards the Grandeur film, hastening to force it into still more abject subservience to its base desires. This is the tendency to entirely smother the principles of montage, already weakened by the 100 per cent talkies, which are none the less awaiting the first powerful example of the perfectly cut and constructed sound film that will establish anew the montage principle as the basic, everlasting, and vital principle of cinematographic expression and creation.

I refer to innumerable quotations, quotations partially accepted even by such great masters of the screen as my friend Vidor and the Grand Old Man of all of us—D. W. Griffith. For example: "Dance scenes need no longer be 'followed' as there is ample room in a normal long shot for all the lateral movement used in most dances. . . ." [The "moving camera" is a means of producing in the spectator a specific dynamic feeling, and not a means of investigation or of following a dancing girl's feet! See the rocking movement of the camera in the reaping scene of *Old and New* and the same with the machine gun in *All Quiet on the Western Front.*—S.E.] ". . . Close-ups can be made on the wide film. Of course, it is not necessary to get as close as you do with the 35 mm. camera, but, comparatively speaking, you can make the same size of close-up. . . ."! [The impressive value of a close-up lies not at all in its absolute size, but entirely in its size relation to the optical affective impulse produced by the dimension of the previous and following shots.—S.E.] "However, with the wide film very few close-ups are needed. After all, the main reason for close-ups is to get over thought [!!!—S.E.] and with the wide film you can get all the detail and expression in a full-sized figure that you would get in a six foot close-up with the 35 mm. film. . . ." [Although preferring, as far as my personal tastes are concerned in *screen* acting, the nearly imperceptible movement of the eyebrow, I none the less acclaim the possibility of a whole body expressing something. Still, however, we cannot admit the expulsion of the close-up—the fixing of attention by the isolation of a desired

During the filming of *Battleship Potemkin*, 1925. Eisenstein in cap and grey jacket; three assistants are seen: Alexandrov at the right of the camera, Levshin in striped shirt, and Antonov at the far right.

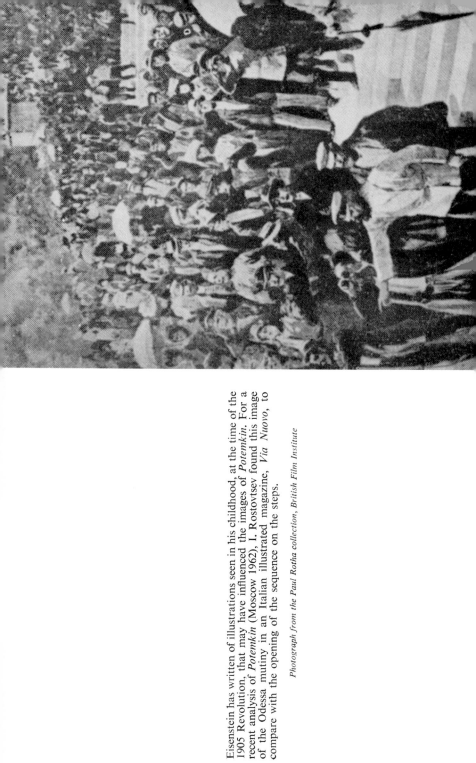

Eisenstein has written of illustrations seen in his childhood, at the time of the 1905 Revolution, that may have influenced the images of *Potemkin*. For a recent analysis of *Potemkin* (Moscow 1962), I. Rostovtsev found this image of the Odessa mutiny in an Italian illustrated magazine, *Via Nuovo*, to compare with the opening of the sequence on the steps.

Photograph from the Paul Rotha collection, British Film Institute

In December 1929, during his stay in London, Eisenstein visited the film-making class conducted by Hans Richter in a studio over Foyle's, in Manette Street, where Richter directed a short improvisation about a London policeman, acted by Eisenstein. Some of the group shown in this photograph have been identified: Eisenstein (in policeman's helmet) is communicating (by cane) with Richter, in the left-hand corner; Mark Segal is playing the warming-pan; Lionel Britton (leaning on the helmet) is feverishly telephoning; Jimmy Rogers (Cavalcanti's cameraman) is smiling at his Debrie; Len Lye is in hat, and the trio behind him, from right to left, are Michael Hankinson, Basil Wright, and Towndrow.

Photograph from British Film Institute

fact or detail, an effect by no means achieved by merely providing the body with disproportionate increase in absolute size.—S.E.]

Close-ups, moving camera shots, absolute dimensional variation of figures and objects on the screen, and the other elements concerned with montage, are far more fundamentally bound up with the expressive means of cinema and cinema perception than is involved in the task of merely facilitating the view of a face, or the "getting over of a thought" on it.

As we have proclaimed (and as Alexandrov tried to show in humble essay form in that piece of irony, *Romance Sentimentale*, so grievously misunderstood in its intentions), with the coming of sound montage does not die but develops, amplifying and multiplying its possibilities and its methods.

In the same way the advent of the wide screen marks one further stage of enormous progress in the development of montage, which once more will have to undergo a critical review of its laws; laws mightily affected by the change of absolute screen dimension, making impossible or unsuitable quite a number of the montage processes of the days of the olden screen, but on the other hand providing us with such a gigantic new agent of impression as the rhythmic assemblage of varied screen shapes, the attack upon our perceptive field of the affective impulses associated with the geometric and dimensional variation of the successive various possible dimensions, proportions and designs.

And, accordingly, if to many of the qualities of Normal Screen montage laws we must proclaim: "le roi est mort!" yet with much greater strength we must cry "vive le roi!" in welcome to the newcoming of the montage possibilities of Grandeur Film, never hitherto envisaged or imaginable.

Santa Maria Tonantzintla, Cholula, Mexico

In 1928, before Eisenstein left for Europe and America, he had experienced his first attempt at teaching the principles of film-making. After he returned to the Soviet Union

*in 1932 a series of frustrated efforts to resume film produc-
tion made him turn again to the profession of teaching. The
combining of this with more continuous theoretical work
than had previously been possible made his work at GIK,
the State Cinema Institute, an experience as rewarding to
himself as to his students. The classroom of the Direction
Course became his studio, his workshop, his laboratory, his
stage and his screen. At the end of 1934, partly owing to
his intense application to its problems, the Institute was
raised to the status of a Higher Institute, VGIK, and Eisenstein celebrated the occasion with a declaration of purpose.*

GTK—GIK—VGIK
Past—Present—Future*

The anniversary of the Cinema Institute has a special importance, for nowhere else in the world is there a film school
on such a scale. There's nothing like our Institute, neither
in the film-Babylon of Hollywood nor in the countless other
Babylons of the world's film industries.

The reason for this strange circumstance should be
obvious. It is not for lack of means in America, nor of raw
film in Germany, nor of the wish to learn in England. Such
an institute could be born and could function only in the
Land of the Soviets. Only here were swept away those basic
barriers that preclude the possibility of a similar institution
in the West. Only here, in a country of socialist competition,
has an end been put to the chaos of capitalist competition.
Only here can that reflection of traditional relationships in
bourgeois society, the traditional concept of success, with

* Written for the fifteenth jubilee of the Cinema Institute ; this
essay, however, does not pretend to deal with the whole history of
the Institute, but only with that period when I was associated with
it—that is, from 1928 to the present [the essay was written at the
end of 1934].

the successful triumphing over the unsuccessful, be regarded with a new understanding.

Two contestants. One beats the other. X is less good, while Y is better. Hurrah for Y. But with us the unprecedented paradox (if examined from the same viewpoint). Two contestants. One is defeated. The other wins. So the other is better. But is the first bad? Nothing of the sort! Both are good. And this is because they are not competing against each other. It is because both of their interests reside in the general good. It is this general good that takes first place. And the loser in a contest can be just as proud as the winner.

For us this has become a—b—c. For us this is now flesh and blood.

But you should see the incredulity, amazement and consternation of European and American film directors when they are told that our master film-makers take their "professional secrets" to the rising young generation. When you begin to tell them about the Institute, you can see their eyes open wide in astonishment; you can see what they're thinking: "They'll snatch the bread out of your mouths. Why do you do it?"

Yet we do it—and we draw others into doing it as well.

There's enough bread in our country for all. Property relationships long ago departed from our psyche. Moreover, through many years of practice and experience, new material or spiritual values have arisen. And there is only one anxiety: will there be enough hands, enough heads, enough creative temperaments to fill the ranks of production in all the increasing scope of our growing cinematography?

In any country engineers instruct engineers. Technicians instruct technicians. The arts also can achieve such a level of personalization. Yet nowhere else can a creative worker teach a younger creative worker in an organized, socialized arrangement.

Elsewhere a "creative talent" is a ticket of admission into the privileged caste of supermen. A creative person does not even "mystically" comprehend his own activity. In the interest of this activity it pays to keep the caste as sparse as possible. A bourgeois collector who finds a duplicate of an object in his collection which is thought to be unique will spend any amount of money to destroy the duplicate and remain the possessor of the "unique" object.

A big artist does everything he can to "lose" the young beginner. All because the demand for creative work is limited. Because theatres and cinemas are not opening, but closing.

Because the demand for skillls does not expand, but contracts. Because beyond the talents of two or three stars the demands do not exceed the narrow channel of petty-bourgeois taste.

We, on the contrary, aim at a broad range and numerous applications for creative activity and creative energy. Theatre and cinema grow wider in subject and in quantity. And basically, there is an increase in demands and requirements for quality, for cultural quality. and for the qualifications of achievement.

And this situation produces a new necessity—to explore scientifically, with research and experiment, the questions of creation, of creative instruction and creative training. To strip away the veils of caste mystique that prevent the study of creative problems, and the theories and practice of creative work.

Only we have made this possible socially. Methodically as well.

No other social structure than ours can establish the social and psychological premises for such activity. Our social system alone possesses the desire and the means of removing all the wrappings of secrecy and mystique from the way things happen. In the matter of perceiving creative problems and processes we can claim to have advanced one step from infancy; we are at least of primary school age.

Already our method of research into certain areas of phenomena has revealed enormous horizons of understanding matters which have always been regarded as some kind of sacred mystery. Having brought such clarity into the field of the analysis and knowledge of art, this method could be applied with even more remarkable success to "practical aesthetics"—constructive creative practice. On the first level, every day adds to the volume of research that enriches the fund of Marxist classics on this question; on the second level, we have taken only the first steps.

It must be frankly acknowledged: the Institute wears me out. I'm worn out by the furious enthusiasm of the research work being done: by the revelation of fundamental laws and proportions in the construction of works, and by the process of their creation. And all this is along a line in the area of film craft that is least known and least investigated: the activity of the director as a composer of the audio-visual complex of a film. This may be terribly harmful for a creative worker. Perhaps this may explain the disappearance of his own creative career. Creative muteness may be the reward of those who allow themselves to introduce the scalpel of analysis into areas where entrance has always been forbidden.

Some even spitefully say: "He who can—creates; he who can't—teaches." Yet this does not take one thing into account. Study has not yet reached the level of automatic teaching. "To teach" in the present stage still means really "to create", for this is almost a bare place where one must form one's system and method for creatively apprehending the art of film direction. And work in this constructive sense is no less and no more than one's own creative tasks.

But on the other hand, what can compare with the feeling of an explorer, a pioneer, who gathers and links the experience of predecessors and contemporaries in the building of a synthetic constructive methodology, absorbing into itself all the highest achievements in the arts!

Only in close contact with those who grow, aspire, extend, achieve, miscarry or fail alongside the creative strivings of the younger generation, is it possible to see into this active application of the principles of the great heritage of scientific Marxism to the creative constructive process.

The old Proletcult view of the spontaneous birth of great artists solely from the ranks of the working class has long since been discarded. A thirst for study in a creative worker, for the study of direction, is obvious to everyone who speaks of creative longings. To meet this creative desire in the younger generation of the victorious working class, to meet the developing of his own experience and the summed-up experience of the older generation of film-makers, to meet it not with stories and anecdotes of production, but with experiment, with the intelligence of precise methods—those are the aims that must stand before those film-makers who can imagine their creative participation in the building of the Soviet cinema as extending beyond the frame of their own films.

For us an anniversary is not an occasion for banquets. To us an anniversary has something of the effect of that poster of the civil war period, with a finger pointing directly at the passer-by: "And what were YOU doing then?" The approach of a jubilee makes everyone accountable to the segment of history just past. And this accounting must always start from a recognition that what has been done is too little. This isn't modesty. This is a natural feeling when comparing either the little or much that has been done with the immense perspectives of what is left to be done in the future.

The Institute has a double account: of people and of the things they have done. Many of our people have been absorbed into film production. In addition to the great masters—Pudovkin (of whom Kuleshov's workshop can be proud), the Vasilievs (of whom my workshop is proud), Golovnya and Volchok (who do honour to the cameramen's course), GTK* and GIK can list many, many workers of various calibres and specialities, who have harmoniously joined the production family.

Nor is the service and task of the Institute confined to this. Its duty extends beyond urgent training of new film-makers. No less important a task is the setting in motion of the very understanding of the method and science of cinematography. The organizing of this work of scientific calculation, within the faculties, seminars, officers, or in special scientific bodies is the work of NIS.† Their job is to provide research forces and proposals reflecting all the immediate themes and problems of current cinematographic practice. They are also responsible for the general methodo-

* The first stage of GIK was as a State Technicum of Cinema: GTK.

† NIS: the Scientific-Research Department of GIK.

logical lines of two of GIK's faculties in particular: direction and photography.

Here we should note the decisive turn taken by the Institute since 1928. Developing from a technicum towards an eventual academy, the direction course has shown two prominent tendencies that were absent from the activity of GIK in its earliest stages.

First, in its adopting a higher educational level than an "artistic" studio, which is often the only ultimate aim of an instructional administration linked with art.

Second, in its relating cinema to the other arts, as distinct from the former tendency to seek cinema specified as "self-born," based on the suspect term of "photogenic" and the special aesthetics of keeping cinema separated from its parentage of other arts.

It is only on the basis of the closest contact with the culture of literature, theatre, painting and music, only in the most serious examination of the newest scientific disclosures in reflexes and psychology and related sciences, that the study of cinema specifics can be co-ordinated in some constructive and workable system of instruction and perception.

The direction course in the academic year of 1932/33 undertook the large task of organizing these conditions into the first detailed programme on the subject of the theory and practice of direction to be issued by the Institute.[1] This document, exhaustive or not, is the first formulation of a "codex" on what a film director must study and know in order to fulfil the great tasks that await him.

This programme also includes the core of the training method which, as the school work has shown us, is the one best adapted for creative education. This "socratic" method is called "directorial practice".

But our work doesn't stop at this. The present programme develops along two further lines. The Institute is directing the formation of a normal college plan of teaching, attached to any given basic discipline. Our work is also proceeding towards the "synchronization" of the whole complex of taught subjects and spheres of knowledge that are necessary to a director for the many facets of his activity. This will be a substitute for the unsystematic accumulation of subjects

71

that is typical of the worst specialized institutions on the college level.

The work projected by the direction course inevitably touches other faculties also. We are at present conducting a basic reconstruction of the cameramen's faculty, based fundamentally on those principles which we have been checking and elaborating in recent years. For the first time in the existence of the Institute friendship and co-operation have been established between the two faculties on the base of a unified theoretical understanding of the subjects taught and a unified method of research and instruction. For the first time, with the combined strengths of both faculties, the question of the cameraman's craft has been raised to the position of highly qualified creative work, as distinct from the attitude, which we can remember all too easily and which remains almost unchanged in the West, of treating the cameraman as a "technical" worker, deprived of creative independence and personality.

The initial difficulty encountered with almost the entire student body was the low general cultural level of students at their admission. Nor has this defect been remedied. It is this general culture and cultural basis in the arts that is, perhaps more than in any other artistic field, required in film direction. Its many sides require a many-sided background. And this is one of the most serious problems facing our young people.

Looking through the lives of artists, we may notice particularly those who have achieved something in the field of cinema arts. The first note struck is almost inevitably, "In childhood his parents' home was often visited by actors, writers, artists . . ."—"The child grew up amidst the lively surroundings of art interests and problems that concerned his parents . . ."—"He moved to the home of his uncle who was a great lover of antiquities and the arts . . ."—"From his earliest conscious years he was accustomed to drawing and music . . .", etc.

But our young creative worker had no such childhood. His mother did not grace a literary salon. His father did not patronize the Muses. During the hardest years his mother worked heroically in a factory. As he grew up his involvement was in the work of liquidating disorder. The young fellow was soon immersed in an atmosphere of feverish construction, liquidation of deficiencies, liquidation of the class enemy. He is filled with the most valuable first-hand experience of participation in forming the most remarkable Socialist actuality. No time for any profound study of Tolstoy or Dickens, like the future poets of a previous generation, whose biographies record their gulping down mountains of "forbidden writers" in their grandfathers' libraries.

Beginning with the warm caresses of the Muses, obligingly bending over their cradles, the lives of the great artists go on to record a feverish ill-digested diet, mad nights, racing through books by the light of a tallow candle—fantastically grabbing at knowledge and culture in maturity, while regretting the lack of opportunity for nurture in their childhood.

Yet there is no way round this. The sleepless nights and long hours of obsessive study cannot be dispensed with. The more knowledge one gains in childhood, the less expenditure of strength later. One way or another the knowledge must be acquired. An elementary accumulation of knowledge is unavoidable and necessary for every single person who wishes by means of self-education to express actuality by this or that path. Without such a cultural basis he will be doomed to pitiable babbling that might be sufficient for primitive circumstances, but shows up miserably when surrounded by those demands that are made by a growing Socialist country.

What should be done? How to start? Such primary conditions of nurture do not exist. You cannot reconstruct them. Besides, in those traditional forms they are quite unserviceable today. One meets many students—or, rather, one used to meet students who grew up amidst Bach and Beethoven, Bryusov and Blok, from their earliest years. All the better —it would seem. But those little pigeons tend to take first place and to forget those who came from factory or farm without ever having read Balzac or Mark Twain. Nevertheless, it's remarkable how "truth" almost always takes sides with the latter. They show creative power, energy, original research, even though there may be less "first-class apprenticeship" or "swift progress". These creative youngsters, representatives of the young class that has taken power into its own hands, can also seize and keep the fortress of knowledge. Their creation can be deeper, more full of sap, more original and powerful than those who, in spite of all the trappings they have picked up, lack these basic conditions of vitality. I say this as the result of several years of work with Soviet youth.

Yet the cultural defect remains painful for both student and instructor. It blocks the course of training. It delays the possibility of associative consolidation of materials in the consciousness and in the senses. No, we can't reproduce the cultural nursery of an "intellectual" or "aristocratic" family. But there is another means. Our genuine family has become our Socialist society. Through the system of social organizations it can link up and fill in this layer of nourishing surroundings, needed both by the growing seed and the forming senses, to shape the consciousness of the future builder of cultural and artistic values.

Obviously we are speaking of linking the first steps of training with a tendency towards the arts. And of creating ties between the lower and middle school links, where alongside a general cultural education a person with a predisposition to art could obtain the necessary complex of information and knowledge.

It would be better in a consistently planned arrangement to re-initiate that type of specialized school for artistically gifted youngsters of middle and senior years who, though perhaps inconsistent and sporadic, nevertheless sprang from the first years of the revolution.

Such schools—the first links of artistic training—would turn out young people at a level approximating to that aimed at by technical colleges, but with a programme heading them in the direction of specialization that is primarily creative. If the technical students at the end of their schooling are well up in the subtle prerequisite knowledge of all types of engineering, then the students predisposed to art would possess an accumulation of those particular perceptions in the area of the humanities and a mastery of basic qualifications in graphic art, music, movement, etc., that would be useful to follow through towards any art. In such schools there need not and cannot be specialization, but their students must be culturally prepared for that which would be suitable for a college of art, architecture, literature, music or cinema.

In his subsequent cinema training the student could expect a normal four-year course at college. At the time of his admittance there would be expected of him no specialized knowledge of the photo-chemical process or of optics. These would be dealt with later in either the director's or the cameraman's course.

But in the second year of the Institute it could suddenly become clear that he had read neither *Dead Souls* nor *Le Père Goriot* (and I know such instances in our Institute). Even so there would be no necessity for such a shameful spectacle as that of a student rattling off in faultless phrases a history of literature with Marxist appraisals of this or that literary-social phenomenon, only to find out later that he had never actually read—or even seen—the works he had talked so fluently about. Such cases also are too familiar to us at the Institute. If our higher authorities were to decree the reorganization of the teaching of geography and history, and the extension of that principle to areas not already covered by decrees, students would not have to stoop to such evasions.

A four-year course, according to the revised and broadened programme of the practical work of our Institute on similar principles, should be more than enough for the education of genuinely qualified trainees in the specialized skills of film direction. Only a few additional practical production tests would be required before the final "ordination" to the status of director.

There is a third level, not yet absolutely necessary, but included for those who want to achieve the highest standards of qualification by specializing in scientific work on film problems: the Academy level.

Here there would be more than the acquisition of knowledge; this would be a place for actively creative, educationally experimental and experimentally scientific work. Practical experience, hitherto accidentally acquired, could be transmuted, in conditions of collective scientific research with laboratory equipment, to methodological generalization. Here such data could emerge from and carry forward the knowledge and style of the Soviet cinema. Two years of such work in an experimental studio, with growing acquaintance with the newest data of creative and theoretical ideas, technical discoveries and accomplishments, would make an excellent preparation for workers of the highest qualifications and could well lift our cinema culture to unprecedented heights.

Here would be realized the slogan on the indivisibility of practice and theory that is needed in such a creative base, relating the Academy to the factory that produces the films. Such an Academy would make it possible for those whose years of practical work had shown them the need for theoretical intelligence and summing up, to take part in further scientific planning of perspectives that evolve from immediate film problems.

Three such links for the cultural formation of cinematographers would, I think, answer the problem of creating basic cadres of film-makers. Child prodigies and naturally talented persons could always find a footing in one of these three links, according to their development and talents, and help in the gleaning of knowledge for their future work.

Such are the outlines of the future. Such, approximately, are the forms and directions developed by our Institute in the years of its most recent formation and maturity. This gives us an approximate outline of those perspectives towards which it is aiming its further growth.

Eisenstein's teaching arrangements at VGIK provided leave of absence for any production project he might begin. At the time of this essay's publication, just when circumstances and his own desires seemed to have committed him to a professorial rather than a production career, Eisenstein announced that he was preparing a new film, Bezhin Lug, *and requested leave from the Institute. The leave was to be temporary and short, the production was to be rapid and efficient, but it was two-and-a-half years later that the production of* Bezhin Lug *was stopped by the film administration. Soon afterwards the film administration itself was totally overhauled and Eisenstein's next project,* Alexander Nevsky, *was as efficiently made as he promised. During the preparation of* Nevsky *and the next project,* Ferghana Canal, *he continued to superintend the progress of the directors' course at VGIK, and to plan a book.* Pushkin and Cinema. *It was during a trip to Uzbekistan for* Ferghana Canal *that Eisenstein drafted the foreword to his* Pushkin book.

Lessons from Literature

The heritage of all mankind is ours to master and apply.—Lenin

It is our responsibility to put into practice Lenin's great directive on our cultural heritage. We must learn how to do it—for too many of us do not know. In our profession it is especially complicated, for the cinema has no *direct* ancestors.

To write "in imitation of Tolstoi" or "in imitation of Hemingway" is, comparatively, easy. Nor is this so silly as it may sound. For everything begins with imitation. We know instances of writers transcribing entire masterworks. This is not a naïve undertaking. This is a way of finding the *movement* of another, perhaps a classical, writer, and of learning by this means the ideas and feelings embedded in this or that system of visual and aural images, in his word-combinations and so forth.

In ascending to the factors that emerge from movement —from this primary gesture of the writer—there is, on the one hand, complexity, for it is always easier to "skin" than to learn. On the other hand, literature can be treated not only directly, as by literary heirs, but in the interests of its *indirect* heirs; for example, the cinema.

77

And here there is another peculiarity, one to which comparatively little attention has been given.

The epoch of victorious Socialism is the only epoch that makes it possible to create a comprehensively perfected work in all its manifold aspects.

It is by this standard that we examine and will continue to examine our classics. The reflection of this standard in literature is and will be as manifold as in the perfection of social conditions, and works will be achieved with a full harmony of all their elements such as has not been and could not be attained in previous epochs.

The accomplishment of this in past epochs was extremely rare and accessible exclusively to creative geniuses (their possession of this feature was one of the conditions that determined their genius). But even in those conditions, each of them, even the greatest of writers, bore elements within himself that stood in the way of perfection, elements that did not reach his highest level. Balzac is accused of slovenly literary language, Shakespeare of negligence in the composition and uneven qualities of *Hamlet*,* Goethe's *Hermann und Dorothea*: "positively impossible to read"; and his *Iphigenie auf Tauris*: "cannot be staged". In the works of Kleist has been discovered side by side with his genius a triviality worthy of Klopstock (Stefan Zweig has written very perceptibly about this), and so on.

The task of the historical-literary critic includes the selection and appraisal of these phenomena. As with Wagner's Beckmesser in *Die Meistersinger*, his duties also include the establishment of categories, as well as critical recommendations of this or that author. It is here that any disproportions in the desired perfection are branded for all to observe. The premises and conditions of similarly emerging phenomena are analysed. Here also there is an especially severe emphasis on any inadequacy in the social reflection of his epoch, resulting from an undue subservience of the writer's conscience in observing the social limitations of his times, and his difficulties in overcoming these pressures.

---

* Theoretical conjectures (Aksyonov's for example) have been advanced about the imperfections of the tragedy as it has been handed down to us.

Lenin's comments on Tolstoi and Engels's strictures on Zola are especially prominent examples of such criticism. But to *learn* from the classics is an altogether different matter. Here the exaggeration of separate features of a work is by no means an invariably negative phenomenon. In this function it can even be thought of as positively useful, for it holds up, as it were, an enlarging mirror to features which in conditions of ideal harmony are so "soldered" into the structural whole that to isolate them for study is an extremely laborious task.

To be brief, one must know what, in each writer, is to be studied. Particularly outside literary study—in study for the purposes of the cinema.

In this connection all arguments about who is the best writer, or about which writer one must attach oneself to, are irrelevant.

What concerns us here is not this or that writer's work as a whole, but the particular features in his creative work that provide illumination on a particular problem—composition or viewpoint, for example. Obviously, "minor" writers will have less to contribute, and the genius of Shakespeare or Tolstoi will have much to teach us in almost every problem with which we have to deal.

I conducted, in 1928-29, a seminar at GIK on Emile Zola. We accomplished a great deal in the examination of several purely cinematic elements in the plastic side of his creative work, drawing attention to a series of compositional peculiarities which in literature are found almost exclusively in this writer, and which are very close in their nature to cinema. Thereupon, without considering why we had chosen the creative work of Zola for study, several comrades, armed with Engels's well-known quotation on Balzac's superiority to Zola, announced a campaign against our project, declaring that we ought to be studying Balzac and that an "orientation" to Zola was "perverse".

In the first place the matter is not one of "orientation", for we were not making an acceptance of the whole canon of Zola's work as a unit; we were studying a series of specific features, illustrated especially instructively in Zola's work. In the second place, Engels's directive on the superiority of Balzac is centred on one specific element: the socio-economic documentation that interested Engels was less conspicuous in Zola—as with many other writers. On the other hand we can find in Zola a huge quantity of elements, extremely important to film-makers, that are quite absent from Balzac's writings. Open Zola at any page. It is so plastic, so *visually* written that according to it a whole "scene" could be prepared, starting with the director's indications (the emotional characteristics of the scene), exact directions to the designer, the lighting cameraman, the set-dresser, the actors, everyone. Here is the kind of scene you can find on every page of Zola; it is the opening of Chapter II of *La Terre*:

Maître Baillehache, notary of Cloyes, lived on the left-hand side of the Rue Grouaise, on the way to Châteaudun, in a small white one-storey house; from a corner hung the solitary street-lamp that lit up the wide paved street, deserted during the week but loud and lively on Saturdays with the influx of peasants on their way to market. The two professional plates were visible from afar, shining against the chalky surface of the low buildings; behind the house, a narrow garden ran right down to the bank of the Loir.

On this particular Saturday, in the room to the right of the entrance hall, overlooking the street, the under-clerk, a pale puny lad of fifteen, had lifted one of the muslin curtains to watch the people passing. The other two clerks, an old man, pot-bellied and dirty, and a younger man, emaciated, ravaged with liver-trouble, were busy writing at a double desk of ebonized deal, the only piece of furniture in the room except for seven or eight chairs and a cast-iron stove which was never lighted until December, even if snow fell on All Saints' Day. The pigeon-holes covering the walls, the greenish cardboard boxes, broken at the corners and bursting with yellowed papers, fouled the atmosphere of the room with a smell of sour ink and dust-eaten papers.[1]

Compare this with any of the most brilliant pages of Balzac: its visual embodiment seems so grandiose, so literary, that it is not *directly* transferable to a system of visual images. Read this opening of *La Peau de Chagrin*:

> Towards the close of October, 1829, a young man entered the Palais Royal at the hour when the gaming houses opened their doors in compliance with the law which protects an essentially taxable passion. Without undue hesitation, he went up the stairway leading to a gambling den known as number thirty-six.
> "Your hat, please sir," a little old man called to him curtly and querulously. His face was cadaverous and he crouched in the shadows behind a railing. Suddenly, he rose, exhibiting a degraded countenance.[2]

That's all very well, I'm told—this is not merely a matter of plasticity; what's basic is the images and characters of people, and in this Balzac is superior to Zola.

Exactly! In seeking characters we turn to Balzac, but for the plastic of film style, to Zola—and first of all to Zola.

But there is another element, closely connected with character, that we can seek in Zola: this is the ability to link man plastically with his environment.

We hear too often of the "incompleteness" of a person as outlined by Zola—compared with the "deep relief" of a Balzac character.

A personage in Balzac, thanks to his manner of exposition, always reminds me of the fat señor painted by Velásquez (perhaps because of a resemblance to Balzac himself!). Old Goriot, and Vautrin, and father Grandet, and Cousin Bette, and Cousin Pons, and Cesare Birotteau all resemble the Velásquez personage—three-dimensional, seen at full height on a pedestal, in boots and sword, characterized to the last ringlet or whisker, mitten or glove.

Zola's characters, as we call them to mind, can invariably be imagined in styles dear to him—expressed by Degas or Manet. Particularly Manet. And, if I may say so, most of all in the manner of his "Bar at the Moulin Rouge".* Their

* Writing from memory, and far from his Moscow library, E. has unwittingly synthesized *two* Manet paintings, the "Bar at the Moulin Rouge", and the "Bar at the Folies-Bergère".—J. L.

incompleteness seems the same as the incompleteness of the painted girl behind the bar. She seems cut in half by the counter. It is also an incomplete figure who looks at her friend, the waitress, from another part of the painting, where the legs are cut short by the picture frame, and the left breast is covered by the round head of a drinking guest.

It would never occur to anyone to think of this girl as, anatomically, a half-girl. Nor do we think of the engulfing shadow on the face of a Rembrandt sitter as being an absence of part of the jaw, the temple, the forehead, or the eye deep in the eye-socket—all this being particularly notable in the etchings.

Obviously, what Manet gives us are "clots" of real detail —the personage in "close-up"—for it is no accident that the painting of Zola's time is linked with those masters of the close-up, the Japanese artists of the wood-block. Though Manet's image may not be fully drawn, it cannot be said to be undetermined. It is rounded off with the counter of the bar, the reflection in the mirror behind the girl, the tankard of beer, and the guest's head, so craftily concealing the girl's breast. Even the image of a subsidiary figure is drawn with the same customary complex of elements that is inseparable from the central personage.

Balzac is no less accurate in defining the elements connected with the habits and actions of a person. But Balzac only *names* these, as if describing the supplying firm, their method of ordering, often with attached prices—you almost expect catalogue numbers. So that Balzac gives you the person and all pertaining to him—objects, habits, setting—all gathered by him into a picture, the legs of his personage hidden by the edge of the table, the personage himself hidden in a detailed description of the wall's upholstery, the objects arranged in methodical order. For our art Balzac's method does not give us much help.

On the other hand Zola takes you *into* the image; for example, Nana at the race meeting—though the race is just as much a race as she is Nana, they cannot be taken apart. And Zola cuts his way into your visual memory with an unforgettable "shot", as when the black figure of Eugène Rougon casts its shadow across the white sculptures in the

Chambre, or when the carnally red tonality flows into Nôtre Dame in the scene of the christening of Napoleon III's son.

Les Rougon-Macquart are not merely providing a commentary on a full socio-economic picture of Napoleon III's epoch; they encourage each of us, as we read—especially with such a purpose as ours—to do our own creative work. This gives us more than the full personality of Nucingen writing to a Sachar.

So we return to our premises: to ask of each writer that quality that makes him a master. And to leave to the literary critic those matters of academic calculation—such as assigning to each writer his place "in the ranks", or defining his degree of greatness.

No, please: don't confuse the addresses. Don't demand of Flaubert the virtues of Gogol—don't seek in Dostoevski lessons in the art of Tolstoi—and vice versa! That's as unreasonable as to want apples in the spring, or snow in the summer.

What we need is a "cinematographer's guide" to the classics of literature. And to painting, too. And to theatre. And music. How fascinating, for example, to define in detail what can be learned in Repin's work as distinct from Serov's work. What can be learned from Bach as distinct from Wagner. From Ben Jonson as distinct from Shakespeare.

We must learn in the way that Busygin writes with such modesty in his autobiography: "At the Industrial Academy the chief thing I'm learning is—how to learn."

We must study how to read.

This is essential in order to write:

for a writer—the pages of a literary scenario (or treatment).

for a director—the sheets of a shooting-script, or the shots in preliminary sketch, or completed images on the canvas of the screen.

Literature *per se* has as many means and circuitous expositions as there are ways of perception. But without our premises these mingled forms remain closed to us.

For film-writing the responsibility is of immeasurable extent.

The greatness of Pushkin is not for films—but how filmic!

That is why we begin with Pushkin.

Kokand, Uzbekistan
13 October 1939

Ferghana Canal was left among the unrealized films, and the planned Pushkin and Cinema was left among the unrealized books. This winter several other films were planned before Eisenstein finally returned to production: among them a film about Pushkin, using an untried colour idea—selected, single, essential colours. While Eisenstein was deep in the problems of fusing the elements of drama, colour, music, movement and space, the Bolshoi Opera Theatre invited him to stage a new production of Wagner's Die Walküre, and he at once accepted this opportunity to practise the theories of greatest concern to him at that moment.

The Embodiment of a Myth

My latest work has been on the production of the opera *The Valkyrie* in the Bolshoi Theatre in Moscow, the largest and finest opera house in the Soviet Union. As a cinema director I was quite surprised when one day the Art Director of the Bolshoi Theatre rang me up and invited me to produce *The Valkyrie*. I had never worked in a musical theatre before, although over twenty years ago I had experimented in the legitimate theatre. Nevertheless, I accepted the offer. Now that, after eight months of work on this production, the date of the première of the opera is approaching, I feel as though I had long been striving precisely towards this work. Wagner proved to be quite a natural step in my creative path.

In Wagnerian opera I particularly appreciate the epic quality of the theme, the romanticism of the subject, and the surprising pictorial nature of the music, which calls for plastic and visual embodiment. But what most attracted me in Wagner were his opinions on synthetic spectacle which are to be found scattered throughout the great composer's theoretical works. And the very nature of Wagner's music dramas confronts producers with the task of creating internal unity of sound and sight in the production.

The problem of the synthesis of the arts is of vital concern to cinematography, the field in which I am principally engaged. Men, music, light, landscape, colour, and motion brought into one integral whole by a single piercing emotion, by a single theme and idea—this is the aim of modern cinematography. Although as yet there are all too few examples of the true cinematography of sound-and-sight consonance (only a few scenes, for instance in Disney's wonderful *Snow White* or individual scenes from *Alexander Nevsky*, such as the "Attack of the Knights"), advanced cinema directors are engrossed in the problem of spectacle synthesis, experimenting in this field and accumulating a certain amount of experience.

Wagner's unusually descriptive music raises particularly keenly the question of seeking and finding the adequate visual image. The solution of the sound-and-sight problems involved in the production of Wagnerian music dramas is of tremendous interest and is capable of enriching the sound cinema, especially at a time when the latter is beginning to become not merely sound-and-sight cinema but colour and stereoscopic cinema as well.

Early cinematography was engendered by the theatre. Subsequently it came into sharp conflict with the theatre, relentlessly discarding everything faintly suggestive of the stage—even going to the point of dispensing with unified dramas and with the persons playing, the actors. But now, after the intensified "rehistrionization" of cinematography and the attempts to "cinematographize" the theatre that may be observed lately, there is again coming to the fore a mutu-

85

ally creative enrichment of both cinematography and the theatre—without the suppression of the spontaneity of either of them—that is leading both to the resolution of new artistic problems.

It is not for me to judge the measure in which success has been achieved in practice by a film director staging a music drama in the theatre.

Wagner's *Ring of the Nibelung* is wholly based on folk epic material. The material from which Wagner shaped his tetralogy holds a place in the epic lore of the German peoples equal to that held by the *Iliad* and the *Odyssey* in antiquity, *The Song of Roland* among the French, *The Knight in the Tiger Skin* among the Georgians, or *Djangar* in Kalmuck folk poetry.

In the splendid and majestic figures of the heroes of ancient folk lore, resurrected by Wagner, and in the very subjects and themes of the myth of *The Ring of the Nibelung*, the composer was able to express in poetic form ideas that are near and dear to us, ideas by which he was himself inspired in the period of the Revolution of 1848, in which Wagner himself took part. This revolution failed to bring liberation to the people, but although its outcome brought disappointment to Wagner, it was here that the composer found the inspiration for his tetralogy on the curse of gold, in which he envisaged not only the conflict of gods, men, dragons, and dwarfs for the possession of treasure, but primarily that curse which property brings down on men, property which inevitably urges men against each other, property which gives rise to all the misdeeds of "mythology and history", as Wagner himself writes.

The last part of the tetralogy, *The Twilight of the Gods,* symbolizes the death of the whole "world of murder and plunder, legalized by falsehood, deceit and hypocrisy", the world that the young Wagner abhorred. As is well known, Wagner subsequently abandoned these sentiments of his youth, but *The Ring of the Nibelung* preserves in the impassioned emotional quality of its music the tragedy of the great conflict between the human feelings of love and self-abnegation and the curse of property; the greatest of all his works, it expresses Wagner's purest and noblest feelings.

Significant in concept, Wagner's work is not a bare scheme based on a preconceived thesis. The heroes of the *Ring* are not abstractions; nor are they megaphones proclaiming the propaganda maxims of the author. The innermost meaning of the events is as much contained in the depths of Wagner's poetry as the very treasure that gives rise to the play of human passions which become so intertwined and grow so involved that we are wholly engrossed in the human side of the destinies of the characters he depicted. And within the limits of *The Valkyrie* their fate is profoundly tragic and human. Allow me to recall the subject of this opera.

In his childhood Siegmund lost his twin sister Sieglinde. He searches for her in vain. And finally, one day, pursued by enemies from whom he had desired to protect a girl as defenceless as his sister, he finds himself in the hut of Hunding. There he finds a beautiful woman languishing in bondage to an unloved husband. They fall in love with each other at first sight. Siegmund wishes to rescue her from her husband. When it turns out that Hunding, who has returned, is Siegmund's sworn enemy and that on the morrow he means to challenge the unarmed Siegmund to battle and to kill him, Hunding's wife administers a sleeping draught to her husband and flees with Siegmund. In an ecstasy of love, in passionate words of endearment, they tell each other the stories of their lives, from which it appears that Hunding's wife is actually Siegmund's long-lost sister Sieglinde for whom he has been searching so long.

In primitive society marriage between brother and sister was a normal and natural thing. But the tragedy of Siegmund and Sieglinde lies in the fact that they live in a transition period, when such love has already come under the ban. Thus their behaviour evokes the wrath of the gods.

Three moral and ethical points of view clash with each other in judgment on the behaviour of Siegmund and Sieglinde. The representative of one of them is Wotan, the ancient German personification of the forces of nature. He takes Siegmund, who, moreover, proves to be his son, under his protection. But he has to yield to the representative of another point of view—to his wife Fricka, the goddess who

87

protects the sanctity of the domestic hearth. He therefore orders the Valkyrie Brünnhilde, the executress of his will, to give Hunding, the injured husband, the victory in his duel with Siegmund.

But here the third point of view comes in: the point of view of Brünnhilde. Touched by the great love felt for Sieglinde by Siegmund, who is ready to give up all blessings hereafter in order to save his beloved, Brünnhilde rebels against the orders of her father, Wotan, and tries to give the victory to Siegmund.

Wotan's interference prevents her from carrying out her intention. Wotan punishes Brünnhilde: he deprives her of her godhead because she allowed human feelings to sway her so powerfully. Brünnhilde only manages to save Sieglinde and her future son, and is herself doomed to slumber on a solitary rock and to become the wife of the first man who wakes her. The only thing to which the wrathful father consents is to surround the rock with flames so that Brünnhilde shall not be won by a coward. Flames thereupon burst from the ground and surround the sleeping Brünnhilde. This concludes the first day of the *Ring*.

In the following musical drama, *Siegfried*, it falls to Siegfried, the youthful son of Siegmund and Sieglinde, the favourite hero of northern folk lore, to awaken Brünnhilde from her long slumber and to become her husband. But this, as well as the subsequent vicissitudes of the drama, falls outside the scope of *The Valkyrie*.

The humanity of the themes, the epic nature of the subject, the dramatic quality of the situations, and the poetical nature of the myth upon which the Wagnerian drama is based cannot but enchant the artist.

"It is harmonious, and let this fact become evident to you on the stage . . ." These words of Wagner's about music are the key to the scenic interpretation of his works.

The main task of the producer lies in the direct perception of the music and in its answering embodiment on the stage, for in no other music but Wagner's do thought and concept so utterly colour the element of music. Listening to *The Valkyrie*, or, rather, immersing oneself in its musical element, one may not only grasp the dramatic structure of the work but also sense the form in which it should be unfolded on the stage. Thus, the sensing of the music dictates the form of the production. Wagner's music calls for visual embodiment, and its visual embodiment must be incisively clear-cut, impalpable, frequently shifting, material.

Everything in *The Valkyrie* is activity and passion, which, even though it may be chained, is not directed inward; passion that strains outward and breaks out; passion that turns into action, into insubordination, into a conflict of wills, into a duel and the thunderous interference of higher powers, into a saturnalia of elemental forces and passions.

That is what Wagner himself wrote to Franz Liszt. *The Valkyrie,* this first day of the *Ring,* dictates the scenic solution of visibility, objectivity, activity, the mobility of men and scenery, the play of light and fire.

The music of *The Valkyrie* is impregnated with the sense of some ancient past—a past that never, it seems, existed. It has no archaisms, no stylization, and yet this atmosphere of the ancient past of mankind which suddenly makes itself felt before us is suggested by a number of miracle-working nuances. And, working on a new interpretation of the Wagnerian drama, we tried to convey this atmosphere of the past not by ethnographically transferring pictures of Nordic life to the boards of the opera theatre, but by delving deep not only into the characters of the personages of the drama, but also into the historical consciousness that gave birth to their system of thinking. Primitive man envisaged nature as an independent living being, now gracious, now austere, at times echoing his own feelings, at others opposing them, sometimes friendly, sometimes hostile to him.

In our production the lives of the heroes of the opera are echoed by the phenomena of nature—by a tree that seems just about to speak, by the mountains that rise up during the duel between Siegmund and Hunding, by the elemental force of the flames that range around Brünnhilde, and in the heavens by the thunder cloud that bears Wotan. That is how ancient man, the author of myths, folk lore, and epics, pictured nature's participation in his personal life.

It was this idea that prompted us to introduce one other element in our production—original pantomime choruses. Our aim was to convey through them the feeling that is typical of the period of epics, legends, and myths. That is the feeling that man is not yet cognizant of himself as an independent unit set apart from nature, as an individual that has already acquired independence within the collective body.

For this reason, in our production many of the characters are at certain moments enfolded, as it were, by these choruses, from which they seem inseparable, which vibrate with one emotion, one and the same feeling with them. Thus Hunding, the representative of the crudest, atavistic stage of the trible—when the tribe is still nothing more than a horde close to the flock, the herd, or the pack—appears surrounded by the myriopod, shaggy body of his pack, a body which on falling to the earth appears to be the hunting pack of a leader, and which on rising to its feet apears to be Hunding's encirclement—kinsfolk, armour-bearers, servants.

In just the same manner Fricka, his patroness and defender, comes upon the stage surrounded by a chorus of golden-fleeced half-sheep, half-men—partly like domesticated animals, partly like men who have abjured their own passions and have voluntarily put on the yoke of the tamed instead. Fricka exercises sole sway over them. Fawning in servile fashion, bent to the ground, whipped on by her, they swiftly pull her wraithlike and victorious chariot from the stage.

And whereas the first two mimic choruses, upon falling to the ground, spread along its surface, the third—the chorus of the Valkyries, indomitable and headstrong as their father Wotan—flies upward into the unclouded distance.

From the purely plastic angle these choruses have still another special task. They serve as something like a group connecting link between the individual human beings and the environment, that is, between the soloist and the substantial arrangement of the scenic space—the decorations. It was our idea that the decorations in this production should serve not merely for the ornamentation or artistic arrangement of the stage, not merely as laconic data on the place of the action, but as the support of the plastic action, just as that inimitable music which calls the performance as a whole into life serves as the sound support for it. In our production the decorations would be that part of the single dynamic whirlwind that engendered the music to whose lot it fell to congeal fast in the scenic space as machines and colours, steps and precipices, surfaces and planes, so as to serve as a support for the actions and deeds of the actors.

There is much I should like to say about the ideas that came from this absorbing work on the production of a Wagnerian opera, but I must not, by my "interpretations" as a theatrical producer, transfer into the sphere of reason that which sprang directly from the emotions.

Let us follow Wagner's behest: "... I believe that a totally true instinct saved me from striving too excessively to be clear: I see distinctly, by feeling, that too open a revelation of the author's concepts only hampers comprehension. ..."

condensed and translated by Bernard Koten

Eisenstein's great project, a book on direction to absorb the materials and ideas of his teaching programme, was continually going forward. The theme of the book was more than technical: this was to channel all his excitement and research in the creative process, in nature and in art—towards the new art of synthesis. In 1939 a fragment of his book was published as On Structure; *a year later another fragment,* Once More on Structure, *appeared. It is revealing to read these within the period of Eisenstein's publication, to listen to him using his powers of persuasion and logic to propose methods and viewpoints that were not then popular nor even acceptable.*

More Thoughts on Structure

In writing my book on direction I have noticed, among other questions, a curious fact. Namely, that in the realm of composition a dialectical position usually, somehow, finds its unity in opposition.

It finds its reflection in this circumstance, that *for any given composition using a direct solution there are also equally correct and impressive solutions that are in direct opposition.*

This phenomenon can also be found in the richest expressive manifestations of mankind—in nature itself.

Thus, for example, in a moment of terror a man not only retreats from the cause of his terror, but just as often, as if bewitched, he is drawn to the very thing that inspires his terror. The edge of a cliff "draws" us to it. The criminal is "drawn" to the scene of his crime, rather than fleeing from it. And so on.

And in composition, that draws its sustenance from the experience of actuality, this circumstance may be swiftly discovered in even the most trifling instances.

If, for example, it is decided that a certain moment in a rôle must lead to a delirious scream, we can say with conviction that that moment will be served just as powerfully— by a scarcely heard whisper. If rage is expressed by maximum movement, then an absolutely stony immobility will be no less impressive.

If Lear is strong in the tempest that envelopes his madness, then no less powerful will be the effect of a directly opposite solution: madness surrounded by the calm of "indifferent nature".*

Of two opposites one is usually more "saleable" and cus-

* This phrase of Pushkin's stimulated one of Eisenstein's most important essays, unpublished in his lifetime. See No. 296 in the Bibliography.—J. L.

tomary. And therefore it comes first to mind. The second acts more unexpectedly and more sharply, bringing with it an unaccustomed freshness. We can recall the stunning effect of Negro syncopated jazz, where the rhythmic principle was usually in contrast to what the European ear had been taught.

In his autobiography[1] Paul Whiteman writes:

... jazz is a method of saying the old things with a twist, with a bang, with a rhythm that makes them seem new ... The first beat in any bar, which normally is accented, is passed over, and the second, third or even fourth beats are accented.

This can be roughly illustrated with a familiar bar of music. Suppose we take "Home, Sweet Home". Here it is in its original form:

Now let us jazz it up:

Jazz quickly won popularity, but often the intrusion of similar "unusual" opposites is not smooth.

See what happened to Dumas *père* at the Théâtre-Français at a period when this theatre was still ignorant of *la poésie de l'immobilité*.

And Dumas shows us a vivid example in action of direct and opposite solutions in the composition of an actor's performance. It is described in his memoirs.

The famous Mlle Mars was to play in Dumas's new play, *Antony*. They could agree on nothing, nor could Dumas agree with the theatre, neither in the understanding of his drama, nor in the handling of its rehearsals. So he took the play to another theatre, where the rôle of Adèle was to be played by another leading actress, the young Dorval. The memoirs tell of the final rehearsals and performance of *Antony*:

> Madame Dorval had made the very utmost out of the part of Adèle. She enunciated her words with admirable precision, all the striking points were brought out, except one which she had not yet discovered. "Then I am lost!" ('Mais je suis perdue moi!') she had to exclaim, when she heard of her husband's arrival. Well, she did not know how to render those few words. And yet she realised that, if said properly, they would produce a splendid effect. All at once an illumination flashed across her mind.
>
> "Are you here, author?" she asked, coming to the edge of the footlights to scan the seats.
>
> "Yes . . . what is it?" I replied.
>
> "How did Mlle Mars say: 'Then I am lost!'?"
>
> "She was sitting down, and got up."
>
> "Good!" replied Dorval, returning to her place, "I will be standing, and will sit down."[2]

In the excitement of the successful première (3 May 1831) the actor Bocage forgot to move the armchair ready to receive Adèle, when she is overwhelmed at the news of her husband's arrival.

> But Dorval was too much carried away by passion to be put out by such a trifle. Instead of falling on the cushion, she fell on to the arm of the chair, and uttered a cry of despair, with such a piercing grief of soul wounded, torn, broken, that the whole audience rose to its feet.

The "opposite" solution justified itself no less powerfully than the "direct" one.

Of course, a purely mechanical opposition, not growing from *a genuine feeling of opposition within the phenomenon itself, or*—to be more exact—not growing from the possible contradictions *within the phenomenon's relationships,* can never be sufficiently convincing.

This would remain a superficial *game of contrasts* in relation to current acceptance, and could not possibly be lifted to the embodiment of a unified theme, if merely presented in the less usual of two equally possible and basic opposites. Yet the "formal" aspect of our first glance at the "opposite" structure in what Mme Dorval did—is only apparently "formal".

In actuality we can find in this little example of two treatments of one and the same movement an opportunity to examine the whole warring contradiction of two styles of acting, a struggle between the classicism of the champions of romanticism, a struggle that reflects the complex social processes of the beginning of the nineteenth century. The opposing solution in our example only reflects the opposing of a tradition, with which the "classical" actress Mars was departing from theatre history just as the "romantic" actress Dorval was arriving.

It is easy "arithmetically" to calculate a third solution that, regardless of its unexpectedness, could seem in opposition at the same time to *both* earlier solutions: to play this scene without a *sweep of movement* upwards or downwards—but, ignoring both, to use restrained movement and rely on intonation. But below the "arithmetic" of this lies a most complicated social process, reflected in that style of acting about which some of the first practitioners of this new theatre wrote to each other:

> Suffering ought to be expressed as it is in life—that is, not by the arms and legs, but by the tone and expression; not by gesticulation, but by grace.[3]

Perhaps it is not astonishing that what now appears to us as a possibly personal variation on a single scenic solution was once a type, the only possible stylistic solution. Actors came to other solutions only through a difficult struggle that was accompanied by the mastery of a new artistic ideology.

Quite unastonishing.

We are the heirs of the whole incredible fund of past human culture.

In its hues, in its stylistic peculiarities, in its genres, and simply in certain of its features, our art embraces all the experience which for the pre-synthetic stage of the history of arts appeared as leading banners for whole epochs, for whole styles, for whole stages of art ideology.

And art ideas that were once shaped on the battlefield of changing styles now appear as the means for variations and hues *within the unity of our style* of Socialist realism. Apart from all that is new and unprecedented in it, its particular works can catch fire from those *hues* that once were obligatory and then were doomed to be the sole possible and exhausted *colours*.

Naturally the conditions for an inner-based choice of this or that hue or this or that opposition within it depend now on what strength is applied and on which particular day. Similarly there can be exchanges with each other. That is what makes the example of Mlle Mars and Mme Dorval so apposite, not only in its circumstances of historic upheaval and changing styles.

Many other cases could be brought in evidence. To find analogies one does not have to stretch so far. In fact the most pertinent cases, available in quantity, are to be found on Soviet screens.

Both *Strike* and *Battleship Potemkin* are instances of stylistic particularity.

I can remember when the cycle *Toward Dictatorship,* though only one film was realized, was worked out stylistically. I can even remember where we discussed this. It was by the curved wall of the now demolished Strastnoi Monastery. Along it ran a path that led to "Kino Malaya Dmitrovka 6", noted for its showings of the most triumphantly successful American films. Here we saw *Robin Hood* and *The Thief of Bagdad, The Gray Ghost* and *The House of Hate.**

How to beat these "giants" of the American cinema—and just as we were taking our first timid steps in film-making?

* *The Gray Ghost* (1917, with Priscilla Dean and Eddie Polo) was the first U.S. serial to reach Russian audiences ; *The House of Hate* (1918) was also a serial, directed by George Seitz, with Pearl White.—J. L.

How could our young cinema be heard with a voice of its own, against the noisy roar of the American-European film industry that controlled all the channels of trade and production? Where could we find stories that would be just as sharp, if not sharper, than the plots of these American successes?

Where should we find native "stars" whose radiance could compete with whole "constellations" from America and Europe? And heroes whose originality would displace the accepted heroes of the bourgeois cinema?

The task was not one merely of making good films. The area of our task was much broader—the whole area of culture: to make an impact on bourgeois culture *by showing a contrasting culture and art.* To compel it to listen to and respect what was coming from the young Land of the Soviets, so enigmatic and so little known in those years to Europe and America.

An impetuous twenty-six-year-old thus sketched a promethean task for himself.

And the solution came—almost "mathematically".

A story sharper than the American ones? What could be sharper than to reject "story" altogether?

"Stars" superior to the American-European ones? How about doing the unthinkable for that time—making films without "stars"?

Individualities more significant than the current film-heroes? What if we should turn our backs on all that and build with quite different materials?

And in "countering" all—abolishing story, discarding stars—to push into the dramatic centre the mass as the basic *dramatis persona,* that same mass that heretofore had provided a background for the solo performance of actors.*

Thus by an almost formally "opposite" direction was formulated that stylistic peculiarity of our cinema which for many years served as its determining image.

Of course it would be naïve to suppose that "mathematics"

---

* In this connection let's not forget the reaction to the completed *Strike* of one of the oldest actors of the Russian cinema, the late Saltykov, whose approving comment after a screening was: "If only, against that background, there could be—me."

alone could give birth to that which was so characteristic and expressive of its time.

The liberation of the consciousness from all that representational structure linked to the bourgeoisie; a new world revealed in the entrance of a new class upon the arena of world history; October—and the rising ideology of the victorious proletariat: these are the premises from which arose the possibilities of a new language in culture and the arts.

And from this came the opposition and interchange of those two class ideologies. Such oppositions always reveal those stylistic peculiarities in which the art of these classes speak at their moment of sharpest impact.

It is quite impossible to find and reveal simply "formal" opposing solutions to these deep inner roots.

This is a far broader phenomenon than is assumed by those who love to draw imaginary pictures of how works of art are created, a fact they could prove for themselves by observing this creation. Many such writers try to expound the history of the creation of a work by fitting it into some rigid formula. Too little is written honestly and frankly about how this or that work was conceived and realized.

Anecdotal details, surprises or apparent accidents need remove nothing from the recognized basic principles of a developing work of art. Such genuine details of creative biographies convey a sense of life in the description of the process of creation. This cannot be an abstract schema, certainly not with such a full-blooded process as creation.

Here is another instance of such a frank page of creative autobiography — Vladimir Nemirovich-Danchenko's — one that is quite near to that which was discussed above:

> During the same season as that of Chekhov's *Sea-Gull* I produced *The Price of Life*—in Moscow in the *benefice* of Lensky, in St Petersburg in that of Savina. In Moscow the success of the play was foreshadowed from the first act, and developed into an ovation.
>
> ... The price of life, the question of suicide, naturally presupposes that the author is consumed with this tremendous moral problem, that he has been seized with the

phenomenon of suicide epidemics, and so forth. Actually, such was not the case. The author, during the summer, sat in his house in the village and said to himself that it was now absolutely necessary to write a play—necessary according to various earthly considerations. What play he himself did not yet know. It was necessary to find a theme. And one day he put before himself the question: "Contemporary plays usually end in suicide, but suppose I take a theme and *begin* with a suicide? A play that begins with a suicide; is it not an engaging idea?"

And then, somehow, I put before myself this problem: "Playwrights always write so that the third act shall be the act of conflict, the most effective act—a big ensemble scene . . . But suppose the most important act should be built on a duet? Yes, so that the entire act might be played, say by Yermolova and Lensky, and yet be thoroughly absorbing . . ."

And when the plot of the play had already been told, suicide still remained the spur for dramatic situations. It must be remembered that two acts had already taken place, yet the author had not yet begun to reflect upon the moral essence of the "price of life"; this problem must of itself rise above the images, the scenes, the fragments of observation, even as the mist rises above the bogs, the hillocks, and the shrubs . . .

The Griboyedov prize—for the season's best play—was awarded to *The Price of Life* . . .[4]

In conclusion I'd like to submit one more example of opposite structure, as a means of simply producing something "original". Here the matter is one of terminology, which often takes a thing to the opposite extreme. The term here is "an opposite generality".

Somehow our conversation moved on to Dostoyevsky. As we know, Turgenev did not like Dostoyevsky. To the best of my recollection this is how he spoke about him: "Do you know what an opposite generality is? When a man is in love, his heart beats faster; when he's angry, his face reddens, etc. But in Dostoyevsky everything is made deliberately contrary. For instance a man is about to

shoot a lion. What does he do? In actuality he grows
pale and tries to run away or hide himself. In any simple
tale, say by Jules Verne, for example, that's the way it
would be told. But Dostoyevsky tells it the other way.
The hunter blushes and stands still. That's an opposite
generality. This is a cheap way to pass for an original
writer."⁵

I'll neither quarrel nor agree with Turgenev. But I know
that some film-makers, in order "to pass for an original",
resort to this same method. Thus, for example, most of
Marlene Dietrich's "mystery" was built by Sternberg exactly
on this principle. In such films as *Morocco*, all the mystery
of her personality was based on the simple device of having
her pronounce all her affirmative remarks . . . in a questioning tone. "You've already dined?" is answered by Marlene's
attenuated "Yes-s-s" in which one can hear the question-
mark. And the audience at once supposes Heaven knows
what secret relationships and a whole multitude of mysterious motives. And this too is only—"an opposite generality"

To penetrate to all the strata that lie beneath this phenomenon is not within the scope of this essay, but I want to
pursue it into one relevant area. For this rule on the correct-
ness of an opposite solution, as observed in the conditions
noted above, is true for more than particular solutions. It
can be justified in whole systems of principles that are connected with certain compositional structures.

The pathos construction as sketched in my previous
essay* would not be complete without presenting an example of an opposite type of structure—leading, however, to
an effect of pathos that is equally strong.

The pathos of a theme can also be resolved through the
two oppositions that are always at the disposal of the
compositional structure.

* This essay, *On Structure,* was translated as "The Structure of
the Film" in *Film Form.* The quotations that follow are from that
translation.
Russian uses of the terms *pathos* and *pathetic* are closer to their
original Greek roots—to suffer, to go through passion—than to
modern English usage.—J. L.

In the example from *Potemkin* I showed the *direct method* in the construction of pathos.

The basic indication of a pathetic composition is that for each element of the work there must be maintained the condition of "going out of oneself" and passing into a new quality. I drew attention to the behaviour of a man in this state:

Seated—he stands. Standing—he collapses. Motionless—he moves. Silent—he cries out. Dull—he shines. Dry—he is moistened by tears . . . etc.

Of his speech I wrote:

The unorganized customary flow of speech, made pathetic, immediately invents the pattern of clearly behaviouristic rhythm; prose that is also prosaic in its form, begins to scintillate at once with forms and turns of speech that are poetic in nature . . . etc.

And, finally, the sequence of the "Odessa steps" was analysed in detail to show these conditions applied to composition. All this demonstrated the "direct method" in constructing pathos.

For an "opposite" structure, producing a similar effect, we can take a quite different example: also a film, one of high socialist pathos—*Chapayev*.

However, if anyone, after reading my previous essay, should try to apply that research on *Potemkin* directly to *Chapayev*, he would place himself in an extremely embarrassing position. A formula doesn't fit. In this case he would find that either the formula would have to be put "under suspicion"—or deny the fact that *Chapayev* is pathetic. Both one and the other would be a mistake.

For the secret lies in the fact that *Chapayev* is built on the *second opposition*, through which can be seen that a unity for both bases is the principle of a pathetic construction.

For such accomplished works as *Chapayev* we are right to expect to find within the work itself a "key" scene, where one of the decisive inner technical and stylistic conditions invariably "bursts through" to the action itself, or to the dialogue or in the dramatic situation. Such a scene or phrase must be one of the most memorable, one of the most "characteristic" for the film.

In such a scene the key must open the base of the theme itself. This should also function as a key to the correct understanding of composition as an embodiment of this particular theme.

This was the justification of the "Odessa steps" in *Potemkin*: the cumulative point of the film's drama, it seemed also the sharpening point for the compositional movements, advancing towards a disclosure of their "secret" and leading to a revelation of the method itself.

I believe that *Chapayev*, notwithstanding all the rich drama of the work, will show its "method" most characteristically in one of its *least* dramatic episodes.

In the episode of *"Where should the commander be?"*

It is precisely in this episode that we see introduced into the practice of our Soviet cinema something new—in principle, in style and in quality.

It is characteristic of the *pathos* of *Chapayev* that its hero is not put on a pedestal. That the hero is shown as not separated from the humans around him, as not standing over other people, not leaping ahead of other people. Here the hero is shown as flesh of his class's flesh; within it; with it; not only *leading* it, but also *listening* to it—a genuine people's hero.

This could be the "ecstatic" image of an ordinary soldier who *from his place in the ranks* breaks *forward*: a hero. In such a hero we can feel that he is—us; that he is each one of us, ordinary soldiers, too. Along with this feeling there is no lowering of the hero, no levelling. The hero remains aware of his relationship to the ranks—and his relationships to all people.

There is a remarkable scene in Abel Gance's *Napoleon*.

Napoleon, still as General Bonaparte, is reviewing the troops after some victory in Italy.

In the front rank there is a rank-and-file former friend (excellently played by Kolin) of Napoleon. He boasts to the soldiers beside him of his intimacy with Napoleon.

He will prove it: he will break discipline by taking a step forward from his rank, and nothing will happen to him.

102

He takes this step forward.

Bonaparte approaches on a galloping horse.

Bonaparte sees the transgressor.

The horse is drawn up short.

Bonaparte recognizes the transgressor.

A dead pause.

A brief, harsh command.

And . . . the whole rank of soldiers takes a step forward.

The horse turns sharply. Napoleon gallops off.

Kolin faints in the arms of his mates . . .

And a film treatment that forces Chapayev to step back, to stand in the same rank with the rest, is essentially a step by which he forces all to sound in key equally with him as heroes. For in Chapayev there is no distinction between the general-Bonaparte and the soldier-Kolin.

We found the key scene of the drama not in a dramatic scene.

This in itself is significant from the viewpoint of those speculations that I presented on the "opposite" solution of pathos in this film. Let us look into that circumstance more intently.

In the episode the argument is about where the commander should be. The argument develops from the group's general agreement that the commander's place is *ahead*, with drawn sabre. Only Chapayev, out of his military wisdom, says that this is *not always so*, that there are times when the commander ought to be *behind*, in order to confront the pursuing enemy—and then once more be ahead.

What a lesson in dialectic struggle!

And the researchers into pathos who wish to propagate a mechanical view on pathos as identical in *Potemkin* and *Chapayev* could learn a lesson in the dialectics of composition from the film of *Chapayev* itself.

In the developing circumstances of the film's battles we see that the commander who should be *ahead* must also be *behind*. And these two opposites of his locations, penetrating each other through the film's action, are finally, to an equal degree, summed up in unity—in the commander's behaviour in battle.

Thus through the inner content of the theme the structure

of pathos must be "tearing along with drawn sabre before him", and also "disposed behind", i.e., developed not through contrasts, as in *Potemkin*, but through contrasting oppositions.

Both, penetrating each other, merge in a unity of that general method of pathetic composition that I described in the previous essay and which remains true, independently of the fact that it is on one of two possible oppositions that the pathetic structure of this or that work can move.

In the previous essay I produced the example of the behaviour of a man in ecstasy, a man consumed by pathos.

I spoke about eyes suddenly full of tears. I spoke about silence bursting into shouts. I spoke of immobility suddenly transformed into applause.

I spoke of *prosaic* prose, unexpectedly changing into the structure of poetry.

But would not a *reversal* of these phenomena also correspond to that formula of "going out of oneself"?

Shining eyes, suddenly dry. A paroxysm of cries, suddenly hushed. Applause, abruptly ceased.

Fully and appropriately elevated poetic speech, suddenly sounding like . . . ordinary prosaic conversational speech.

Doesn't this remind us of the time when Russian names unexpectedly appeared in the pages of novels, hitherto peopled by Héloïse, Clarissa, Aline, Pauline and Céline?

. . . Tatyana was her sister's name:
For the first time in any novel
It humbly asks romantic fame . . .[6]

There is, of course, no analogy here in content. We are speaking of a completely different historical matter.

As for the high images in pathetic films of the first type one cannot say that our cinema behaved like Tatyana's mother:

She used a sing-song voice; and, posing,
Praskovya she would call "Pauline" . . .

It would be just as untrue and offensive for our cinema to say that with the arrival of *Chapayev* our cinematography

. . . called "Akulka" the former Céline . . .

Yet if we wish, however ironically, to equate the poetic speech of our cinema with "Céline", and its high prose, humbly, with "Akulka", then we may have found *Chapayev's* place.

Actually *Chapayev* speaks of things that we are used to hear only with the structures of a hymn, of elevated speech, of verse—but says them in simple conversational speech. The heroics of its story might have sounded the drum; but composition forced its exposition from the "elevated writing" that would have been natural and appropriate for it —into an everyday prosaic structure.

Engels popularized the memory of M. Jourdain who was quite astonished to realize that he had always spoken prose.

It could be said of *Chapayev*'s story that, though it does not pursue that aim, its essence is poetic.

Poetry for such an inner-excited subject is just as obvious and usual as a prosaic structure of speech for an unexcited person.

And the shift from a naturally anticipated elevated style to a deliberately prosaic quality—this is the same sort of jump from quality to quality as in the more customary reverse order, a leap from spoken prose into the dimension of oratory.

Here are examples of two orators:

One of them snatches a certain phenomenon from life. In itself this would be quite normal. It seems natural and requires no extra thought. It seems contemporary and commonly prosaic. And then he discloses the power of pathos in fiery speech as he plucks all coverings from the phenomenon, sublimating this particular thing, this solitary instance on to the plane of a universal generalization, revealing all the significance concealed at its core.

We can't imagine this first orator without pathos—even with so "natural" a phenomenon as the exploitation of one class by another—or even with such a decisive moment as: to take or not to take power in one's hands. This is the fiery pathetic style of the speeches and editorials of Lenin.

Then let us take an opposite case. The revolution is now victorious. Socialism is being constructed. We are making the transition to Communism. The fulfilled thousand-year dream of generations of oppressed peoples is written into the unforgettable articles of the Stalin Constitution.

These very lines blaze, resound, glow with enthusiasm. And their high pathos is achieved when they are uttered . . . in a low voice, with even intonation, almost devoid of gesture.

This is the pathos style of a conquering October.

This is the pathos style of a victorious October.

This is the pathos style in the report of the Central Committee preceding a congress.

The pathos style of a conquering October is reflected in the compositional structure of *Potemkin.*

The pathos style of a victorious October is reflected in the compositional structure of *Chapayev.*

Just as the victories of Bolshevism before October and after are united in method, so the pathos structures of *Potemkin* and *Chapayev* are equally united in method.

Once more let us recall that the opposite is *not chosen arbitrarily by the author.* It is always historically dictated by the epoch, by the moment.

There was a time when I was much abused because I divided the first fifteen years of Soviet cinema into three five-year periods, each with its specific traits and sharply distinguished in physiognomy from the others.*

Regardless of whether I was right or wrong, it is now established that there must be a detailed new treatment of the history of our cinema.

But the unity of stylistic principles in whole groups of films, "leading" the specific periods—that is now beyond question. So this matter makes some progress, especially in regard to those indications of pathetic style that I've now outlined in these two essays.

Strike, Potemkin, Mother, Arsenal are films of the first type of pathos.

Chapayev, the *Maxim* trilogy, *Baltic Deputy* are vivid examples of another, *opposite* pathetic composition.

In considering this it is interesting to note with what

* In his essays, "The Middle of Three" and "At Last!" (Nos. 116 and 114 in the Bibliography).—J. L.

degree of firmness this or that film is attached to this or that stylistic method.

In the fine *Baltic Deputy*, for example, one observes that when it departs from the characteristics defined by its manner of pathetic style, it becomes compositionally helpless. For this reason the film's finale—the departure for the front —insoluble by the "second method", seems incomparably below the rest of the film.

Something similar can be detected in *We From Kronstadt*. In the scenario the scene of the landing was splendidly conceived, but in execution it was unable to rise to the necessary pathetic power of a composition of the "first order". Incidentally, of this film as a whole it can be said, paradoxically, that its scenario attaches it to the first method, but through its director's sympathies and tendency it leans to the second.

In the fourth five-year period that is now closing (1935–1940) it is interesting to note that alongside high examples of the second type of pathetic style—in *Lenin in October* and *Lenin in 1918*—it also returned to enrich the first type of pathetic composition. Both *Alexander Nevsky* (1938) and *Shchors* (1939) provide new aspects for the tradition of pathetic style in the pre-*Chapayev* era of *Potemkin* and *Arsenal*.

We can detect in this that some historical "principle" must have "powered" this change. And the historical determination of the stylistic peculiarity of both these films is now clear. The climactic creative period of their production coincided with a tremendous patriotic surge of our whole country—with that flaming patriotism that is bound in our memories to the heroic battle at Lake Hassan. This militant pathos, touching all the people of the U.S.S.R., determined the methodological direction that embodied the pathetic style of both films.

Built by the patriotic enthusiasm of millions of people, these two films—*Nevsky* and *Shchors*—stand as the pylons of a gate through which, in the next five-year period, will newly surge towards us films of a great unfolding of the first type of pathos.

*　　*　　*

Many films of this type are mentioned by title in the thematic plans of the studios. Many are already in the scenario stage—and some in production. They do not interfere with films of the second type—they don't even engage in polemics with them. They compete with them, and successfully, in attracting the interest of the spectator.

And they immeasurably broaden the diapason of our cinema's stylistic possibilities.

The next four years were years of war. In the autumn of 1941 the Mosfilm studio was evacuated to Alma-Ata, in Soviet Asia, and with it went Eisenstein with his preparations for an historical tragedy, Ivan the Terrible. *In the difficult circumstances of the temporary studio, work went very slowly and the film was unfinished when the studio returned to Moscow in 1944. Moreover, the plan for the film had grown larger; begun as a two-part film, it was now to be in three parts. Part One was released on 30 December 1944 with success. While Part Two was being completed, Eisenstein contributed essays to two volumes on* The History of World Film Art: *these were his estimates of the work of Griffith and of Chaplin.*

Charlie the Kid

The Kid. The name of this most popular of Chaplin's films is worthy to stand beside his own name; it helps to reveal his character just as the names, "The Conqueror", "The Lion Heart", or the "Terrible", themselves designate the spirit of William who conquered the Great Britain of the future, the legendary courage of Richard of the Crusades, or the cunning Moscovite Tsar, Ivan IV Vasilievich.

Neither Direction; nor Method; nor Tricks; nor Comic

Technique: none of these things move me. I do not wish to probe these things.

In considering Chaplin, one's main aim must be to fathom that structure of thought which sees phenomena in so strange a fashion and responds to them with images of equal strangeness. And within that structure to discern that part which exists as a perception of the outside world, before it becomes a concept of life.

In short, we shall not concern ourselves with Chaplin's world outlook but with that perception of life which gives birth to the unique and inimitable conceptions of what is called Chaplinesque humour.

The fields of vision in a rabbit's eyes overlap behind the back of his head. He sees behind him. His lot being to run away rather than track down, he doesn't complain about that. But these fields of vision do not overlap each other in front. In front of the rabbit is a piece of space it does not see: a rabbit running forward may bump into an obstacle right in front of it.

The rabbit's outlook on the world is different from ours. The sheep's eyes are placed in such a way that its fields of vision do not overlap at all. The sheep sees two worlds—the right and the left, which do not merge into a visual whole.

Thus, a different kind of vision produces a different kind of picture-image.

Not to speak of the higher transformation of *vision* into a *perception* and then to a *point of view* which comes about the moment we rise from the sheep and rabbit to Man, with all his accompanying social factors. Till finally all this is synthesized into a world-outlook, a philosophy of life.

How those eyes see.

Extraordinary eyes.

The eyes of Chaplin.

Eyes able to see in the forms of careless merriment an Inferno as fierce as Dante's or the *Caprichos* that we were shown in *Modern Times*.

That is what excites me.

That is what interests me.

That is what I wish to find out.

With what eyes does Charlie Chaplin look on life?

The peculiarity of Chaplin consists in the fact that, despite his grey hairs, he has preserved a "child's outlook" and a spontaneous perception of events.

Hence his freedom from the "manacles of morals" and his ability to see in a comic spectacle that which causes others' flesh to creep.

Such a trait in an adult is called "infantilism".

Hence, the comedy of Chaplin's situations is based mainly on their infantile treatment.

To this point, however, there are two reservations:

This is not the only mode of treatment Chaplin uses.

And he is not the only one who uses it.

True, we were not trying so much to find his modes of treatment as to find out "the secret of his eyes", the secret of his outlook, the embryo from which any type of treatment can grow.

But first let us discuss the reason why, out of all the means available to him, Chaplin chooses this particular method of achieving a comic effect, and by this choice becomes the most representative figure of American humour.

Particularly because, through this trait of infantile humour, he becomes the most American of all American humorists. And I don't mean by this that, as is often said, the mentality of the average American is no higher than that of a 14-year-old!

In his *Dictionnaire des idées reçues* Flaubert did not include the word "infantilism".

Otherwise he would have written, as he did of Diderot: "Diderot—always followed by d'Alembert."

Infantilism is always followed by "escape" from reality.

In this case it is particularly to the point, for the same impulse to run away, driving Rimbaud from Paris to Abyssinia or Gauguin to Tahiti is, of course, able to drive one from the New York of today, only much further.

The fetters of "civilization" are now spread over such a wide area that one meets with exactly similar Ritz Hotels (and not only hotels) in all the great centres of Europe and the United States, and even in the most secluded corners of the island of Bali, in Addis Ababa, in the tropics, and amidst the eternal snows. The wings of "geographical" escapism have been cut by the busy air-routes. Only "evolutionary" escapism is left: a downward course in one's own development. All that is left is a return into the circle of ideas and feelings of "golden childhood", a regress into infantilism, an escape into personal childishness.

In a strictly regulated society with strictly defined canons this urge to escape to freedom from the fetters of "the-once-and-for-all strictly laid down and established" must be especially strong.

Remembering America, two things come to my mind: the test for a driving licence; and a story from a students' magazine. In both cases: an examination.

In the first you are given a questionnaire.

The questions are to be answered simply "Yes" or "No".

The questions are put not like this: "What is the maximum speed at which you should drive past a school?" but like this: "Should one drive past a school at a higher speed than 30 miles an hour?"

The answer expected is "No".

"Should one approach a main road from a secondary road and cross it without waiting at the crossing?"

The answer expected is "No".

Similar questions are also given demanding "Yes" for an answer.

But nowhere will you find a question: "On approaching a main road from a side road, what do you do?"

The examinee is nowhere expected to think independently or to arrive at an independent conclusion.

Everything is reduced to automatic memorizing, to a reply of "Yes" or "No".

No less interesting is the automatic way the exam papers are checked.

Over the questionnaire a graph paper is placed with a perforated square matching wherever the answer "yes" should be placed.

Then a second perforated graph paper, punched to match the answer "No".

111

Just two glances by the examiner are enough:

Do the punched-out squares of the first graph show only the positive answers? And the second, negative answers?

A wonderful invention, one would think, for standardizing the issue of driver's licences.

But . . .

Here in a students' magazine is a funny story about how a class is examined at a University.

Everyone holds his breath and listens.

They listen to the sound of a typewriter . . . being typed by a blind student.

There are two taps. Then—three.

The whole room writes furiously.

In the first case the two letters mean "No".

In the second case the three letters mean "Yes".

Here is the same driver's test system. The same graphic grid. The same play on "Yes" and "No".

The mechanical grid and the blind student—the guide to the seeing ones—combine into one symbol.

The symbol of a whole mechanical and automatically intellectual system.

A kind of intellectual conveyor-belt system.

It is only natural to long to escape from it.

If Chaplin's physical exit from the single-track of machinism reaches its leaping representation in *Modern Times*, he achieves an intellectual and emotional exit by means of the *infantilism* method, with a similar liberating leap from the confines of intellectual machinism.

And in doing this Chaplin is a hundred per cent American. A general system of philosophy and its applied interpretation always reflects the basic nostalgia hidden in the heart of a people or a nation, existing in a definite social system.

"By their theories shall ye know them" might be said just as truthfully as "by their deeds".

Let us look at the typical American interpretation of the secret of comedy. And let us make clear that all theories and explanations of the comic are local and relative.

But here we are not interested in how much objective truth there is in his interpretation of the "secret of comedy".

We are interested in the specific American attitude to the problem of the comic, just as we are interested in the interpretations of Kant and Bergson primarily as personal and social "documents of the epoch", and not as universal truths and theories of the comic, objectively embracing absurdly tiny spheres of interpretation.

Our aim therefore will be to find out the most typically American *source* of the basic theory of the comic.

In searching for the "German" attitude to the comic we would turn to metaphysics. In search of the "English" attitude we would turn to the essayists who, through the mouth of George Meredith, consider humour to be the privilege of select minds, etc., etc.

In searching for the "American" approach and the most typical "American" understanding of humour, we shall not turn to metaphysicians or satirists, nor to philosophers or essayists.

We shall turn to—practice.

American pragmatism in philosophy reflects this avid search for what is, above all, *useful and applicable*—in everything that interests an American.

Hence countless books on methods of "conditioning people by means of humour".

I have read pages upon pages on the use of wit to arouse interest in a lecture or sermon, to increase the church collection; or the countless jokes with which a good salesman can inveigle a customer into buying a vacuum cleaner or a washing machine he doesn't need.

The recipe is strong, infallible and successful.

It all comes down to flattery, in one form or another, if not to pure bribery!

Often the recipe is supplied with a short theoretical introduction.

I will quote from a typical American book giving the perfect "American" approach to the basic appeal of humour.

We shall see that the method of the typical "American" comedian (despite his international fame) comes completely within this interpretation.

I shall not be sparing of quotations. Apart from their content, the very publication of such books is the clearest evidence of "Americanism", reaction to which gives birth to a particular form of comic treatment: that of escape from this kind of "Americanism".

There is a book written in 1925 by Professor H. A. Overstreet, Head of the Department of Philosophy, College of the City of New York. It is called *Influencing Human Behaviour* and is a symposium of lectures delivered at the request of a group of students.

As the author points out in his foreword, this request in itself was "unusual" and "significant".

And, indeed, the request was intelligent and businesslike and meant listening to a "course [of lectures] indicating how human behaviour can actually be changed in the light of the new knowledge gained through psychology". The authors of the request

> ... have in common an interest in understanding and improving social conditions. Besides this, and perhaps first of all, we desire to utilize as a part of our everyday technique of action such knowledge as modern psychology can furnish us. Our interest is not academic. We wish actually to function with such knowledge as we may gain.

In his preface the practical psychologist gives an answer in keeping with the technical nature of the request:

> The object of these chapters is to discover how far the data of modern psychology can be put to use by each of us in furthering what is really the central concern of our lives. That central concern is the same whether we be teachers, writers, parents, merchants, statesmen, preachers, or any other of the thousand and one types into which civilization has divided us. In each case the same essential problem confronts us. If we cannot solve it, we are failures; if we can, we are—in so far, at least— successes. What is this central problem? Obviously, it is to be, in some worthwhile manner, effective within our human environment.
> We are writers? Then there is the world of publishers, some of whom we must convince as to our ability. If we succeed in doing that, then there is, further, the reading

public. It is a bit of sentimental nonsense to say that it makes no difference at all if a writer convinces not even a single soul of his pertinence and value, so be it only that he "express" himself. We have a way of being over-generous with so-called misunderstood geniuses. True, this is a barbarian world; and the fine soul has its hard innings. . . . At any rate, as his manuscripts come back, he might well cease putting the blame on philistine publishers and public long enough to ask himself whether, indeed, he is not deficient in the very elementary art of making the good things he has to say really understandable.

We are businessmen? Then there are the thousands of potential customers whom we must induce to buy our product. If they refuse, then bankruptcy. . . .

We are parents? It may seem somewhat far fetched to say that the chief concern of a parent is to be accepted by his children. "What!" we cry, "aren't they *our* children; and aren't children required to respect their parents?" That, of course, is all old philosophy; old ethics; old psychology as well, coming from the day when children, like wives, were our property. Nowadays children are persons; and the task of parents is to be real persons themselves to such an extent that their children accept them as of convincing power in their lives. . . .

We need not specify further. As individuals, our chief task in life is to make our personality, and what our personality has to offer, effective in our particular environment of human beings. . . .

Life is many things; it is food-getting, shelter-getting, playing, fighting, aspiring, hoping, sorrowing. But at the centre of it all is this: it is the process of getting ourselves believed in and accepted. . . .

How are we to become intelligent about this? . . . Not by talking vaguely about goals and ideals; but by finding out quite specifically what methods are to be employed if the individual is to "get across" to his human fellows, is to capture their attention and win their regard, is to induce them to think and act along with him—whether his human fellows be customers or clients or pupils or children or wife; and whether the regard which he wishes to win is for his goods, or ideas, or artistry, or a great human cause. . . .

To become skilled artists in the enterprise of life—there is hardly anything more basically needful than this. It is to this problem that we address ourselves.[1]

Only by a great effort I restrained myself from placing numerous exclamation marks after each pearl of this hymn to pragmatism, bringing together a writer, a businessman and a parent in one category, and uniting a customer with a wife, or goods with ideas!

However, let us peruse further Professor Overstreet's guide, which at times reads like some of the best pages of Labiche or Scribe.

For example, the section on the "Yes-Response Technique":

The canvasser rings the door-bell. The door is opened by a suspicious lady-of-the-house. The canvasser lifts his hat. "Would you like to buy an illustrated History of the World?" he asks. "No!" And the door slams.

. . . in the above there is a psychological lesson. A "No" response is a most difficult handicap to overcome. When a person has said "No", all his pride of personality demands that he remain consistent with himself. He may later feel that the "No" was ill-advised; nevertheless, there is his precious pride to consider! Once having said a thing, he must stick to it.

Hence it is of the very greatest imporance that we start a person in the affirmative direction. A wiser canvasser rings the door-bell. An equally suspicious lady-of-the-house opens. The canvasser lifts his hat. "This is Mrs. Armstrong?"

Scowlingly—"Yes."

"I understand, Mrs. Armstrong, that you have several children in school.

Suspiciously—"Yes."

"And of course they have much home work to do?"

Almost with a sigh—"Yes."

"That always requires a good deal of work with reference books, doesn't it—hunting things up, and so on? And of course we don't want our children running out to the library every night ... better for them to have all these materials at home." Etc., etc.*

We do not guarantee the sale. But that second agent is destined to go far! He has captured the secret of getting, at the outset, a number of "yes-responses". He has thereby set the psychological processes of his listener moving in the affirmative direction. ...[2]

On page 259 of this "guide" is a businesslike presentation of the key, not to an abstract understanding of the principles of humour in general, but to an American understanding of the secret of humour, or rather, to that understanding of the nature of humour which is most effective in its application to an American.

Professor Overstreet starts with a correct observation:

... it is almost the greatest reproach to tell a person flatly that he has no sense of humour whatever. Tell him that he is disorderly, or lackadaisical, or homely, or awkward, he will bear up under these. But tell him that he has no sense of humour: it is a blow from which even the best of us find it difficult to recover.

People have a most curious sensitiveness in this regard.

I can confirm the truth of this observation by the most perfect example in the sphere of humour—Chaplin himself.

I am least of all interested in writing a theoretical treatise, and that is why I take any opportunity to leap to the sphere of personal reminiscences.

An evening in Beverly Hills. In Hollywood.

Chaplin is our guest.

We are playing a popular Hollywood game.

A cruel one.

This game is characteristic of Hollywood, where, in the small area of a few square miles, there is concentrated so much self-esteem, self-love and self-infatuation—deserved and undeserved, well-founded and unfounded, over-estimated and under-estimated, and all morbidly over-strained—enough to suffice for at least three-quarters of the globe.

This game is a variation of the popular game "Opinions". With this difference, that here the opinion is expressed in answers to a questionnaire, which give "marks", i.e. "cleverness": 5; "wit": 3; "charm": 4, etc.

The one who is chosen as the subject for such a questionnaire, must fill up his own, giving himself marks accordingly.

"A game of Self-Criticism" we would call it in Moscow.

The more so, as the whole point of the game is not the guessing, but simply the degree of divergence of marks between the general opinion and the subject's own opinion of himself.

A cruel game!

Especially, as the column "Sense of Humour" occupies an important place in it.

"The King of Humour" goes quietly to the kitchen, and putting on his glasses, somewhere near the refrigerator, fills up his questionnaire.

Meanwhile a surprise is being prepared for him.

Public opinion has rated his sense of humour as low as 4.

Does he see the humour of the situation?

He doesn't.

The guest is offended.

The distinguished visitor lacked a sense of humour when it touched himself; so the mark of 4 was well-deserved! . . .

Why is it, asks Professor Overstreet, that people are so sensitive when their sense of humour is in question?

Why is there this all but universal wish to be possessed of humour?

Apparently, the possession of humour implies the possession of a number of typical habit-systems. The first is an emotional one: the habit of playfulness. Why should one be proud of being playful? For a double reason. First, playfulness connotes childhood and youth. If one can be playful, one still possesses something of the vigour and the joy of young life. If one has ceased to be playful, one writes oneself down as rigidly old. And who wishes to confess to himself that, rheumatic as are his joints, his mind and spirit are really aged? So the old man is proud

118

of the playful joke which assures him that he is still friskily young.

But there is a deeper implication. To be playful is, in a sense, to be free. When a person is playful, he momentarily disregards the binding necessities which compel him, in business, morals, domestic and community life. . . . Life is largely compulsion. But in play we are free! We do what we please. . . .

Apparently there is no dearer human wish than to be free.

But this is not simply a wish to be free *from*; it is also, and more deeply, a wish to be free *to*. What galls us is that the binding necessities do not permit us to shape our world as we please. They hand out the conditions to us. We must take them or leave them. What we most deeply desire, however, is to create our world for ourselves. Whenever we can do that, even in the slightest degree, we are happy. Now in play we create our own world. . . .

To imply, therefore, that a person has a fine sense of humour is to imply that he has still in him the spirit of play, which implies even more deeply the spirit of freedom and of creative spontaneity.[3]

All subsequent practical recipes stem wholly from these premises.

As regards the specifically American notion of humour, the observations of Professor Overstreet are very apt and very correctly derived from the basis of specifically American psychology.

Legions of American comedians fit into the limits of the framework laid down for them.

And the most perfect of them fits it to absolute perfection, for he carries out these principles not only through infantilism, gags and tricks as such, but through the subtlety of his method, by offering an infantile pattern for imitation, psychologically infecting the spectator with infantilism and drawing him into the infantile paradise of the golden age of childhood.

The leap into infantilism also serves Chaplin as a means of psychological escape from the limits of the regulated, ordained and calculated world around him. It is insufficient.

Merely a palliative. But it is the utmost he can do with the possibilities available to him. In his longing for freedom, Chaplin has defined the only means for the complete escape of an artist from all limitations through his art, in his comments on—animated cartoons.

...in my opinion the cartoon is the only real art of today, because in it and only in it the artist is absolutely free to use his fantasy and to do whatever he likes to do with the picture.[4]

This, of course, is a cry: a cry of longing for the most perfect form of escape from the inhibiting fetters of just such conventions and necessities of reality as Professor Overstreet has so obligingly enumerated above.

Chaplin finds a partial satisfaction of his nostalgia for freedom by plunging psychologically into the golden age of infantilism.

Similarly, satisfaction is found by the audience whom he takes with him on his magic journey into the world of fiction, light-heartedness and tranquillity, which hitherto they knew only in the cradle.

The businesslike formality of America is in many ways a younger brother of the primness of Dickens's Mr. Dombey. And it is not surprising that England too, in its own style, had the inevitable "infantile" reaction. On the one hand it is expressed by the entry of the child into subject and plot: for it was in England that the child was first introduced into the sphere of literature, and whole novels or large parts of them are dedicated to representing the psychology of little children. Passing into the pages of a novel, Mr Dombey becomes "Dombey & Son", and many pages are dedicated to little Paul, David Copperfield, Little Dorrit, Nicholas Nickleby, to name but a few characters from this most popular British author alone.

England was also fertile soil for the profuse growth of infantilism in what is known as *nonsense* literature. In the immortal *Alice* of Lewis Carroll and in Edward Lear's *Book of Nonsense* are preserved the finest examples of that style, although it is well known that Swinburne, Dante

Gabriel Rossetti, and even Ruskin have left amusing examples of poetic nonsense in the form of limericks.

"Flight from reality . . ."

"Return to childhood . . ."

"Infantilism . . ."

In the Soviet Union we don't like these words. We don't like these concepts. We don't sympathize with the fact of their existence. Why?

Because in the very practice of the Soviet State we have approached the problem of the liberation of man and the human spirit from a completely different angle.

At the other end of the earth people have only one alternative: to flee, psychologically, fictitiously, back to the carefree abandon of childhood.

At our end of the world we do not flee from reality into fairy-tales; we make fairy-tales real.

Our task is not as grown-ups to plunge into childhood, but to make the children's paradise of the past accessible to every grown-up, to every citizen of the Soviet Union.

For no matter what paragraph of the Constitution we take, we are struck by the fact that here, systematically presented and state-legalized, are actually the very things which constitute the ideals of the golden age.

"The right to work."

What an unexpected conception was brought by this apparently paradoxical formula to those in whose minds work was inevitably linked with the idea of a heavy burden and an unpleasant necessity!

How new and unexpected the word "work" sounded in the company of words like "right", "glory", and "heroism"!

And yet this thesis, reflecting the real state of things in our country, the complete absence of unemployment and the ensuring of work for every citizen, is psychologically a wonderful resurrection, on a newly perfected—the most perfect—phase of human evolution, of just that premise, which at the very dawn, the Childhood of Mankind, in the past Golden Age seemed to man in his primeval, natural, and simple condition to be the natural conception of work and the rights and obligations involved therein.

We are the first to have completely cleared the road, so that all creative strivings can move along the path which the spirit of every individual thirsts for.

One does not need aristocratic connections to take up a diplomatic career.

To become a Civil Servant one doesn't have to be signed up at birth to a privileged public school, outside which such a political career is inevitably closed to him.

To achieve a high position in the Army one doesn't need membership of a caste or social position, and so forth.

Nowhere in the world hitherto has this happened, either in this fashion or on this scale.

And this is why from time immemorial man has had this dream, cast in the form of longings, myths, legends and songs, of the possibility of becoming whatever he wished.

Even more has been done in our country: the wise measures for the security of old age lifts from the backs of our citizens one more terrible burden—the burden of eternal fear of the future, feelings unknown to beasts, birds, flowers, or little children, who are completely free from care—the burden of worry about this much-vaunted "security" which weighs down every American, no matter what his material position or place in the social scale.

And that is why the genius of Chaplin could only be born at the *other* end of the earth, and not in the country where everything is done so that the golden paradise of childhood can become reality.

That is why his genius had to shine there, where the method and type of his comedy was a necessity, where the realization of the child's dream inevitably ends for the grown-up in nothing but disappointment.

"The Secret of his Eyes" is undoubtedly revealed in *Modern Times*. As long as he was concerned with the pleiad of the most beautiful of his comedies, of the clash of good and evil, of big and little, his eyes, as if accidentally and simultaneously lighting on the poor and the rich, laughed and cried in unison with his theme. But they apparently went contrary to their own theme when in the most modern times of American depression the good and evil "Uncles" turned out to be the real representatives of uncompromising social groups, at which the eyes of Chaplin first blinked, and then narrowed; but continued obstinately to look at modern times and phenomena in the old way. This led to a break in the style of things: in thematic treatment, to the monstrous and distorted: in the inner aspect of Chaplin himself, to a complete revelation of the secret of his eyes.

In the following discussion I do not wish by any means to say that Chaplin is indifferent to what is happening around him or that Chaplin does not (even though partly) understand it.

I am not interested in *what* he understands.

I am interested in how he perceives; how he looks and sees, when he is lost "in inspiration"; when he comes across a series of images of phenomena, which he is laughing at, and when laughter at what he perceives is remoulded into the forms of comic situations and tricks; and with what eyes one must look at the world, in order to see it as Chaplin sees it.

A group of delightful Chinese children are laughing.
One shot. Another. Close up. Mid shot. Again close up.
What are they laughing at?
Apparently at a scene taking place in the depths of the room.
What is taking place there?
A man sinks back on a bed. He is apparently drunk.
And a tiny woman—a Chinese—slaps him on the face furiously.
The children are overcome with uncontrollable laughter.
Although the man is their father. And the little Chinese woman their mother. And the big man is not drunk. And it is not for drunkenness the little wife is hitting him on the face.
The man is dead. . . .
And she is slapping the deceased on the face precisely because he has died and left to a hungry death her and the two little children who laugh so merrily.

That, of course, is not from one of Chaplin's films. These

are passing strokes from that wonderful novel by André
Malraux, *La Condition Humaine*.*

In thinking of Chaplin, I always see him in the image of
the Chinese children, laughing merrily to see how comically
the slaps of the little woman make the head of the big man
wobble from side to side. It is not important that the
Chinese woman is—the mother. That the man is—the
father. And it is not at all important that in general he is
dead.

In that is the secret of Chaplin.

In that is the secret of his eyes.

In that is his inimitability.

In that is his greatness.

*To see things most terrible, most pitiful, most tragic
through the eyes of a laughing child.*

To see the images of these things spontaneously and suddenly—outside their moral-ethical significance, outside
valuation, and outside judgement and condemnation—to see
them as a child sees them through a burst of laughter.

In that Chaplin is outstanding, inimitable and unique.

The sudden immediacy of his look gives birth to a comic
perception. This perception becomes transformed into a
conception. Conceptions are of three kinds:

A phenomenon genuinely inoffensive. And Chaplin's
perception clothes it with his inimitable Chaplinesque
buffoonery.

---

* The difference between this "quotation" and Malraux's text may
have an interesting explanation. Here is the passage, as translated
by Alastair Macdonald in the Penguin edition:

> Like the starving Russian, living almost next door to him, who
> one day found life as a factory-hand a little more intolerable
> than he could bear, and committed suicide; and whose wife,
> mad with anger, had slapped the corpse which was leaving her
> to her fate; with four children crouching in the corners of the
> room, and one of them saying: 'Why are you fighting?'
>
> (*Man's Estate*, p. 168)

As Eisenstein began this essay on Chaplin soon after Malraux
visited him to discuss their collaboration on a film to be based on
La Condition humaine, E's free quotation may be the only surviving fragment of the lost script prepared at that time. On the other
hand, and equally revealing, E's quotation may represent the way
he recalled the passage.—J. L.

A phenomenon personally dramatic. And Chaplin's perception gives birth to the humorous melodrama of the finest images of his individual style—the fusion of laughter with tears.

The blind girl will call forth a smile when, blindly, she douses Charlie with water.

The girl with her sight restored might appear melodramatic when, in touching him with her hand, she does not fully realize that before her is the one who loves her and gave her back her sight. And then within that very incident the melodrama may be comically stood on its head—the blind girl repeats the episodes with the *bon vivant*, saved by Charlie from suicide: in which the *bon vivant* only recognizes his saviour and friend when he is "blind" drunk.

Finally, *socially tragic phenomena*—no longer a childish amusement, not a problem for a mind, not a child's plaything—the comical-childish vision gives birth to a series of terrible shots in *Modern Times*.

The ability to *see as a child*—is inimitably, irrepeatably inherent in Chaplin personally. Only Chaplin sees this way. What is astonishing is this very power of Chaplin's sight to see piercingly and immutably through all the workings of professional cunning.

Always and in everything: from the trifle, *A Night at the Show*, to the tragedy of contemporary society in *Modern Times*.

To see the world thus and have the courage to show it thus on the screen is the attribute of Genius alone.

Though, incidentally, he doesn't even need courage.

He can *only* see it that way, and no other.

Maybe I stress that point too much?

Possibly!

We are people with a "conscious purpose", "conscious tasks".

And inevitably "grown-ups".

We are grown-ups and may have lost the ability to laugh at the comic without taking into consideration its tragic significance and content.

We are grown-ups who have lost the lawless age of childhood, when there were as yet no ethics, morals, higher standards of judgements, etc., etc.

* * *

Chaplin plays up to actuality itself.

It is the bloody idiocy of war in the film *Shoulder Arms*. The modern era of the most modern times in *Modern Times*. Chaplin's partner is by no means the big, terrible, powerful and ruthless fat man, who, when not filming, runs a restaurant in Hollywood.

Chaplin's partner, throughout his repertoire, is another. Still bigger, still more terrible, powerful and ruthless. Chaplin and actuality itself, partners together, a pair in harness, play before us an endless string of circus acts. Actuality is like a serious "white" clown.

He seems clever and logical. Observant and foresighted. But it is he finally who remains the fool and is laughed at. His simple, childlike partner Charlie comes out on top. Laughing carelessly, without being aware that his laughter kills his partner.

And like a young chemist who for his first analysis is unsuspectingly given a glass of pure water, and finds in it all kinds of conceivable and inconceivable ingredients, so in this pure water of infantilism, of spontaneous comic perception, everyone sees what he wishes.

As a child I saw a magician. He moved across the darkened stage like a faintly visible phosphorescent ghost.

"Just think of someone you want to see," cried this circus Cagliostro from the stage, "and you will see him!"

And in this merry little fellow, who is himself a magician and a wizard, they also "see". See what he had never put there at all.

An evening in Hollywood. Charlie and I are going to Santa Monica, to the local Lido Venice festival by the sea. Presently we are taking pot-shots at mechanical pigs. Taking cock-shies at coconuts and bottles. Chaplin, putting his glasses on in a businesslike fashion, will add up the score, so that he can take one big prize instead of a lot of small ones, an alarm clock instead of say, plaster casts of Felix the Cat.

And the boys will slap him on the back with a familiar "Hello, Charlie!"

Later, as we are sitting in the car, he pushes over a book to me. It's in German. "Tell me what it's all about," he says. For he doesn't know German. But he knows the book says something about him.

"Please explain."

It is a German expressionist booklet[5] and at the end is a play, dealing, of course, with a cosmic cataclysm: Charlie Chaplin pierces through the revived chaos with his stick, and points the way of escape beyond the world's end, politely touching his bowler as he does so.

I had to admit I got stuck in interpreting this post-war delirium.

"Please tell me what it's all about" is what he might have said about much that is said about him.

It is extraordinary how much metaphysical nonsense sticks to Charlie Chaplin.

I remember one more anecdote.

It belongs to the late Elie Faure, who wrote of Chaplin:

As he hops from one of these feet to the other—these feet so sad and yet so absurd—he represents the two extremes of the mind; one is named knowledge and the other desire. Leaping from one to the other he seeks the centre of gravity of the soul which he finds only to lose it again immediately.[6]

However, irrespective of the will of the artist, the social fate of his environment brings forth an unerringly true interpretation.

And so, one way or the other, Truth in the West chooses this little fellow with his comic outlook in order to replace what is comic for him with something that is by itself often beyond the category of the comic.

Yes, Chaplin's partner is reality.

What a satirist must introduce into his works on two planes, Chaplin the comedian presents on one plane. He laughs spontaneously. Satirical interpretation is achieved by the fade-in of Chaplin's grimace on the conditions that gave rise to it.

*   *   *

"You remember the scene in *Easy Street* where I scatter food from a box to poor children as if they were chickens?"

This conversation took place aboard Chaplin's yacht when we spent three days off Catalina Island, in the company of sea lions and flying fish, with underwater gardens that you could watch through glass-bottomed boats.

"You see, I did this because I despised them. I don't like children."

The author of *The Kid*, which made five-sixths of the globe shed tears over the fate of a neglected child, did not like children. Was he—a monster?

But who *normally* does not like children?

Why, children themselves.

The yacht plunges on its way. Its movements remind Chaplin of the rolling gait of an elephant.

"I despise elephants. To have such strength and to be so meekly submissive."

"Which animal do you like?"

"The wolf" came the unhesitating answer. And his grey eyes and the grey eyebrows and hair seemed wolf-like. His eyes peer into the sunny flickering of the Pacific Ocean sunset. Over the flickering ocean glides a destroyer of the U.S. Navy.

A wolf.

Obliged to live with the pack. But always to be alone. How like Chaplin that was! Always at war with his own pack. Each an enemy to the other and to all.

Maybe Chaplin doesn't really mean what he says. Maybe it's a bit of a "pose".

But if it is a pose, then, no doubt, it's that pose by which Chaplin with his inimitable and unique perception illuminates the world.

Six months later, on the day I was leaving for Mexico, Chaplin showed me the rough cutting copy, as yet without sound, of *City Lights*.

I was sitting on Chaplin's own black oilcloth chair. Charlie himself was busy: at the piano and with his lips, he was filling in the missing sound of the picture. Charlie (in the film) saves the life of a drunken millionaire who is trying to drown himself. The saved one only recognizes his saviour when he is drunk.

Funny?—tragic.

That is Saltykov-Shchedrin. That is Dostoievski.

The big one beats the little one. He is beaten up.

At first—man by man. Then more—man by society.

Once, long ago, there was a widely popular photograph in either the London *Sketch* or the *Graphic*.

"His Majesty the Baby," was the title under it.

The photograph depicted a surging flood of street traffic, in Bond Street, the Strand or Piccadilly Circus, suddenly freezing at the lift of a "Bobby's" hand.

Across the street goes the child, and the flood of traffic humbly waits, until His Majesty the Baby has crossed from pavement to pavement.

"Stop for His Majesty the Baby!" one wants to shout to oneself, when attempting to approach Chaplin from a social-ethical and moral position in the widest and deepest sense of these words.

"Stop."

Let's take His Majesty as he is!

* * *

Chaplin's situations, after all, are just the same as those children read about in fairy stories, where an array of tortures, killings, fears and terrors are inevitable accompaniments.

Their favourite heroes—the terrible Barmaley ("He eats little children"), the Jabberwocky of Lewis Carroll, Baba Yaga and Kashei the Immortal.*

Stories take time to read. And their quintessence, for lighter reading, is distilled from verses.

Thus in the nurseries of England and America persists through the ages a merry obituary of "Ten Little Nigger Boys", who one after the other, in verse after verse, die all kinds of deaths.

* Russian folk-tale characters: Barmaley is the equivalent of the "Wicked Ogre", Baba Yaga to the "Horrid Witch" and Kashei the Immortal to the "Superman Hero".—H.M.

And, what is more, without any guilt at all and without any reason whatsoever.

 a bumble bee stung one, and then there were five.

five little nigger boys going in for law:
one got in chancery, and then there were four.

four little nigger boys going out to sea;
a red herring swallowed one, and then there were three.

three little nigger boys walking in the zoo;
the big bear hugged one, and then there were two.

two little nigger boys sitting in the sun;
one got frizzled up, and then there was one.

one little nigger boy living all alone;
he got married, and then there was none.

Incidentally, it may be that this last line contains the "significance" of the whole nursery rhyme; Marriage is the end of childish infantile existence—the last little boy dies and an adult emerges!

However, the tendency we are discussing is still more clearly seen in the collection of Harry Graham's *Ruthless Rhymes for Heartless Homes* (the last London edition was the nineteenth!).

This dedication serves it as a foreword:

With guilty, conscience-stricken tears,
I offer up these rhymes of mine,

To children of maturer years
(From seventeen to ninety-nine)
A special solace may they be
In days of second infancy.

The verses, addressed to those who have fallen into the r second childhood, are made according to all the canons dear to—first childhood.

The Stern Parents
Father heard his Children scream,
So he threw them in the stream,
Saying, as he drowned the third,
"Children should be seen, *not* heard!"

Mr Jones
"There's been an accident!" they said,
"Your servant's cut in half; he's dead!"
"Indeed!" said Mr Jones, "and please
Send me the half that's got my keys."

One could write a whole dissertation on Anglo-Saxon humour as compared to the "Slavonic Soul", if, in connection with the last example, one remembers the dramatic treatment of Chekhov's short story "Sleepy". There a girl-nurse—herself only a child—chokes a child given her to look after, because the child cries at night and won't let her sleep. And all this under the warm peaceful reflections of the green-shaded oil lamp. . . .

But one way or another—in the dramatic description of the adolescent girl, in the fantastic structure of the Grimms' Fairy Tales or in the careless amusement of *Ruthless Rhymes*—all have grasped the most important thing in child psychology and the child soul, that which Leo Tolstoi long ago pointed out.

Maxim Gorky recorded Tolstoi's words:

. . . [Hans] Andersen was very lonely. Very. I don't know his life. It seems to me he lived, travelled a lot, but this only confirms my feelings—that he was lonely. And for that very reason he turned to children, although mistakenly, as if children would feel sorry for a person more grown up. Children don't feel sorry for anything, they are incapable of feeling sorry . . .

And all specialists in the child soul say the same.

And it is interesting to note that it is this particularly which lies at the bottom of children's jokes and stories. Yelena Kononenko writes of Moscow children: 'Grandad, will you see the New Moscow? What do you think, will you still live to see it?' . . . Vladilev asked cruelly. 'And I see that presently he is confused, understanding a little that he should not have asked the old man that question. Obviously he is a little ashamed and sorry for Grandad. But speaking generally he is not sorry for old men and, when kids in the yard said that old people would be made into glue, he laughed till the tears ran and asked me slyly how much glue could be made out of Grandad. . . .'

Kimmins writes about English and American children. His conclusions are based on a colossal quantity of statistic material. In the section of his work dealing with "What Young Children Laugh At" we read:

> The misfortunes of others as a cause of laughter are frequently referred to by young children, and form the basis of many funny stories. With children of 7 years of age, about twenty-five per cent of the boys' stories, and sixteen per cent of the girls' are of this nature. At 9 years of age there is a decrease to about eighteen and ten per cent respectively.[7]

But this concerns only *stories*. A description of similar *facts* continues to retain their mirth-invoking effect: they are "in special favour during the period of rapid growth from 12 to 14 years of age".

In another work Kimmins, in dealing with "The Child's Attitude to Life" on the basis of an analysis of children's stories, quotes this typical story, attributed to the medium-aged groups:

> "A man was shaving, when a sudden knock was heard at the door; this startled him, and he had the misfortune to cut off his nose. In his excitement he dropped his razor, which cut off one of his toes. A doctor was called

in and bound up the wounds. After some days the bandages were removed, when it was found that the nose had been fixed on to the foot and the toe on to the face. The man made a complete recovery, but it was very awkward, because every time he wanted to blow his nose he had to take his boot off."[8]

This situation is exactly in the spirit of the English pantomime Pierrot (so typically English), which so amazed Baudelaire, accustomed to the French Debureau. Here is what he wrote:

These were the dizzy heights of exaggeration.

Pierrot passes a woman who is washing her door-step: after rifling her pockets, he tries to bag the sponge, broom, bucket and even the water. . . .

For some misdeed Pierrot finally had to be guillotined. As it is England, why not a hanging rather than the guillotine? I do not know—the choice was doubtless determined by what was to follow. . . . After struggling and bellowing like a bullock that scents the slaughter-house Pierrot met his destiny at last. The head was detached from the neck, a big red and white head that rolled noisily to the edge of the executioner's pit, showing the bloody disc of the neck, the severed vertebrae and all the details of a butcher's joint just carved up for display. And suddenly the shortened trunk, moved by its irresistible mania for robbery, stood up, triumphantly snatched up its own head like a ham or a bottle of wine, and, more wisely than the great St Denis, stuffed it into its pocket![9]

To complete the "bouquet" one might call to mind a "fable" by Ambrose Bierce. The ruthless "humoresque" of this author is very apt, for the Anglo-American type of humour, which we are discussing here, arises completely from this same general source!

A Man was plucking a live Goose, when the bird addressed him thus:

"Suppose that you were a goose, do you think that you would relish this sort of thing?"

"Suppose that I were," said the Man; "do you think that you would like to pluck me?"

"Indeed I should!" was the natural, emphatic, but injudicious reply.

"Just so," concluded her tormentor, pulling out another handful of feathers; "that is the way *I* feel about it."[10]

The gags in *Modern Times* are completely in this spirit!

"Only children are happy, and that not for long," says wise Vassa Zheleznova in Gorky's play of the same name.

And not for long; because the stern "You mustn't" of tutors, and future standards of behaviour, begin to lay their interdiction on children's unrestricted desires from their very first steps.

He who is unable in time to subordinate these bonds and force their limitations to serve himself; he who, having become a man, continues to remain a child—will inevitably be unable to adapt himself to life, will always be placed in a ridiculous situation, will be funny and provoke laughter.

If the method of the child eyes of Chaplin determines the choice of his theme and the treatment of his comedies, then in the way of plot—it is nearly always the comedy of situations, the childish naïve approach to life clashing with its stern grown-up reprimands.

The genuine and touching "Simple Soul in Christ", over whose image dreamed the ageing Wagner, turns out to be not the Wagnerite *Parsifal,* surrounded by Bayreuth pomp and confronted by the Holy Grail, but none other than Charlie Chaplin, amidst the gutters and alleys of Kennington!

The amoral ruthlessness of the child's approach to phenomena in Chaplin's outlook appears, with all the other accompanying disarming traits of childhood, within the very characters of the personages of his comedies.

From this arises the genuine touchingness of Chaplin, almost always able to hold back from pre-conceived sentimentality.

Often this touchingness is able to achieve genuine pathos.

The finale of *The Pilgrim* has an effect of catharsis, when the Sheriff, losing his patience, kicks Charlie in the behind

—only after Charlie has not understood the good intentions of the Sheriff—to give him, the escaped convict, the possibility of escaping over the frontier into Mexico.

Realizing the goodness of the child-soul of the escaped convict Charlie, who passes himself as a parson and thereby saves the money of the little village church, the Sheriff does not wish to be out done in good deeds.

Taking Charlie along the frontier of Mexico, on the other side of which lies freedom, the Sheriff does all he can to make Charlie understand that he should take advantage of this proximity to escape.

But Charlie just cannot understand it.

Losing his patience, the Sheriff sends him to gather flowers on the other side of the frontier. Charlie obediently passes over the ditch dividing slavery from freedom.

Satisfied, the Sheriff goes off.

But then the childishly honest Charlie overtakes him with the flowers he has gathered.

A kick in the behind unties the dramatic knot.

Charlie is freed.

And the most brilliant finale of all his pictures—a work of genius—Charlie running from the camera with his hop, skip and jump as the iris closes.*

Along the line of the frontier—one foot in the United States, the other in Mexico.

As always, the most wonderful details or episodes in the films are those which, apart from everything else, serve as an image or symbol of the author's method, arising from the peculiarities of the author's make-up.

So here.

One foot on the territory of the Sheriff, the law, shackled feet; the other foot on the territory of freedom from law, responsibility, court and police.

The last shot of *The Pilgrim* is almost a blueprint of the inner character of the hero.

The blueprint of every conflict in all his films: a graph of the method by which he achieves his extraordinary effects.

* The diaphragm in front of the camera lens produces the effect of the picture being slowly encircled, smaller and smaller till it is totally obscured. Also known as the Iris out.—H. M.

The running away into the Iris Out is almost a symbol of perpetuity for a grown-up half-child in the environment and society of the full grown-up.

Let's dwell on this! Though the shade of Elie Faure stands in our path, a threatening warning against the insertion of superfluous metaphysics into the Tap-dance of Chaplin's boots!

Particularly because we interpret that drama more broadly, as the drama of the "Little Man" in the conditions of contemporary society.

Fallada's *Little Man, What Now?* is, as it were, a bridge linking these two interpretations.

However, Chaplin himself interprets his own finale; for the little man in contemporary society there is no way out.

Exactly the same as for the little child, who cannot remain as such for ever.

It is sad, but step by step it is necessary to cast off all attractive traits. . . .

— There goes naïveté. . . .

— There goes trustfulness. . . .

— There goes lightheartedness. . . .

. . . and similar traits out of place in cultured society. . . .

There goes unwillingness to consider the interests of a neighbour. . . .

There goes unwillingness to abide by the generally accepted rules. . . .

There goes a curb on the immediacy of a childish egoism. . . .

"Laughing, we part with our past",[11] and so here.

Laughing and sorrowing. . . .

But now let us for a moment imagine that a man has grown up and has, at the same time, retained unrestrained infantile traits in their fullest.

The first and most important of them—complete egoism and a complete lack of moral restraints.

Then before us is a shameless aggressor, a conqueror, an Attila. Chaplin, who has since branded the contemporary Attila could not help in the past wanting to play—Napoleon.

For long he has considered this thought and this plan.

In this scenario Napoleon does not die on St Helena. He

136

turns pacifist, succeeds in escaping from the island and secretly returns to France. There he gradually succumbs to temptation and prepares a *coup d'état*.

"However, when the revolution has to start, news comes from St Helena that Napoleon died. It was his double, you know, but all and everybody believe that the real one died. All his plans are ruined and Napoleon dies of sorrow. His last words will be: It is the news of my death that has killed me."[12]

This line surpasses the immortal telegram of Mark Twain: "The news of my death is somewhat exaggerated."

Chaplin himself describes the film as tragic. The film was conceived but not made.

Napoleon would have stood in the gallery of other Chaplin characters, an image of the broken ideal of infantilism.

*　　*　　*

Corresponding to the "Modern" times of fascism, taking the place of the epoch of Chaplin's *Modern Times,* a significant move takes place in Chaplin's art.

The method of comic effects of Chaplin, unerringly triumphant over the means of his infantile approach to phenomena, suddenly makes a basic change in the character of the persons portrayed, in *The Great Dictator*.

No longer broken as before, but now triumphant, unrestricted and impulsive.

The author's method becomes a graph of the characteristics of his hero.

And at the same time a hero whom the author himself brings to life on the screen by his own acting.

There he is—the "infantile" hero at the height of his power.

Hynkel examines inventions submitted to him by successful inventors.

Here is the "bullet-proof" jacket.

Hynkel's bullet pierces it without hindrance.

The inventor is killed instantaneously and falls like useless lumber.

Here is the man with an intriguing parachute-hat who jumps from the top of the palace.

The dictator listens.

Looks down.

The inventor has crashed.

His remark is superb.

"Again you palm off bad quality rubbish on me!"

Isn't that a scene in childhood?

Children's freedom from morals is what is so astonishing in Chaplin's vision.

Formerly Chaplin always played the side of the suffering only, the little barber from the ghetto, which he plays as a second role in *The Great Dictator.*

The Hynkels of his other films were first of all policemen; then the giant partner who wants to eat him under the guise of a chicken in *The Gold Rush,* then many, many policemen; the conveyor in *Modern Times,* and the image of the terrible environment of terrible actuality in that film.

In *The Great Dictator* he plays both.

He plays the two diametrically opposite poles of infantilism; the triumphant and the defeated.

And therefore, no doubt, the effect of this particular film is astonishing.

And no doubt particularly because in this film Chaplin speaks with his own voice.

For the first time it is not he who is in the power of his own method and vision, but method and consciously willed, purposeful presentation are in his adult hands. All this is because here from first to last speaks civil courage, clearly, ringingly and distinctly, the courage not just of a grown-up, but of a Great Man with capital letters.

And thereby Chaplin stands equally and firmly in the ranks of the greatest masters of the age-long struggle of Satire with Darkness, alongside Aristophanes of Athens, Erasmus of Rotterdam, François Rabelais from Meudon, Jonathan Swift from Dublin, François Marie Aroues de Voltaire of Ferney.

And even, maybe, in front of the others, if one bears in mind the scale of the Goliath of Fascist Baseness, Villainy and Obscurantism who is crushed by the sling of laughter

from the tiniest of Davids—Charles Spencer Chaplin from Hollywood.
  Hereinafter named:
  Charlie, the Grown-Up.

translated by Herbert Marshall

"Charlie the Kid" appeared in the World Film Art volume on Chaplin and "Dickens, Griffith and the Film Today" appeared in the Griffith volume, but a change in cultural policy stopped the series. Among the cancelled volumes was one on John Ford, for which Eisenstein wrote the following tribute, published posthumously.

Mr Lincoln by Mr Ford

Suppose some truant Good Fairy were to ask me, "As I'm not employed just now, perhaps there's some small magic job I could do for you, Sergei Mikhailovich? Is there some American film that you'd like me to make you the author of—with a wave of my wand?"

I would not hesitate to accept the offer, and I would at once name the film that I wish I had made. It would be *Young Mr Lincoln,* directed by John Ford.*

There are films that are richer and more effective. There are films that are presented with more entertainment and more charm. Ford himself has made more extraordinary

* *Young Mr Lincoln* was released in the United States by 20th Century-Fox on 9 June 1939; *producer,* Darryl F. Zanuck; *associate producer,* Kenneth Macgowan; *scenario,* Lamar Trotti; *direction,* John Ford; *photography,* Bert Glennon; *design,* Richard Day and Mark-Lee Kirk; *costumes,* Royer; *music,* Alfred Newman; *editor,* Walter Thompson. With Henry Fonda, Alice Brady, Marjorie Weaver, Arleen Whelan, Eddie Collins, Richard Cromwell, Eddie Quillan, Donald Meek.

films than this one. Connoisseurs might well prefer *The Informer*. Audiences would probably vote for *Stagecoach*—and sociologists for *The Grapes of Wrath*. *Young Mr Lincoln* didn't even get one of those bronze Oscars.

Nevertheless, of all American films made up to now this is the film that I would wish, most of all, to have made. What is there in it that makes me love it so?

It has a quality, a wonderful quality, a quality that every work of art must have—an astonishing harmony of all its component parts, a really amazing harmony as a whole.

I believe that our age yearns for harmony. We look back on the past with envy, and we've made the sunny harmony of the Greeks into an ideal. And our yearning already has brought us some result. Especially in one-sixth of the earth our century has shaped positive ideals. And more: this is a century in which we have realized ideals.

Yet as a whole our globe is experiencing a century of lost harmonies. And a world war that has crushed our gardens and monuments of culture is a most germane phenomenon of this age.

That is why a word of harmony is especially attractive to our epoch. Through such a creation can be expressed active opposition to our discordant times, a force to help people hope for peace, to send representatives to conferences, to form national bodies and to unite nations together.

Among those few works of our time that possess a nearly classical harmony *Mr Lincoln* by Mr Ford occupies a place of honour.

This film is distinguished by something more than its marvellous craftsmanship, where the rhythm of the montage corresponds to the timbre of the photography, and where the cries of the waxwings echo over the turbid flow of muddy water and through the steady gait of the little mule that lanky Abe rides along the Sangamon River. And there is something here more than the skill of filming in a stylized daguerreotype manner that is in unison with the moral character of Lincoln's sentences, or the eccentricity of Henry Fonda's performance that keeps the genuinely moving situation from sliding into sentimentality, and instead reaches a rare degree of pathos, as in the stunning departure of Lincoln into the landscape at the end of the film.

There is a deeper thing here—in those fundamentals and premises from which craftsmanship and harmony grow. Its source is a womb of popular and national spirit—this could account for its unity, its artistry, its genuine beauty.

Historically Lincoln came from the depths of his people, absorbing into himself its most typical and fascinating features. And the film also seems to grow wholly from the fascinating image of this man who embodied the best and highest progressive traditions of America. The harmony of the work of art could be a reflection in images of those great principles that are common to all mankind, and this reflection shows us one of the loveliest aspects of mankind's creativity.

Thus through the image of his historical protagonist John Ford touches the principles whose bearer was the historical Lincoln, not only through the sentences spoken by his Lincoln character, but in the very structure of his film.

Here before us is a miracle—daguerreotypes come to life. Here are those dresses of "unspeakable" checks, tight in the waist and immense below, those ringlets peeping out from dainty caps, those earrings that vie in their perfect forms with the ringlets, those frock-coats and beaver hats, walking-sticks and waistcoats, beards and moustaches and various tufts of hair, fanciful military uniforms—no longer frozen on the metal daguerreotypes, but now with the vital breath brought to life. These gods of antiquity (though not in plaster casts) are suddenly not only living, but running through a gay country fair.

Here's a tug-of-war, with a rope stretched across a well-prepared mud puddle, into which the group at each end of the rope is trying to pull the other. At the last minute, joining the group that seems about to lose, comes one more to help pull—a gaunt and gawky youngster, just stepped from a gallery of daguerreotype portraits of American country youths.

With his long arms he comes very close to cheating: at a critical moment he catches hold of the wheel of a wagon standing nearby. Yet his absolutely innocent look bespeaks only resourcefulness in a moment of decision. And the cluster of opponents at the other end of the rope are swept into the mud puddle with the enthusiastic shouts of the bettors and bystanders.

Our tall rustic is already well into a home-made pie, baked by one of the town's ladies for an eating contest—an indispensable feature of American country fairs.

Image after image of the daguerreotype era is thus brought magically to life in the reality of its great-grandchild —the cinema era. These are the living screen images of the first reels of film about Abraham Lincoln, filled with a feeling for the epoch, atmosphere and national character, and thrown on to the surface of the screen by the sure hand of John Ford.

Through all this moves a giant child, the young Lincoln. There he is involved in a tug-of-war, pulling as if his life depended on it. Here he is devouring pies in an eating contest. And there he is outstripping all the others in the art of rail-splitting. He looks awkward and even lazy, but he always seems to be where he is needed, with a resourceful gesture at the right moment. You sense in him the most practical skill in all sorts of work, the greatest endurance, with the greatest awareness and alertness in struggle.

From the beginning of the film he stands before us as an ideal warrior. He's as clumsy as the young Ilya Murometz, with his deliberate, drawling speech and slow gestures—all in order to gain time for a keen glance to seek a gap in the defences of the opponent, a careless movement of a rival, a weakness in the enemy forces. He reminds me of the anecdote of the stammering bargainer who employed his stammer as a business method, a persuasive tactic in a quarrel or a duel of wits.

The events of the film do not go as far as Lincoln's nation-wide struggle for the unity of the country—we don't even see the violent election campaign in which Lincoln's slogan of freedom was ranged against the slogans of reaction. Yet from the very first glimpse of young Abe's horseplay in the contests at the fair, you sense the fighter in him, a man of insatiable will and energy. Here is a simple and deep lad of the people, an embodiment of Karl Marx's favourite quotation from Terence: "Nothing that is human is alien to me,"—for only one to whom everything human is not alien can to the end maintain his intimacy with all that can be judged human.

Even if Ford did not intend this as a prelude to a later part of his film showing Lincoln's political struggles on the way to the presidency, or to a later indication of President Lincoln's articulation of the ideals of democracy within the nineteenth-century horizons of America, there is no doubt that Ford, always a clever master of his medium, wanted to make us conscious of all these scenes and details of a sketch necessary to any future film about Lincoln.

His informal plot, almost plotless or anecdotal, little more than a chapter in the biography of a man with a great future, looks on closer inspection like a thoroughly composed image synthesizing all those qualities that shone in the historical-political role played by this American giant.

Yet, strictly speaking, what do I know about Mr Lincoln historically? Very likely, nothing more than any more or less educated person knows about him.

We all know of some crafty figures of foreign history: Catherine de' Medici, Mazarin, Fouché ...; some sly diplomats: Talleyrand, Metternich . . .; some downright villains: Cardinal de Retz, Cesare Borgia, Marquis de Sade . . .; some great conquerors: Attila, Caesar, Napoleon.

The great humanists whom we know are notably fewer. Among these and in one of the first places is the Illinois lawyer who became President of the United States—Abraham Lincoln.

We attach to his name the emancipation of the Negro slaves, and the fortunate conclusion of the fratricidal war between the North and South. Reading history in closer detail, we learn that in these matters Lincoln conducted himself somewhat less decisively and courageously than we might have wished, and considerably more slowly and cautiously than now—looking back—would seem necessary. And we learn that the leadership of the Northern cause was not ultimately disinterested. We also know that after the war many of these liberators took their revenge by enslaving and exploiting not only Negroes but white slaves as well.

Despite these contrary factors in his history we are right to think of Lincoln as not only a bearer but a living embodiment of the positive ideals of freedom and justice for future generations of America. It is this that leaves with us a powerful image of a tireless fighter for freedom, justice, unity and democracy—and we know that he was murdered at Ford's Theatre in Washington on 14 April 1865.

There is an almost faultless criterion in establishing the historical relation of the people with their governments and leaders. By what nicknames do the latter go down in history?

The Carolingian dynasty ended in the tenth century with the characteristic figure of Louis V—"the Sluggard." The last Duke of Burgundy goes into history as "the Bold." With a reflection of evil and cruelty the popular memory of Henry VIII's first daughter is preserved as "Bloody Mary".

One of the wisest of names was that given by the people to the Moscow Tsar, Ivan Vasilyevich. The feudal forces destroyed by him howled about his bloodthirstiness, cruelty, mercilessness. The people dubbed him Grozny—"the Terrible".

The image of Lincoln, from the surface of his historic role, to its depths, is caught by the American nicknames for him that have come down to us. Here is the way he was painted by his contemporaries: The Great Emancipator, The Martyr Chief, The Sage of Springfield, Man of the People, The Great Heart, Honest Old Abe, Father Abraham, Uncle Abe, The Smart Lawyer, The Rail-Splitter. And there were the hostile names given him by the South: The Tyrant, Spindleshanks, The Crow. These last two remain on the surface. But what was there on the surface?

American film directors show a wonderful ability in choosing the people to whom they entrust the characters of literature or their own fantasies.

John Ford especially has this gift in abundance; he can bring to life so many and such unexpectedly varied aspects —look at the actors who play the roles of the passenger in the white hat (in *Stagecoach*), of Casey, the itinerant preacher (in *The Grapes of Wrath*), or the prison governor (in *The Prisoner of Shark Island*). And Victor McLaglen in *The Informer*, or Thomas Mitchell who played the drunken doctor in *Stagecoach* and in *Hurricane*.

All of these actors—and Ford himself, of course—could be students of American history, for in embodying their imagination with such striking and artistic flair they chose the particular image and figure of Lincoln!

When the world press reported Papanin's expedition, someone wrote that it would be impossible to invent a more suitable image of a man who could place an administrative foot on the North Pole.

But give any master of "personifying" historical monuments the task of inventing an appropriate figure, devoid of false pathos, for a bearer of the ideals of American democracy, and he would never think of creating such an extravagant figure—an exterior reminding one simultaneously of an old-fashioned semaphore telegraph, a well-worn windmill, and a scarecrow, clothed in a long, full-skirted frockcoat, and crowned with a shaggy top-hat in the shape of a stovepipe.

In all probability it is precisely through these external features that this historical figure can be shown as heroic and full of pathos, for he is so obviously free from all pose, free even from the slightest concern with himself. The business of this life was the most disinterested service in the interests of his people.

Outside films I know the image of Lincoln through the dozens of photographs gathered in one volume[1] by the conscientious hand of an emigrant from fascist Hungary who was received hospitably in America. Stefan Lorant did this in answer to his ten-year-old son's question, "What was Lincoln like?" From every page of the album this fanatic looks at us, changed and stooped by the years.

You are surprised to observe what accurate intuition and skill were shown by the pleasant-looking young Henry Fonda in transforming himself into this Don Quixote, whose armour was the U.S. Constitution, whose helmet was the traditional top-hat of a small-town lawyer, and whose Rosinante was a placid little mule that he straddled, his long legs almost touching the ground. This is a portrait finished with strength, pathos and life. The man has been reconstructed and passes alive before us on the screen.

The truthfulness of this image and figure in the film could be verified by the millions of pages that have been written in America about Lincoln—and there must be several hundred plays about him.

But it was enough for me to check it against three vivid glimpses of him, preserved in my memory, to be satisfied that before us moved a miraculous reincarnation of an image of the past in a living film-image of today.

The first is a first impression of the arrival in New York of the new President, elected by a provincial majority despite the antipathy to him in this already powerful city.

The second is an anecdote from the time when this man already held the reins of power with an iron hand.

And the third is a fragment of reminiscence, attached to life in the White House while the fate of the American nation, state and people was being decided in the Civil War.*

... I shall not easily forget the first time I ever saw Abraham Lincoln. It must have been about the 18th or 19th of February 1861. It was rather a pleasant afternoon, in New York city, as he arrived there from the West, to remain a few hours, and then pass on to Washington, to prepare for his inauguration. I saw him in Broadway, near the site of the present Post-office. He came down, I think from Canal street, to stop at the Astor House. The broad spaces, sidewalks, and streets in the neighborhood, and for some distance, were crowded with solid masses of people, many thousands. The omnibuses and other vehicles had all been turn'd off, leaving an unusual hush in that busy part of the city. Presently two or three shabby hack barouches made their way with some difficulty through the crowd, and drew up at the Astor House entrance. A tall figure stepp'd out of the centre of these barouches, paus'd leisurely on the sidewalk, look'd up at the granite walls and looming archi-

* The printed text of this essay must have been condensed, for only two of the three promised glimpses follow.—J. L.

146

tecture of the grand old hotel—then, after a relieving stretch of arms and legs, turn'd round for over a minute to slowly and good-humoredly scan the appearance of the vast and silent crowds. There were no speeches—no compliments—no welcome—as far as I could hear, not a word was said. Still much anxiety was conceal'd in that quiet. Cautious persons had fear'd some mark'd insult or indignity to the President-elect—for he possess'd no personal popularity at all in New York city, and very little political. But it was evidently tacitly agreed that if the few political supporters of Mr Lincoln present would entirely abstain from any demonstration on their side, the immense majority, who were anything but supporters, would abstain on their side also. The result was a sulky, unbroken silence, such as certainly never before characterized so great a New York crowd.

Almost in the same neighborhood I distinctly remember'd seeing Lafayette on his visit to America in 1825. I had also personally seen and heard, various years afterward, how Andrew Jackson, Clay, Webster, Hungarian Kossuth, Filibuster Walker, the Prince of Wales on his visit, and other célèbres, native and foreign, had been welcom'd there—all that indescribable human roar and magnetism, unlike any other sound in the universe—the glad exulting thunder-shouts of countless unloos'd throats of men! But on this occasion, not a voice—not a sound. From the top of an omnibus (driven up one side, close by, and block'd by the curbstone and the crowds), I had, I say, a capital view of it all, and especially of Mr Lincoln, his look and gait—his perfect composure and coolness— his unusual and uncouth height, his dress of complete black, stovepipe hat push'd back on the head, dark-brown complexion, seam'd and wrinkled, yet canny-looking face, black, bushy head of hair, disproportionately long neck, and his hands held behind as he stood observing the people. He look'd with curiosity upon that immense sea of faces, and the sea of faces return'd the look with similar curiosity. In both there was a dash of comedy, almost farce, such as Shakspere puts in his blackest tragedies. The crowd that hemm'd around consisted I

147

should think of thirty to forty thousand men, not a single one his personal friend—while I have no doubt (so frenzied were the ferments of the time), many an assassin's knife and pistol lurk'd in hip or breast-pocket there, ready, soon as break and riot came.

But no break or riot came. The tall figure gave another relieving stretch or two of arms and legs; then with moderate pace, and accompanied by a few unknown-looking persons, ascended the portico-steps of the Astor House, disappear'd through its broad entrance—and the dumb-show ended.

I saw Abraham Lincoln often the four years following that date. He changed rapidly and much during his Presidency—but this scene, and him in it, are indelibly stamp'd upon my recollection. As I sat on the top of my omnibus, and had a good view of him, the thought, dim and inchoate then, has since come out clear enough, that four sorts of genius, four mighty and primal hands, will be needed to the complete limning of this man's future portrait—the eyes and brains and finger-touch of Plutarch and Eschylus and Michel Angelo, assisted by Rabelais . . .

This vivid account is by a man whom we know and love for his extraordinary poems and poesy. It is from a lecture about a man whom he loved and saluted. Himself an enthusiast for the Coming Century of Democracy he could not but salute, he could not but love Lincoln.

Walt Whitman wrote this. It is a lecture[2] that he delivered in New York on 14 April 1879, the fourteenth anniversary of the president's assassination.

My earliest recollected encounter with the image of Lincoln was in a book whose title I've forgotten, an old collection of stories about the American Civil War.

The President was supremely simple and modest in his personal habits. He even cleaned his own boots—about which someone sarcastically remarked to him:

"A perfect gentleman never cleans his own boots!"

So Lincoln asked him, "And for whom does the perfect gentleman clean them?"

You can see the calm, unblinking, wise eyes raised to the sarcastic gentleman—and you can imagine that poor fellow fidgeting and wishing that the floor would open up and swallow him.

Here in the film, with wonderful imagery, is seized this exact gaze, a gaze of cosmic reproaches to worldly vanities, a gaze that does not miss the least trifle, a gaze that does not permit the least trifle to obscure the great meaning of all that stands beyond life's trifles, errors, blunders, sins, crimes—the evils of conditions and habits, all the accepted evils that must be changed for the sake of Man.

The film's story is limited to the youth of Lincoln. But Henry Fonda manages to convey much more than this fragmentary (on the surface) episode from the legal practice of Lincoln. Behind these visible events can be sensed the universal pathos with which Lincoln burned—as head and leader of the American people, elected President at the most critical moment of United States history. . . .

I first saw this film on the eve of the world war. It immediately enthralled me with the perfection of its harmony and the rare skill with which it employed all the expressive means at its disposal.

And most of all for the solution of Lincoln's image.

My love for this film has neither cooled nor been forgotten. It grows stronger and the film itself grows more and more dear to me.

By October 1945 most of the evacuated film industry had moved back from its temporary Asian bases to the former film centres, and in Moscow the important journal of film theory and criticism, Iskusstvo Kino (Art of the Cinema), was revived. Its first post-war number contained several brief statements by film leaders; Eisenstein's contribution, "In Close Up", on the defects and ideals of film criticism, was regarded as so offensive that the entire editorial board was reprimanded and thereafter this journal remained closed to Eisenstein until his death.

A Close-Up View

Everyone knows—though many forget—that cinema offers various camera positions, known as:

long shot, medium shot, and *close-up*

And we know that these shot-dimensions express varying viewpoints on phenomena.

The long shot conveys the general scope of the phenomenon.

The medium shot places the spectator in an intimate relationship to the players on the screen: he feels in the same room with them, on the same divan beside them, around the same tea-table.

And finally, with the help of the close-up (the enlarged detail), the spectator plunges into the most intimate matters on the screen: a flinching eye-lash, a trembling hand, finger-tips touching the lace at a wrist . . . All these at the required moment point to the person through those details in which he ultimately conceals or reveals himself.

If one can look at the phenomena within a film in these three different ways, then it is exactly thus—in three ways—that one can look at a film as a whole. Or I should say, it must be looked at in this way.

In this way, "in long shot" can stand for the view on the film as a whole: on its thematic necessity, on its contemporary quality, on its correspondence to the needs of the day, on the ideologically correct presentation of the questions it touches, on its accessibility to the masses, on its usefulness, on its fighting significance, on its evaluation in relation to the high reputation of Soviet film work.

Such is a broadly social appraisal of our film productions. And, basically, it is the reflection of this viewpoint that one finds in the central organs of our press.

The normal spectator, whether a member of the Young

Communist League, seamstress, general, student at the Suvorov school, metro-builder, academician, cashier, electrical technician, deep-sea diver, chemist, pilot, typesetter, or shepherd, looks at a film "in medium shot".

Before all other considerations this spectator is moved by the living play of emotions: his human nearness to the images on the screen; whether he is agitated by a concept or by feelings close to him, by the circumstances of a man's fate in his milieu, in the phases of struggle, in the joys of success and the sorrows of adversity. Man, filmed in medium shot, would appear to symbolize in himself this intimacy and the nearness of the spectator to the screen image.

The general characteristics of the theme enter the spectator's consciousness *en passant*. The generalized concept of the event is embedded in the spectator's feelings.

Merged with the hero through his experiences witnessed on the screen, the spectator gives second place to the important and indispensable general idea presented by the film.

Thus the spectator is, before all else, in the grip of the story, the event and the circumstances.

It's quite unimportant to him who wrote the scenario.

He sees the setting of the sun, not the skill of the cameraman.

He weeps with the heroine of the film, not with an actress who plays her role well or poorly.

He is immersed in the emotions of the music, and is often unaware that he is listening to music going on in the "background" of the dialogue that is engrossing him.

From the spectator's viewpoint there can be no higher appreciation than this.

This can happen in fullest measure only with films of perfect truth and artistic persuasiveness.

In the press it is the review-article that corresponds with this point of view. It is that type of synopsis-article, in which the screen images are not spoken of as actors in certain roles, but the behaviour and fates of their film images are appraised as if they were the actions of living beings, living completely real lives that have been somehow accidentally thrown on to a screen along with whatever else may be flowing past in the vicinity of the film theatre.

In this type of synopsis-article we are moved by the correct or incorrect behaviour of the characters—we take sides with one character against another, we seek a revelation of their inner motives, we really wish to read about the characters on the screen as people moving in genuine actuality. If such an article does not slide into being simply a synopsis, it can reflect the stimulated thoughts of a spectator under the immediate impression of the work.

And there is a third way to examine a film.

Not only can there be a third way—there *must* be this third way.

This is an examination of the film itself *in close-up*: through a prism of firm analysis the article "breaks down" the film into its parts, resolves its elements, to study the whole just as a new model of construction is studied by engineers and specialists in their own field of technique.

This must be the view of the film from the standpoint of a professional journal.

There must be an appraisal of the film from the positions of both "long shot" and "medium shot"—but firstly it must be an examination "in close-up"—a close-up view of all its component links.

Though in "long shot" view we can form a sharply accurate, even merciless social judgement of a film, and we can be occasionally lifted above the simple, uninvolved synopsis-article by a stimulated and thoughtful selection of a film's events and images, we are also obliged to give a firmly professional, *critical* look at the values and short-comings of what is done. We must make the highest demands upon the production before us—and in this we are far from perfection.

Without this "third criticism" neither development nor progress nor a persistent heightening of our working level is possible.

A high social appraisal must not serve as a shield, behind which with impunity can be concealed poor editing or a low quality of enunciating those words which, in any final accounting of a film, also determine its value.

The spectator's interest in the story must not serve in mitigation of poor photography, nor should a record box office for a film divest us of responsibility for a poor musical accompaniment, a poorly recorded sound-track, or (so often!) bad laboratory work, especially in the release prints.

I recall those days long past of screenings in the early years of ARRK,* when, shaking and trembling, a director would bring his production before a professional gathering. His trembling was not for fear that after the screening he would be called ugly names by this or that colleague. He was trembling for the same reason that a singer trembles before an audience of singers, or a boxer before other boxers, or a matador before *aficionados* of bull-fighting—knowing that an untrue note, a false modulation, an incorrectly aimed blow or faulty timing *would be noticed by all*. The smallest fault against inner truth, the smallest slip in an editing join, the smallest defect of exposition, the slightest flaw in rhythm: any of these would instantly arouse a sharp reaction of disapproval from the professional audience.

This was because, to render the film as a whole its due, to participate in its events with ideas and feelings, the spectator-professional could not forget that he was not only a spectator—he was also a professional. He knew that the success of the film as a whole does not invariably mean the perfection of all its connected parts: the theme thrills or the acting satisfies, and this takes precedence over the plastic imperfections of the work. Yet this did not prevent him, pleased as he was by the truth of the work, from being harsh and demanding towards those parts that came short of perfection.

Then came a strange period.

The acceptance of a film as a whole began to be regarded as making up for all its particular sins and defects.

I recall a different era, during a decadent period of ARRK, when, in discussing a film that had turned out well, it was forbidden to say, for example, that its photography was pale or that graphically it was not sufficiently inventive. If you dared to go as far as that, all the blame and discredit of Soviet film errors would be heaped on you. Bugaboos

---

* Association of Workers in Revolutionary Cinema.

would be waved frighteningly before you—especially that you were denying "the unity of form and content"!

This may sound now no more than a story, but it is a bad story.

This dulled the sharpness of demand for film quality. It cooled the passion for more exacting standards of art. It undermined the sense of responsibility in the film-makers themselves. In many ways it bred indifference to the values of the separate components. The brilliant clarity and ideals of cinematic style grew dim and tarnished.

But now we have peace again.

The perfection of professional quality in what we are called to do, regardless of time, place and conditions—that is our sacred duty. And the struggle for conditions under which the desired quality may be achieved—is no less our duty.

The facilities to perfect the production conditions of our work, the capacities to secure this necessary quality for our productions—this is our fighting task, as well as the supreme service to the ideal, the struggle for artistic form and quality in our works. It is to this that we here summon all on the threshold of our new peace.

To show "in close-up" what we are called to do, to perceive, to criticize and to press forward—this must become the fighting line of the newly re-born journal, *Iskusstvo Kino*.

Bowing (where necessary) before certain films "in long shot", thrilled (where possible) like the rank-and-file spectator "in medium shot"—we, "in close-up", will be professionally relentless in our demands on all the components of a film.

Acting thus, we will not be frightened by the shouts of the weak-sighted uncritical folk, trying to scare us with the ghost of "a divided unity of form and content": and we will continue to point out qualitative divergences between a theme and its visualization.

Because a genuine unity of form and content also demands *a unity in the qualitative perfection of both*.

Only perfected art deserves to flash from the screens of our victorious era of post-war constructive creation.

Notwithstanding the success and honours achieved by Part I of Ivan the Terrible, *the continuation of Eisenstein's last film was so abruptly halted as to bring his film-making career to an end. When Part II was condemned and shelved, and the completed portions of Part III were destroyed, Eisenstein, now in very poor health, returned to theory and teaching for his last years. In this respect 1946 and 1947 were productive years. After his first heart attack he tried to hurry books and ideas to completion that had long waited for this attention. He worked on the memoirs that he planned only for posthumous publication and resumed his lectures to the direction course at VGIK. The following lecture (preserved in a stenographic record) was delivered to his class of student-directors on Christmas Day 1946.*

Problems of Composition

In this semester we have touched the most varied questions of composition. We have spoken about the general significance of composition, about the rôle of imagery in composition, and we have studied it in passages from Pushkin's works, where we tried to translate his poetry into montage-lists or into detailed plans for action. What should be our next problem?

Scenario material as received by directors often has a certain compositional fragmentation that tends to reduce its expressiveness. How can we take scenario material of such compositional friability and give it a firm structure and a compositional style?

I want to show you this process in an extract from V. Nekrasov's novel, *Stalingrad.**

* E. refers to the first version of this novel, as published in *Znamya* (Nos. 8–9, 1946); its later publication was entitled *In the Trenches of Stalingrad*, a title that the author had used in his first sketches. The published English translation by David Floyd is entitled *Front-Line Stalingrad* (Harvill Press, London 1962).

But let us first agree on our viewpoint in examining the compositional question in relation to this extract. We can approach the question in its most narrow, one might even say, its most "operative" sense, that is, how to treat the material, how to arrange it and how to juxtapose its several elements.

We should not forget that the literal meaning of the term "composition" is, firstly, "to compare", and "to arrange". It is in that narrow sense that we shall examine this chosen material, in order to learn how to establish its proportions and the links between the separate parts of the work, its separate episodes and the separate elements within the episodes.

There are several methods and approaches by which one can determine the constructional firmness and wholeness of a work.

One of the simplest methods of establishing compositional ties and links between the separate parts is in finding *repetition*, the use of which we have repeatedly noticed in examples from the works of Pushkin.

The factor of repetition plays an important part in music. In music you will always find certain thematic material which penetrates the whole work at regular intervals of time and is subjected to various treatments.

Similarly, we find in poetry the repetition, with or without alteration, of a certain image, a certain rhythmical pattern, a certain element of subject or melodic arrangement.

Such repetition helps, more than anything else, to create a sense of the unity of the work.

The use of repetition can sometimes be found in the subtle outer structure of the work, for example, where the distance and intensity of separated accents can be discovered in familiar and strictly defined mathematical relationships—within the total rhythm.

It seems obvious that such elements of compositional connectives belong to a category of the simplest means for establishing the unity of a work, along with the usual proportional correlations of its parts.

Now we must speak of the simplest features of composition and show how it is achieved in the actual treatment of specific material. Such constructions can be of various kinds. One kind of construction can be completely arbitrary and unrelated to the real proportions of life. What elements will you find in such a construction?

Such a work, in so far as it employs a certain proportion, can to some degree affect the spectator. But, its "laws" of construction, in so far as they are accidental, cannot penetrate to the depths, nor in the right way; they cannot take possession of the spectator, nor will they convey to him a sense of reality, or the realization of the theme.

These works are inevitably formalistic, for they are not based on an aspiration to reflect in its totality the phenomenon of actuality and its inherent natural laws. And thus arises an artist's arbitrariness, completely without foundation.

A man who does not know how to find the exact rhythmic proportion that expresses the flow of the inner content of the theme will turn to some other solution: if he is an editor he might say, "Let's cut this sequence according to a waltz pattern", that is, in a rhythmic figure made of three beats.

Why? Based on what? For what reason?

It's just this sort of approach that can be found in the graphic arts when, for example, a young painter will suddenly, for no reason at all, decide to compose his painting in the form of a triangle. Now we know very well that the compositional base of many classical paintings is a triangle —but we also know that the authors of those works "arrived" at such compositional forms from the inner necessities of graphically expressing their themes.

Even without such an inner necessity it is possible for a picture to give an impression of proportional harmony, but even at its best it can only entertain the spectator as a play of formal abstractions.

It is an entirely different matter when the compositional structure emerges from the content and imagery of the work.

The classical structure of musical works, of dramas, of films or paintings is almost invariably derived from a struggle of opposites, linked by the unity of conflict.

Normally in drama there are two contending factors from

the beginning, where the emergent progressive element struggles with surviving elements of reaction.

Music ordinarily employs the collision of two themes, or one theme that divides into two. In development these themes interpenetrate each other, move alongside each other comparatively, or intertwine their lines of movement.

It is difficult to find examples of dramatic art having any genuine impact in which this basic condition for an overall compositional structure is not observed.

It is important for you to comprehend the need for making the composition strictly depend on the content and the aim of the work. Only then can veracity of the story and the whole work be achieved.

If the work follows a pattern that does not flow from the general pattern of the action, determined by its content, then it will always be perceived as contrived, stylized, formalist. I want to emphasize that such elements as the repetition of theme and the composition of its development will never seem contrived if every nuance of such composition comes, not from formal demands, but from concepts that express the theme and the author's relationship to the theme.

For this let's take an example from the classics. When we speak of Pushkin's tragedy, *Boris Godunov*, it is impossible not to recall its famous conclusion: "The people are silent."

Literary history tells us that this conclusion appears only in the printed copy of 1831, and that in the two authentic manuscripts of Pushkin, one in the Lenin Library and the other in the Public Library of Leningrad,* the play ends with the people shouting: "Long live Tsar Dimitri Ivanovich!"

Now which of these two conclusions genuinely responds to the wishes of Pushkin?

Literary research workers have offered many conjectures on this matter. It can be argued that the ending, "The people are silent", was inserted in the text under the pressure of the censorship that could not permit the people being shown taking the side of a Pretender instead of the rightful successor, "God's Anointed". From the censor's

* At present all Pushkin manuscripts are housed in the Pushkin House, Leningrad.

viewpoint any ending, other than that of the people in silence, would undermine the authority of Tsarism.

Nevertheless it is also granted that Pushkin is never known to have expressed dissatisfaction with this revision of the ending. And it is easy to believe that the ending in the printed copy of the tragedy gives a more menacing tone to the final moment than if the people had shouted, "Long live Tsar Dimitri Ivanovich!" In "The people are silent" one can sense not only a smouldering, threatening judgement on events, but even more noticeably, the ominous alertness of the people that takes its own time to say a weighty, decisive, historical word.

In citing this ending I want to show that an apparently outer compositional shift from one variant to another produces a totally different understanding of the work.

In examining the behaviour of the people through scene after scene of the tragedy we can discover that, without showing any initiative of their own, they somehow express their relation to events.

At the beginning the people quite apathetically go to beg Boris to assume the throne; their apathy is emphasized by the rubbing of onions in their eyes to bring tears, and in answer to someone's question, why they appeal to Boris particularly, they say, "The Boyars will manage him".

In this way Pushkin clears the enthusiastic summons of Boris to the throne of any suspicion of genuine feeling, alleged by Karamzin in his description of the scene. A comparison of Karamzin's description with Pushkin's text provides an excellent example of the reworking of material that is required when the author's attitude diverges from the ideological attitude of his source.

Later in the course of the tragedy, when the Pretender calls to the people to come to his side, they open the city gates to him and tie up the voyevod (Shuisky informs Boris of this).

And later—at the Place of Execution—Grigori Pushkin comes to deliver greetings and a summons to the people from the Pretender. The people respond to this ("Long live Dimitri, our father") and following a shout from a peasant

159

in the pulpit ("Take Boris's pup") rush into the apartments of the Godunovs.

In the finale of the tragedy Mosalsky, after informing the people that "Maria Godunova and her son Fyodor have taken poison," turns on them with the question, "What makes you silent?"—and demands, "Shout! Long live Tsar Dimitri Ivanovich!" It is here that we have the two variant endings: according to the printed edition—*The people are silent*; according to the manuscripts—*The people: "Long live Tsar Dimitri Ivanovich!"*

If you bring together these separated scenes and the manuscript finale, it is possible to read the picture they present thus: the people are apathetic; the people don't want Boris Godunov, but they ask him to take power; at the call of the Pretender the people open the gates for him; the people run to "take Boris's pup"; when they learn from Mosalsky's word that Fyodor is dead, the people, according to Pushkin's direction, "are silenced by horror", and after this they obediently shout: "Long live Tsar Dimitri Ivanovich!"

With such a conclusion the whole action of the people, it would seem, corresponds to the words of Shuisky, that "the rabble . . . instantly obeys any suggestion . . ."

A quite different picture is gained from the second ending: the direction, "The people are silent." Now it would appear that the people, who throughout the tragedy have submissively followed orders, at the last moment do not do what they are told.

But can this "reverse repetition" of the end be regarded as simply a formal compositional twist? No, because if you read through the whole action of the people with the new ending, you find that it permits a total re-understanding of the characteristics of the rôle and meaning of the people in the tragedy.

Throughout the tragedy we see the people as witnesses of the struggle between Godunov and the Pretender, with its own viewpoint on this struggle, and even taking part in the struggle on that side that seems necessary at each moment—but what is most important is that after watching these events, the people, in the course of the tragedy, develop an

Eisenstein at Chichen-Itza.

Photograph by Alexandrov

During the making of *Que Viva Mexico!* Eisenstein and Tisse experimented with the use of extreme depth of focus. These two photographs by Alexandrov show a familiar "deep" composition and how it was made.

A photograph taken during the filming of *Ivan Grozny*. Eisenstein stands

awful power. They have grown, and by the last moment they adopt by their silence an active judgement on the events before them.

We can see that the compositional turn of one element gives us evidence for a re-orientation of the treatment of a whole line of action within the tragedy.

It is curious to note that another type of solution has been proposed, not by Pushkin and not by a director staging the tragedy, but by an historian. The commentaries in one edition of *Boris Godunov* contain the suggestion that for a scenic interpretation the most correct choice would follow neither the first nor the second variant, but would give an "individualized" crowd—that is a broken mass, in which one would shout "Yes", another, "No", and a third would say nothing. According to the author of the commentaries, this would be the most correct and plausible solution for the end of the tragedy.

What would be the result of his solution? Under the banner of an "individualized" *crowd* this professor of history de-individualizes the *people*. Any real and active rôle of the people would be altogether lost in such an interpretation. The result would be what Gogol loved to define in the formula: neither this nor that. Here the rôle of the people as one of the leading characters of the tragedy is brought to naught.

A treatment of the people as "instantly obedient to a suggestion" is for us inadmissible. Therefore that ending in which the people hail Dimitri is also questionable.

The alternative treatment is determined by the ending: "The people are silent." Here the people's character is drawn as growing and beginning to feel its mission, its historic rôle.*

* At the end of Meyerhold's life he was rehearsing a production of Pushkin's *Boris Godunov*. Here is his comment at a rehearsal on the final stage direction: "When he complied with the censor's demand and substituted for the people's cheers of "Long live Tsar Dimitri Ivanovich!" the famous direction, "The people are silent," he outwitted the censor because instead of reducing the theme of the People he strengthened it. After all, between a people shouting long live this or that tsar and a people expressing its opinion by silence there is a world of difference. What is more, Pushkin gave

The "treatment" proposed by the aforementioned commentaries tells us nothing and as motivation for the behaviour of the whole people it only says, "thus it came to pass."

Such "reasons"—"it is always thus" and "anything is possible"—these make up that dreadful swamp of inexpressibles in which you sink when you have no clear aim or when your purpose is not cast in a firm compositional form, expressing one basic idea.

And thus we come to the conclusion that every apparently abstract compositional movement and method itself expresses an ideological and political purpose in relation to the formation of the subject.

There are various paths to the exposure and formation of the basic idea in the compositional structure of a work. There can be instances when, before determining the treatment of a work, it is mechanically divided into specific theses, and on the basis of those theses a solution is "worked out". Such a bookish way almost always leads to an abstract solution. ·

Organically and genuinely a different path offers itself, when in the process of work an understanding and a vital perception of the idea gradually begin to enter the material and determine the work's own compositional proportions. With such an approach all that we have said about the compositional growth of a work, about the establishment of its inner links and proportions, will organically flow from the ideational conception with which you approach any theme, any material.

These are the preliminary considerations on composition which are important to keep in mind before examining the task in hand.

---

the Russian theatre of the future a fascinating and extremely difficult task: how to act silence so that it sounds louder than shouting. I have found a solution to this problem and I thank the foolish censorship for spurring Pushkin to make his wonderful find." Meyerhold also had an explanation for the direction: "Obviously this is not merely a pause but a musical indication for the director. In Pushkin's time the art of theatre direction did not yet exist, but he had the genius to foresee it." (Alexander Gladkov, "Meyerhold on Theatrical Art", *Soviet Literature*, No. 1, 1962).—J. L.

Victor Nekrasov's novel *Stalingrad* received extremely favourable notices from the critics. At the same time there was noted, as an essential flaw in the novel, the circumstance that the author writes of the defence of Stalingrad from the viewpoint of a man who finds himself in the thick of events, but unable to comprehend events beyond those matters in which he directly participates; the author does not always generalize the separate facts that fall within his vision, and this prevents him from giving a full picture of the heroic action at Stalingrad.

The author might, of course, object that it was the editors of *Znamya* who gave his work the title, *Stalingrad*, though Nekrasov had called his work "sketches" and had entitled it *In the Trenches of Stalingrad*. Nevertheless his work has come to the critics and to us as a "novel" called *Stalingrad*.

It is curious to note that the same charge that was brought against the novel can be with equal consistency also levelled at its composition as a whole, and in its separate parts. If the historical-thematic plan of the novel is limited to a scrutiny of individual facts, outside the scope of the whole, then this very feature also distinguishes its compositional structure.

Perhaps the task of the author did not cover more than making sketches of separate passing events, in which he figured as witness or participant. If that is the case then it is necessary for us to estimate how, with the use of parallel cases, an impressionistic sketching of material can raise the combined elements of an artistic work to a certain level of thought.

The content of the novel is the activity of a young lieutenant—the author—in the conditions and surroundings of the Stalingrad struggle, and it is the story of how he, on receiving his assignment, comes to Stalingrad, takes part in its defence and in the defeat of the Germans.

We are to work on one fragment of the novel—the first bombing of Stalingrad by German planes. In our discussion of it I shall try to show not only how the composition in general is built, but also, to a certain degree, to look into what work must always be done in developing a shooting-script—for a shooting-script must have, besides all the

163

usual things, a film work's definite compositional structure. Some consider that the writing of a shooting-script consists in breaking up the treatment (or literary scenario) into separate lines. On the left-hand side of the page we put the numbers of the shots, and at the right we list the usually fantastic figures for the footage. Nor do I imply that one can take the question of footage either irresponsibly or frivolously. Everyone must train himself to sense the length and time of sequences in order to be conscious of establishing clearly the future film in its footage-time factor.

But the basic and chief task of the shooting-script is in forming that compositional spine along which must move the development of the action, the composition of the episodes and the arrangement of their elements. In our example from *Boris Godunov* I tried to show that this compositional spine is simultaneously one of the sharpest of expressive forms in relation to a fact and also what is usually called the treatment of a work.

In the novel our fragment is preceded by a description of the weary days when the city, now virtually under siege, maintains an atmosphere of expectation and alarmed inactivity. Two young lieutenants—the author and his friend Igor—find themselves in this city and in this atmosphere; with them are Valega, the author's orderly (one of the most successful images in the novel) and the other lieutenant's orderly, Sedykh. Both young lieutenants kill time as best they can. In the local library one reads old numbers of *Apollo*, the other is enthralled by *Peruvian Tales*. But the library is closing. It is working only one shift—not enough staff. In saying good-bye, the librarian tells them that she has some more volumes of *Apollo*, for 1912 and 1917—and she asks them to come back tomorrow.

And then the passage[1] that we are to work on:

We say goodbye and go. Valega is probably grumbling already—the dinner would be cold.

Near the entrance to the station a square black loud-speaker wheezes hoarsely:

"Citizens, an air-raid warning has been sounded in the city. Attention, citizens, an air-raid warning . . ."

In the last few days air-raid warnings have been sounded three or four times a day. Nobody pays attention to them any longer. There's some shooting—you can't see the aeroplane anyway—and then they give the all-clear.

Valega meets us with a sullen scowl.

"You know very well we've got no oven. I've warmed it up twice already. The potatoes have gone all soft and the borshch is quite . . ." He waves his hand in a hopeless gesture and uncovers the borshch which is wrapped in a greatcoat. Somewhere on the other side of the station the anti-aircraft guns begin to bang away.

The borshch is really good. With meat and sour cream. And plates—rather pretty ones, with little pink flowers—have appeared from somewhere.

"Just like in a restaurant," Igor laughs. "It only wants knife-rests and triangular napkins in the glasses."

And suddenly the whole lot goes flying—plates, spoons, windows and radio-receiver on the wall.

What the devil!

From behind the station the planes come in a steady stream, just as they do in a fly-past. I never saw so many of them. There are so many it is difficult to make out from where they are flying. The whole sky is studded with puffs of anti-aircraft fire.

We stand on the balcony gazing into the sky. Igor, Valega, Sedykh and I. We can't tear ourselves away.

The Germans fly straight at us. They fly in triangular formation, like migrating geese. They fly so low you can see the yellow tips of their wings, the white-bordered crosses and under-carriages exactly like claws . . . Ten . . . twelve . . . fifteen . . . eighteen . . . They draw themselves up in a line right opposite us. The leading one turns upside down, with his wheels in the air and goes into a dive. I can't take my eyes off him. He has red wheels and red cylinder heads. He switches on his siren. Little black spots begin to fall from beneath the wings. One, two, three, four, ten, twelve . . . The last one is white and big. Instinctively I shut my eyes and clutch at the rail. No earth in which to take cover. But you have to do something. A

165

singing sound seems to come from the diving plane. Then it is no longer possible to distinguish anything at all.

An uninterrupted roar. Everything shakes with a horrible tremor. I open my eyes for a second. Nothing to be seen. You can't tell whether it is smoke or dust. Everything is covered in something continuous and thick . . . Again more bombs shriek and more noise. I hang on to the rail. Somebody pinches my arm as if with pincers—above the elbow . . . Valega's face—caught motionless as if by a flash of lightning . . . white, with big round eyes and open mouth . . . Then it vanishes . . .

How long can it go on? An hour, or two hours, or fifteen minutes? There is neither time nor space. Only the thickness and the cold, rough rail. Nothing else.

The rail disappears. I lie on something soft, warm and uncomfortable. It moves under me. I clutch at it. It crawls away.

No thoughts. The brain has been switched off. There remains only instinct—the animal desire to live, and expectation. Not even expectation, but something like—Get it over, get it over quick. . . Whatever it is—only get it over!

Then we are sitting on the bed and smoking. How that happened I don't quite know. Dust all around—just like a fog. And the smell of pitch. In our teeth, in our ears and down the backs of our necks—sand everywhere. On the floor are pieces of plates, puddles of borshch, cabbage leaves and a hunk of meat. In the middle of the room sits a lump of asphalt. Every single window smashed. My neck aches as though somebody had struck it a blow with a stick.

We sit and smoke. I see Valega's fingers shaking. Mine doing the same probably. Sedykh is wiping his leg. Igor has an enormous bruise on his forehead. He tries to smile.

I go out on to the balcony. The station is burning. The little house to the right of the station is also on fire. That's where some sort of editorial office was or a political department—I can't remember. To the left, towards the grain elevator, a continuous glow. The square is empty. There are a few craters in the torn up asphalt.

Somebody is lying behind the fountain. An abandoned ramshackle cart looks as though it had sat down on its hindquarters. The horse is still struggling. Its belly has been ripped open and its intestines are scattered in a pink jelly over the asphalt. The smoke gets thicker and darker. It spreads over the square in a solid cloud.

"Will you want to eat?" Valega asks. His voice is quiet, not his own, rather shaky.

I don't know whether I want to eat, but I say Yes. We eat the cold potato straight from the frying-pan. Igor sits opposite me. His face is grey from dust, like a statue. The evil-looking purple bruise has spread over his whole forehead.

"Oh, to hell with the potato—it just won't go down my throat . . ." He goes out on to the balcony.

As you see, the situation is typical of the circumstances of war. Many have experienced such a situation and can recall it from their own personal point of view. Regardless of this fact, the fragment does not evoke the feeling that it should. The reason for this failing is that the purely compositional expressiveness has been left unfulfilled.

Here we have, rather poorly presented, a description of an aerial attack, stage by stage, with quite well observed individual details. Yet this account is given without "prodding" the means of literary possibilities. The description does not spring dramatically forward, but is content to be a narrative. Such accounts are occasionally found in literary texts as well as in scenarios.

Compare the account of this event, for example, with the representation by Pushkin of the Battle of Poltava. You will see to how large an extent dynamic, rhythmic and structural elements are employed to achieve that compositional relentlessness (remember that word—a composition must be *relentless*) that unswervingly expresses Pushkin's intention, gives three dimensions to the exposition of the subject matter and the author's attitude to it.

From our point of view the defect in the passage chosen from the novel is that the necessary emphases are not made in the material, nor are the high points of tension brought into relief by correspondingly expressive means. Notice the skill with which Pushkin, echoing the varying action of the Battle of Poltava, alters the compositional and rhythmic outlines. The smooth, long phrases of the opening change in rhythm with interjected scenes, which in turn, at the culminating points of the battle, are swiftly transformed into "chopped" lines; "Swede and Russ—stabbing, mangling, slashing". Furthermore, these lines that portray action and behaviour are emphasized with sound images: "Drumbeats, cries, gnashings". Here is not only a choice of characteristic sounds of battle and characteristic action; here, no less, is an inexorable staccato rhythm, a wisely calculated correlation of visual and aural impressions.

We are not demanding that Nekrasov should be a Pushkin. We wish to emphasize the need for choice and a conscious mastery of the medium of expression being used— and we note that the account in the fragment is diffuse, which derives from the almost uniform level of the description, both of the air-raid and of the characters after the attack and the landscape of the blazing city.

Nor is there any variation, either in compositional approach or in inner rhythmic treatment, of the individual parts of the narrative (before the air-raid, the planes, the bombing, after the raid, the burning city, end of scene). This weakens the impression of the fragment which, essentially, has an extremely powerful scene to convey.

As an event entered in a diary, purely for information, we might be satisfied with it, but from the point of view of emotional excitement this treatment of the scene doesn't come up to our demands.

Our task is to translate this material into cinematically striking form and to judge how to arrange it for compositional efficiency.

There is something more to be said about the choice of this fragment.

It is very likely that given a free range of choice of material for this purpose you might not have selected this. Quite understandably, for as treated by the author this fragment draws no attention to itself—the account is not dramatic enough, nor is it particularly thrilling, nor does it seize the imagination.

As for its position in the novel, it is one of the decisive points—for it is from here, from this moment that the epic of Stalingrad begins: this is the first air attack, the first bombing, and here begins the basic thematic line of the novel.

What must be done in order to translate the material of this fragment into a genuinely effective form? That is our present task. How do you think it is necessary to begin?

VOICE FROM THE CLASS: *Divide it into montage pieces!*

To divide it into montage pieces is not difficult. But what will control this division? What is to emerge from a breakdown into a montage list?

VOICE: *The montage pieces are clearly visible in the description of the scene.*

I am in complete agreement with you: the details here are described fully—the phrase is "well seen". However, what we need is to be not only well seen, but also "exposed", *revealed* in such a way that it will act upon our feelings and thoughts.

From this viewpoint what is lacking in this account? What is lacking here is a clearly accented aim or direction which would govern the grouping of its separate elements. The material now is set down in a rather crumbly way. Despite this, are there sequences that convey something deep and substantial which, according to their own nature, could serve as an organized starting-point for shaping the comprehension of the scene as a whole?

VOICES (simultaneously): *Of course, there are!*

When the planes appear — "Ten — twelve — fifteen — eighteen—"

You consider this place the strongest in depth of impression? You really do? But I am asking you to choose a place on which a compositional comprehension of the whole episode can be based. Such conception not to be a "piling up" of details, but primarily the expression of some idea, that continues through the whole sequence.

Could such a purely descriptive picture of an air-raid serve as the means of an inner comprehension of the whole scene? Of course not. This could be an effective scene, but in it there is no key to the compositional solution of the whole.

More suggestions, please.

VOICES: *"We sit and smoke . . ."*
I consider it to be the beginning of the bombardment—
"Instinctively I shut my eyes . . ."
"No earth in which to take cover. But you have to do something . . ."

Why? Why? And again— Why?

In the material of the episode isn't there even one detail that could be ranked beside such "details" as the famous "The people are silent", to which we gave so much attention at the beginning of this lecture? Pushkin's phrase is good, not merely as a stage direction (soundless), or a remark, but above all for the deep idea it contains.

And, as you approach composition, you must seize not only "effective material", but you must find details that touch you deeply, that "touch you to the quick".

Or perhaps the question could be put more clearly: In our material is there something, even a hint of something, through which the idea of the whole scene could be revealed?

VOICE: *It seems to me that the strongest place is when the siren is switched on—the culmination is here . . .*

I'm not against the blare, but is that really capable of revealing the idea of the scene?

VOICE: *But I think such a capacity is in the moment when the blare produces a blow.*

Isn't there a heavier blow to be seized for the comprehension of the episode?

VOICES: *"Somebody pinches my arm as if with pincers— above the elbow . . ."*
"From behind the station the planes come in a steady stream, just as they do in a fly-past."

None of this goes beyond the frame of the purely visual, the impression of pure action. In the next stages of the work these could, with a larger or smaller effect, fill out the separate pieces, but they give us nothing for the definition of the "spine", from which the episode as a whole unfolds.

But perhaps what I'm aiming at is not yet completely clear? Let me explain.

The way to "kindle" the creative fantasy of the artist confronted by an episode cannot be by exterior impressions, but by those containing the most broadly generalized idea of the work. It is that kind of detail that I ask you to find, within this material that has been offered to you. You say: "The planes fly." Where do they fly? We know they are flying towards Stalingrad. But what is the significance of their flight within our composition? Is there some indication how they should be filmed? Is there some line of treatment for the imagery of their action? Can one really draw from this one fact—that they are flying to the city— an understanding of how they are to be represented in this particular episode?

VOICE: *Airplanes with swastikas, hostile to us, are flying over our city. The city is against them, they are against the city—here you have a collision or interaction of opposites.*

How is the city acting against them?

VOICE: *With anti-aircraft guns.*

Is that so? And is that the most significant characteristic in the defence of Stalingrad? And this information of the defence of Stalingrad as an interaction of attacking planes and sharp-shooting anti-aircraft guns—wouldn't this lower the struggle from the level of great pathos to an almost documentary-technical description of separate though very important facts? That's how it seems to me.

So as not to worry you any longer, I'll point to the place that moved me and which meets the conditions in choosing this extract for our work. You may not agree with me, but here is the place:

The smoke gets thicker and darker. It spreads over the square in a solid cloud.

"Will you eat now?" Valega asks. His voice is quiet, not his own, rather shaky.

That is the impressive phrase that caught my attention amidst the general material of the passage.

Why did it catch my attention? And are there grounds for being carried away by such a phrase?

VOICE: *In my opinion, perhaps it was because we see here the first man who did not lose himself in the circumstances of attack.*

Are there possibilities for our work that can grow from this piece?

VOICE: *Certainly, because it shows that a Human Being is always a Human Being and will always remain one.*

Any other considerations in favour of this piece?

VOICE: *I like the transition: after the terrible explosions, when everything flies apart, everything is broken, all is in ruins, comes the question: "Will you eat now?" I don't see here just a man asking a question. And this is because his question, as it were, brings to naught all the efforts of the Germans: the Germans smashed everything, even shattering the very asphalt, but through that question shines one idea: no matter how much the Germans hammer away, they can't beat us.*

Absolutely correct. This piece focuses attention on a magnificent clash: the spreading flames of the ruined city, with hell all around, and suddenly, in the face of all that, the orderly asks in a quiet voice: "Will you eat now?"

This question really has the sound of something "cosmic" overcoming the enemy. Though not yet conscious or deep there is already, as you correctly noted, a sense of elemental invincibility in those the enemy is advancing against. This is more than anti-aircraft guns shooting at bombers. Here is the conflict on a completely different scale and range.

From one side comes the enemy, moving with all the thundering and bursting of cannonades, planes, guns and bombs—and placed in opposition to all this is the intonation of an Altai orderly, speaking in a quiet, frustrating voice: "Will you eat now?" This question, in effect, already "negates", by means of its inner conceptual line, all the horror of the impending.

But is this as definite as we wished? Is there enough in this image of a conscious, purposeful opposition to the enemy, and a conscious will to overcome him?

No. For the present this is elemental inertia, an inertia

"common to all mankind": no matter how many will be killed, no matter how many of us will die, life will look after itself. Is such a motif adequate for us? Is this how we understand the defence of Stalingrad? Of course not.

And here we should ask ourselves whether there is also material in our episode that can reveal the defence of Stalingrad not only as an image of the inertia of life that overcomes death, but above all as a victory of conscious, purposeful Soviet people.

For this let us examine another aspect:

"I don't know whether I want to eat, but I say 'I will'."

What can be sensed in this line? Here is the first sound of a new motif—the incredible obstinacy and tenacity that characterized both the defence of Stalingrad and the defence of Leningrad, and all our other cities that were surrounded but never lost their resolution to defend themselves. Beneath these lines one may easily place another, which expresses its profound, innermost idea: "I don't yet know how we'll manage to defend the city, but I know that we will defend it."

As soon as you add to Valega's words the unspoken thought of the lieutenant, you gain a completed image of the invincibility of our people, possessing indestructible vitality as well as invincible purposefulness. The elemental sound of the orderly's question acquires its final definition in the conscious stubbornness of the officer's words. And both, put together, give a genuine meaningful culmination to the conflicting turns of the episode.

Where is the author's mistake? He is at fault in that he doesn't carve out compositionally these two decisive lines from the general narrative tone; instead, he lets them sound so indistinctly that a whole class of young people didn't catch their particular significance, and "missed" altogether this piece in the whole. It is possible, of course, that the fault lies with the class, but I believe that it is the author's presentation that is to blame. If a film should present these remarks as Nekrasov does, I believe they would never catch the attention of the spectator.

Here we have a typical example of insufficient sculptural

relief in the compositional presentation of the most significant element in the episode.

VOICE: *I like it that this remark is given in a quiet, frustrating voice, and not as a declamation.*

Do you believe that the emphasizing of this remark can be done only through declamatory underlining? Our discussion is not on intonation, but on finding that the most important element of an episode is allowed to be swamped in the general course of the narrative, and that the author by means of compositional structure did not single it out as the most meaningful and significant.

The solution does not lie in making an "exhaustive" treatment of the element itself, but in making a reasoned calculation of the resulting impression. We have seen how the mere extraction, no more, of the remark itself, without the slightest addition of declamation, makes it sound convincing and expressive against the background of the flaming and ruined city.

What causes this most important material to be so submerged that it drowns in the chaos of secondary material?

First of all, because these important remarks are given in exactly the same way as insignificant details of a purely genre order. See what the author writes immediately afterwards:

> We eat cold potatoes straight from the frying pan. Igor sits opposite to me. His face is grey with dust just like a statue. A blue bruise spreads all over his brow, evilly-violet. "To hell with it," he waved his hand. "It sticks in my throat." He goes out on to the balcony.

Are these details necessary? I believe they are completely unnecessary. To add such elements, and to present them in such a matter-of-fact descriptive detail, seems to me simply like the inability to halt the episode at a vital point and place a full stop just where you have the maximum impressive strength.

The art of placing a period where it must be—that is a great art.*

---

* E. often quoted Babel's remark (in his 'Maupassant') that "there is no iron that can enter the human heart with such stupefying effect as a period, placed at the right moment".—J. L.

It's clear enough that the life of the characters is not broken off at this point. Dinner will go on, someone will get up, go out on the balcony, and do all sorts of things. But why do we need all this? It begins to resemble one of the commentator's proposals for the interpretation of the finale of *Boris Godunov*, with an aimless "individualization" of the crowd.

After making a remark about food play a role of great conceptual significance, it is tossed back once more, drowned in a chaos of genre details about food sticking in someone's throat but not in another's, while a third doesn't wish to think about food at all, etc. From this arrangement of the materials we must extract the theme of the birth of stubbornness in the future defenders of Stalingrad—and let nothing throw into shadow the distinctness of its expression.

If you want genre details they can be added *ad infinitum*. One could tell how Valega stands at attention by the table, and Sedykh rubs his leg, and make a string of observations on the fate of the evil-looking purple bruise on Igor's forehead—all is possible. But such a swamping of the essentials with a host of unnecessary, incidental particulars, contributes to the burial of the main thought, and the vital piece itself loses so much of its impressiveness that it seems uninteresting material even for a compositional étude!

I think we have now determined, though with considerable difficulty, the starting point which will permit us to organize the material harmoniously from a definite point of view. Let this serve as an example that the so-called "Breaking down into Units" and the "distribution of acting objectives" (terms used in the Stanislavsky method of Analysis), need not be reckoned from the beginning of an episode but are determined by the point of its maximum significance.

The compositional solution of any scene must be launched from that unit which more than any other impresses one with its content and originality. It must also be kept in mind that ordinarily the unit that strikes with greatest force is not only the most immediately effective, but also the one that contains the inner dynamic expression of the theme.

In the analysed scene with Valega we are moved and struck by the collision of two elements, two rhythms. When you begin to take apart the actual content of these impressions, you'll detect that such a clash of two elements is not accidental; through it is revealed, or can be revealed, a deep inner idea. In this clash, under the most acute conditions, are presented those elements of the conflict in the composition of which would be the dramatic working out of the whole episode.

Here we move on to the second chief method of extracting the essential compositional elements that we need. (As we have just said, the first method is to sift out the significant from the incidental.)

The method that I wish to present is the timely preparation for the extraction of the essential. The most effective means of doing this is to lead to the culmination point through a fixed line of recurrences, uncovered from somewhere near the beginning, and conducted through a series of distinctly memorable points.

We have already said that our chosen scene is very important for Nekrasov's book as a whole. We grow more convinced of this when we look into it intently. And not only because we see beginning here the theme of stubbornness, resistance, contempt for danger, and obstinacy. But also because in this episode's situation we are given, as it were, a vivid anticipation of one of the most serious motives within the general theme of the whole work.

The theme touched on in our chosen episode is resumed three chapters later:

Not long ago some soldiers had marched by. I was on duty at the telephone and went out to have a smoke. As they marched they sang, quietly, in low voices. I didn't even see them—I only heard their steps on the asphalt and the quiet, rather sad song about the Dnieper and the cranes. I went across to them. The men were resting along the roadside on the trampled-down grass under the acacias. The half-concealed lights of the cigarettes twinkled. And a young, quiet voice reached me from somewhere under the trees:

"No, Vasya . . . don't say that. You'll never find any better than ours. Honestly, the soil's like butter, rich and good." He even smacked his lips in a special way. "The corn will come up, it'll be over your head . . ."

Meanwhile the town was burning, and the red reflection of the flames flickered over the walls of the factory, and, somewhere quite near, machine-guns rattled—sometimes more and sometimes less frequently—and Very lights went up, and ahead was uncertainty and an almost inescapable death . . .

I never saw who said that. Someone shouted: "Get ready to move!" There was a clatter of mess-tins and they were off. They went off slowly with the heavy gait of the soldier.[2]

The same theme and almost the same circumstances: the burning city and here a conversation about growing corn:

And in that song and in those simple words about the soil as rich as butter, about the grain growing higher than your head, there was also *some*thing . . . I don't even know what to call it. Tolstoy called it the secret warmth of patriotism. Maybe that was the most accurate definition. Maybe that is the miracle that Georgi Akimovich is waiting for . . .

Even that intonation of Valega's ("his voice is quiet") continues in the speaking of the words or the twinkling of cigarettes:

As they marched they sang, quietly, in low voices. . . .
The half-concealed lights of the cigarettes twinkled. . . .
. . . a young, quiet voice . . .

There also continues what is for us the essential motif of convinced tenacity, as in: "I don't know whether I want to eat, but I say 'I will'." In answer to Georgi Akimovich's harsh words Igor says:

"They will go no further. I know they won't." And he walks off. It can't be . . . That is all we can say for the moment.

And this motif appeared even earlier—thirty pages before our episode:

177

"So long, Ma, we'll see you again, believe me, we shall meet again . . ."
And I have that faith . . . That is all we have now—faith.

Thus individual themes or leitmotifs run endlessly through scene after scene, developing, intertwining, intersecting, each carrying its own deposit in creating the image required by the whole work.

In what respect doesn't this equal the "classics"?

It is true that all these facts are actually present—but present within the material and as material, not in a conscious measure of juxtaposition, not in construction, not in compositional calculation, ensuring their faultless, clear-cut influence.

Individual links do not react to one another nor are sensed as a whole. Nor are the separate lines combined one with the other. Indeed the very lines themselves, in essence, do not exist. The author does not give them any significant form.

Instead we have a scattering of points; admittedly they are brilliant, but they do not fuse into a line. There are sometimes huge gaps. There is sometimes so much material between the thematic lines that we get a "disrupting" effect. Sometimes the reciprocal arrangement is simply chaotic.

In the novel the hero and Georgi Akimovich walk at length, seemingly endlessly, to check the cables linking the charges placed for the demolition of the power station. But the author does not do as much in relation to the thematic lines that run through his novel. Here the lines are torn apart. And the final explosion can't come off. The charges seem to be individually correct, but are not placed properly. The circuit is interrupted and the explosions misfire.

Only when we extract the chief points from the general flood of narrative, and stand them side by side, only then are these lines drawn together and seen as the main line of action in clearly traced contours. But in the novel they are so arranged that unity and connectives between the separate links cannot be perceived; motifs are lost in the flow of genre details that should be attached to the work itself as stubbornly as the resolution of the heroes of the novel.

In one place the author sets forth an idea that is neither new nor unexpected:

There are some little things that you remember all your life. And more than remember. Small and seemingly insignificant, they somehow eat into you, grow into something big and significant, absorbing into themselves the whole essence of events, and become a sort of symbol.[3]

Yet the author's own details remain only memorable particularities, only seeds, unconverted into sprouts that might bring the particularities to a generalized image.

Nor should one lapse into the other extreme—a naked schematic framework in which alone consists the unity of the work. This is just as shocking as the scanning of verses by "beating out" their metres, instead of the living pulsation of the rhythm gliding along the dead bones of the metre. That is a skeleton in place of a living body!

You have no right to count on the "inexorability" of the influence of your work, if its beautiful elements, its construction materials, are not fused into an architectural entity, an engineered, worked out juxtaposition of all its parts. Your separate "bricks" may occasionally be very good, but their only hope of life is in a unity, arranged in a clear architectural form, as we have tried to show—and beyond the limits of "our" episode.

Involuntarily the questions arise: Are all these individual details consistently and consciously finished according to the mould of the chosen thematic lines?

What part does intuition play in making one's theme advance along all its graphic and perceived elements to complete the work?

Isn't the play of the living, perceptible, full-blooded musculature of a sportsman, under the integument of the living body, equally unlike the lymphatic, brittle non-muscularity of an untrained body, as it is to the over-developed system of muscles often transforming a living gymnast into the resemblance of an exhibit in a theatre of anatomy?

Nekrasov's work does not achieve that indispensable degree of inner graphic proportions. Here good "building

179

materials" have not yet been brought together in a convincing architectural whole. In many places the material has been left in stacks. And our job is to sweep away the litter stuffed between the structurally related elements.

Our present task, of making a montage-list or shooting-script from the material of Nekrasov's novel, consists in doing just the opposite of what happened, for example, to the stage adaptation of *Anna Karenina*.

Though Tolstoy's novel with inimitable brilliance and finish images the ever tightening ring of the implacability of society which finally pushed Anna beneath the train, such an inexorably tragic course is absent from its theatrical adaptation. Instead we are given a chain of individual, independent genre episodes in the fate of Anna Karenina, which, though they have connections in them and subject, with those which pushed her to suicide, nevertheless lack the general sense of unrelenting pressure, of ever-diminishing encirclement, so strongly and irresistibly depicted in the novel.

Not only in our episode from Nekrasov's novel but throughout the entire novel there seems to be a single "mood" of the author, a scattering of separate genre and war episodes. But this mood is nowhere raised to a clean-cut purposeful conception that fuses separate elements into a unified, inviolable, interlocked organism, such as we have tried to indicate for the composition of our chosen episode, attempting to shape it into a unity of a strict musical style.

I find myself coming back to music again and again—though I must remind you that I am no musician.

A composer's creative work has long interested me. Not so much what is taught in the Conservatoire, that is, the subtleties of "treatment" of the composer's idea—nor the categories of musical form and general laws of musical construction taught there.

I have always been intrigued by the "mystery" of the birth of a musical image, the emergence of melodies and appearance of that captivating harmony and unity which arise from the chaos of the temporary correlations and disconnected sounds that fill the world around the composer.

I have always wondered how Prokofiev, knowing only

the number of seconds allotted to him and having seen the edited material twice (or thrice, at the most), can have the music ready on the very next day, music which corresponds unerringly and precisely in all its caesuras and accents not only with the general rhythm of the entire episode, but with all the subtlest nuances of the montage development.

Correspondence here is not a "matching of accents"—that primitive method of establishing a correspondence between pictures and music, but the astonishing contrapuntal development of music which fuses organically and sensually with the visual images.

Any composer setting out to write music for the screen, as well as any director with an ambition to work in the sound film, to say nothing of the chromophone film (that is, working with both music and colour), must possess this ability, although not necessarily so highly developed as in the case of Prokofiev.

I shall confine myself at present to analysing the methods by which Prokofiev finds structural and rhythmical equivalents for the edited piece of film that has been brought to him.

The projection-room is darkened . . .

The picture runs on the screen . . .

And on the arm of the chair, nervously drumming, exactly like a Morse telegrapher, tap the relentlessly precise, long fingers of Prokofiev.

Is Prokofiev beating time?

No. He is "beating" something more than that.

He is detecting the structural laws governing the lengths and tempo in the edited pieces, harmonizing these with the actions and intonations of the characters.

On the following day he will send me the music which will permeate my montage structure, the structural laws of which he will carry into the rhythmic figure that his fingers tapped out.

The situation is somewhat different when the composer has to work with unedited material. Then he has to discover the potentialities of structural laws inherent in it.

What should not be lost sight of is the circumstance that

the structure of the separate pieces shot for any scene is not accidental.

If it is really a "montage" piece, that is, not disconnected but meant to produce an image together with other pieces, it will, at the very moment it is shot, be infused with elements which characterize its inner content and at the same time contain the embryo of the structure most suited for the fullest possible revelation of this content in the finished compositional form.

And if the composer is faced with (for the time being) a chaotic agglomeration of pieces with such structural potentialities, his task will not be to discover the finished structure of the whole but to find in the individual elements the embryos of the future structure and, proceeding from these, to set down the compositional form into which the pieces will fit organically.[4]

Our apparent digression, directly related to the work of Prokofiev, closes with what we are doing in our fragment of the *Stalingrad* novel.

When we worked on a Pushkin poem, endeavouring to transpose its lines into adequate rhythmic and visual pictorial elements, we started with *discovering* the basic rules on which Pushkin had constructed them, so that we could transpose those rules into a base for our audio-visual structure.

Nekrasov's material, on the other hand, approximates to the second type of film composer's work that we described above. It bears more resemblance to the selection of pieces that are not yet organized into a final montage composition.

Our task in converting this material is to "listen" to the individual structural potentialities of each of the pieces, to extract them, to define their structure for ourselves, and, according to the compositional demands, to understand, treat, arrange, and group the separate pieces and details.

To be fair to Nekrasov, we must note that the weak montage combination of elements make up an authentically impressive whole and contain separate pieces that are not only excellent, but are also correctly perceived. Correctly in the sense that they are subordinated to a basic mood, corresponding to the author's basic conception and answering to that intonation in which the author senses its fullest expression.

At the same time one cannot help noticing a certain monotony in this intonation, which in my opinion results not so much from an inability to master a diversity of rhythmic styles as from the personal emotional colouring that his own memories and impressions have for the author and which in the novel he shares with his readers.

It is very curious that despite all the objective heroism described by the author the tonality of his exposition is unexpectedly in a minor key. "Musically" it goes contrary to the author's intention, adding to the whole novel a certain extra coating of "intellectualism", and "smoothing out" the expressiveness of the theme's rhythmic turns and the expressiveness of the whole composition.

So, when you take up this existing composition with all its defects and merits, you must do all in your power to make it effective.

Daumier said that "one must belong to one's own time". We can interpret this more profoundly by keeping in mind that we belong not only to our own time, but above all to the great ideas that our people are bringing to life. Therefore both our thoughts and our creative intentions and the concrete embodiments of our thoughts must be determined by our ideological direction.

In order to express organically our ideas in images, we must take care to master the practical skill of craftsmanship, so as to bring out the images inherent in the material.

And this is the most correct path by which to approach composition. It protects the "builder" against formal arbitrariness, as well as abstract preconceptions, and gives him each time the possibility of approaching the living material of the work afresh, and avoiding routine, stereotypes and clichés.

Sources and Notes

A Personal Statement
  see Bibliography, No. 14

The Method of Making Workers' Films
  see Bibliography, No. 8
  1. Alexander Belenson, *Cinema Today* (Moscow 1925).
  2. E. cites these censorship laws as from a New York book of 1911, "The Art of the Motion Picture", but I cannot identify this reference.

The Soviet Cinema
  see Bibliography, No. 68
  1. Though E.'s manuscript refers to Griffith's film *America*, the editors of *Voices of October* revised this to refer to *The Birth of a Nation*, a film that E. may not have known at that time; it is for this reason I have restored the original reference.

The New Language of Cinema
  see Bibliography, No. 52

Perspectives
  see Bibliography, No. 61
  1. G. V. Plekhanov, Foreword to the third edition (Moscow 1914) of *For Twenty Years*.
  2. George Berkeley, Bishop of Cloyne, *A Treatise Concerning the Principles of Human Knowledge;* cited here from a reproduction of the 1710 and 1734 editions (London 1937). These passages from Berkeley's Introduction were translated into Russian by E. from a German text cited by E. Cassirer in *Philosophie der symbolischen Formen*, Vol. I (Berlin 1923).
  3. G. V. Plekhanov, *Fundamental Problems of Marxism*, translated by Eden and Cedar Paul (London 1929),

quoting von den Steinen, *Unter den Naturvölkern Zentral-Brasiliens* (Berlin 1894).

4. The citation of Renan's *La Réforme intellectuelle et morale* was found in Plekhanov, *Art and Social Life*, translated by Eleanor Fox (London 1953), p. 190.

The Dynamic Square
see Bibliography, No. 74

1. This memorandum was compiled by Lester Cowan in preparation for the discussion on 17 Sept. 1930; all of E.'s quotations are from this memorandum, which can be consulted at the Academy of Motion Picture Arts and Sciences, Hollywood. Loyd A. Jones's paper, "Rectangle Proportions in Pictorial Composition", was published in *Journal of the Society of Motion Picture Engineers*, Jan. 1930; this issue contains other relevant papers.

GTK—GIK—VGIK
see Bibliography, No. 119

1. This reference is to E.'s first version of his teaching programme, published in *Sovietskoye kino*, Nos. 5–6, 1933, as "The Granite of Film Science". This programme, tested and enlarged, was later published in *Iskusstvo kino*, No. 4, 1936. For translations of this "second" programme, see Bibliography, No. 145.

Lessons from Literature
see Bibliography, No. 267

1. *Earth*, translated by Ann Lindsay (Elek Books, London 1954).

2. *The Fatal Skin*, translated by Cedar Paul (Hamish Hamilton, London 1949).

The Embodiment of a Myth
see Bibliography, No. 202.

More Thoughts on Structure
see Bibliography, No. 200

1. Paul Whiteman and Mary Margaret McBride, *Jazz* (New York 1926), p. 119.
2. Alexandre Dumas, *My Memoirs*, trans. by E. M. Waller (London 1908), vol. V., pp. 235, 245.
3. *The Letters of Anton Pavlovitch Tchehov to Olga Leonardovna Knipper*, translated by Constance Garnett (Chatto & Windus, London 1926), p. 33.
4. Vladimir Nemirovich-Danchenko, *My Life in the Russian Theatre*, translated by John Cournos (Geoffrey Bles, London 1937), pp. 67–71.
5. S. Tolstoy, "Turgenev at Yasnaya Polyana", in *Golos minuvshevo*, 1919, Nos. 1–14, p. 233.
6. Pushkin, *Eugene Onegin*, in translation by Babette Deutsch (*The Works of Pushkin*, Random House 1936).

Charlie the Kid
see Bibliography, No. 250
1. H. A. Overstreet, *Influencing Human Behaviour* (Jonathan Cape, London 1926), pp. 11–15.
2. Ibid, pp. 26–27.   3. Ibid, pp. 260–62.
4. Chaplin's interview with A. J. Urban, "I Talked with Charlie Chaplin", *Intercine* (Rome), October 1935.
5. Possibly Ywan Goll's *Die Chaplinade* (Dresden 1920), or *Das Chaplin-Drama*, by Melchior Bischer (Berlin 1924).
6. Elie Faure, "The Art of Charlie Chaplin", in *The Art of Cineplastics*, translated by Walter Pach (Boston 1923), pp. 62–63.
7. C. W. Kimmins, *The Springs of Laughter* (Methuen, London 1928), p. 95.
8. C. W. Kimmins, *The Child's Attitude to Life* (Methuen, London 1926), p. 60.
9. Charles Baudelaire, "De l'Essence du Rire," in *Curiosités esthétiques* (Editions de la Nouvelle Revue Française, Paris 1925).
10. *Fables from "Fun"* (these Bierce fables appeared in the London *Fun* in 1872–73); reprinted in *The Monk and the Hangman's Daughter* (New York 1926); E.

found "The Man and the Goose" in *Mark Twain's Library of Humour.*
11. Karl Marx, *Towards a Critique of Hegel's Philosophy.*
12. Urban's interview in *Intercine.*

Mr Lincoln by Mr Ford
see Bibliography, No. 283
1. *Lincoln, His Life in Photographs* (New York 1941).
2. "Death of Abraham Lincoln", in Walt Whitman, *Complete Poetry and Selected Prose and Letters,* ed. by Emory Holloway (The Nonesuch Press, London 1938), pp. 752–62.

A Close-Up View
see Bibliography, No. 249

Problems of Composition
see Bibliography, No. 266
1. Victor Nekrasov, *Front-Line Stalingrad,* translated by David Floyd (Harvill Press, London 1962), pp. 81–84. I have tampered with Mr Floyd's vigorous translation to bring it closer to the *Znamya* text used by Eisenstein; my chief alteration, here and in subsequent citations, is the restoration of the present tense of the original.
2. Ibid; Chap. XVI. 3. Ibid.
4. E. quotes his essay on Prokofiev, at that time not yet published in the Soviet Union (see Bibliography, No. 251).

The Published Writings (1922-1982) of Sergei Eisenstein

with notes on their English translations

This list is based on the bibliography (prepared by Venyamin Vishnevsky and Pera Atasheva) published in *Izbranniye stat'i*, edited by R. Yurenev; interviews, both in Russian and in English, have been omitted.—J. L.

If no place of publication is given, Moscow is to be understood.

1922

1 Letters to the Editors of *Zrelishcha*, 1922, No. 6, p. 26. The letter, commenting on an article by I. Aksyonov on Tairov, is signed by N. Foregger, V. Mass, S. Yutkevich, S. Eisenstein.

1a THE EIGHTH ART on expressionism, America and, of course, Chaplin (written with Sergei Yutkevich). In *Echo*, No. 2, 1922, pp. 20–21.

1b [Notes on Meyerhold's production of *Tarelkin's Death*, unsigned], in *STINF Bulletin*, 21 November 1922. Reprinted in V. E. Meyerhold, *Essays, Letters, Speeches, Interviews*, Vol. 2, 1968, p. 533.

1923

2 MONTAGE OF ATTRACTIONS, in *Lef*, 1923, No. 3, pp. 70–75. Translated excerpt in *The Film Sense*, pp. 230–233; a fuller translation in *The Drama Review* (New York), March 1974.

1924

3 ABOUT WEST, in *Zrelishcha*, 1924, No. 83–84. On Kuleshov's new film, *Adventures of Mr West in the Land of the Bolsheviks*.

1925

4 Letter to the Editors of *Kino-nedelya*, 1925, No. 2. A polemic with V. Pletnyov on 'E.'s departure from Proletcult.

5 Letter to the Editors of *Kino-nedelya*, 1925, No. 10. Continuing the polemic.

5a Letter to the Editor of *Kinogazeta*, 17 February 1925.

6 ARE CRITICS NECESSARY?, in *Novyi zritel*, 1925, No. 13, p. 6. Reply to a questionnaire.

7 ON THE QUESTION OF A MATERIALIST APPROACH TO FORM, in *Kino-zhurnal ARK*, 1925, No. 4–5, pp. 5–8. On the experience of *Strike*, and the theories of Dziga Vertov. Translated in *The Avant-Garde Film*, ed. P. Adams Sitney (New York 1978).

8 THE METHOD OF MAKING WORKERS' FILMS, in *Kino*, 11 August 1925. Translation in *Film Essays*, pp. 17–20.

1926

9 WHAT THEY SAY ABOUT "BATTLESHIP POTEMKIN", in *Sovietskii ekran*, 1926, No. 2, p. 10. A reply to a questionnaire.

10 WHAT WAS SAID ABOUT "BATTLESHIP POTEMKIN", in *Vechernaya Móskva*, 1 February 1926. A brief reply to a questionnaire.

11 "POTEMKIN" THROUGH THE GERMAN CENSORSHIP, in *Sovietskoye kino*, 1926, No. 3, pp. 14–15. E.'s and Tisse's account of their visit to Berlin.

12 NOT AT ALL ODD, ABOUT KHOKHLOVA, in *Kino*, 30 March 1926, reprinted in the brochure, *A. Khokhlova*, 1926, pp. 5–9.

13 GERMAN CINEMA, in *Vestnik rabotnikov iskusstv*, 1926, No. 10, pp. 8–9.

14 S. EISENSTEIN ABOUT S. EISENSTEIN, in *Berliner Tageblatt*, Berlin, 7 June 1926. An autobiographical statement written for this newspaper. Translation in *Film Essays*, pp. 13–17.

15 FIVE EPOCHS, in *Pravda*, 6 July 1926. On the project for *The General Line*.

16 ON THE ROAD OF SOVIET FILMS, in *Rabochaya Moskva*, 15 July 1926. Reply to a questionnaire.

17 ON THE POSITION OF BELA BALAZS, in *Kino*, 20 July 1926. An answer to Balázs's article, "on the future of the film".

18 BELA FORGETS THE SCISSORS, in *Kino*, 10 August 1926. Continuing the discussion with Balázs. Translated in *The Battleship Potemkin*, ed. Herbert Marshall (New York 1978).

19 THE TWO SKULLS OF ALEXANDER THE GREAT, in *Novyi zritel*, 1926, No. 35, p. 10. A reply to a questionnaire on "Theatre or Cinema?".

20 Letter to the Editor of *Molot*, Rostov-na-Don, 26 November 1926. Thanks to those who took part in the filming of *The General Line*.

1927
21 Letter to the Editors of *Novyi zritel*, 1927, No. 2. Protesting against their editorial commentary on E.'s letter to *Molot*.

22 WHAT THE DIRECTORS SAY, in *Komsomolskaya pravda*, 21 September 1927. A reply to a questionnaire on the libretto contest organized by this paper.

23 THE FUTURE OF SOVIET CINEMA, in *Krasnaya panorama*, Leningrad, 1927, No. 40, pp. 7–8.

24 FILM AND THE DEFENCE OF THE COUNTRY, in *Sovietskoye kino*, Leningrad, 1927, No. 7, p. 6. A reply to an anniversary questionnaire.

25 TO EACH HIS OWN, in *Krasnaya gazeta*, Leningrad, 20 October 1927. About the party conference on film questions.

26 WHY "OCTOBER" IS LATE, in *Kino*, 20 December 1927. Translated excerpt in *Kino* (London 1960), pp. 238–239.

27 S. M. EISENSTEIN ON "OCTOBER". In the brochure, *October*, 1927, pp. 7–8; reprinted in the brochure, *October* (Vladivostok 1928).

28 GIVE US A STATE PLAN, in *Kino-front*, 1927, No. 13–14, pp. 6–8. Reprinted in *Izbranniye stat'i* (1956).

1928
29 WHAT WE EXPECT FROM THE PARTY CONFERENCE ON FILM QUESTIONS, in *Sovietskii ekran*, 1928, No. 1, p. 6.

30 LITERATURE AND CINEMA, in *Na literaturnom postu*, 1928,

No. 1, pp. 71–73. A reply to a questionnaire on the interrelations between the two arts.

31 FOR A SPECIAL SECTION, in *Kino-front*, 1928, No. 1, pp. 2–5. An argument for the formation of a special section for film affairs.

32 IN THE BATTLES FOR "OCTOBER", in *Komsomolskaya pravda*, 7 March 1928.

33 HOW WE MADE "OCTOBER", in *Vechernaya Moskva*, 8 March 1928. Signed by E. and Alexandrov.

34 FOR WORKERS' FILMS, in *Revolutzia i kultura*, 1928, No. 3–4, pp. 52–56.

35 OCTOBER, in *Kino*, 13 March 1928. Extracts from the scenario, signed by E. and Alexandrov. Translated in the *Daily Worker* (New York), 3 November 1928.

36 OUR "OCTOBER", ACTED AND NON-ACTED, in *Kino*, 13 and 20 March 1928. The second instalment signed by E. and Alexandrov.

37 FOR A SOVIET CINEMA, in *Na literaturnom postu*, 1928, No. 4, pp. 15–18.

38 WE'RE WAITING, in *Komsomolskaya pravda*, 1 April 1928. On the forthcoming release of *October*; signed by E. and Alexandrov.

39 "GENERAL LINE", in *Komsomolskaya pravda*, 30 April 1928. Signed by E. and Alexandrov.

40 THE FUTURE OF SOUND FILMS, A STATEMENT, in *Zhizn iskusstva*, Leningrad, 1928, No. 32, pp. 4–5, and *Sovietskii ekran*, 1928, No. 32, p. 5. Signed by E., Pudovkin, and Alexandrov. Translations in New York *Herald Tribune*, 21 September 1928; in New York *Times*, 7 October 1928; in *Close Up* (Territet), October 1928; in New York *Sun*, 5 June 1930; and in *Film Form*, pp. 257–259.

41 THEATRICAL TRASH AND NEW WEAPONS OF CULTURE. QUESTIONNAIRE: HOW CAN WE USE THE SOUND FILM, in *Sovietskii ekran*, 1928, No. 34, p. 6.

42 THE UNEXPECTED JUNCTION, in *Zhizn iskusstva*, Leningrad, 1928, No. 34, pp. 6–9. Translation in *Film Form*, pp. 18–27.

43 HOW WE ARE MAKING "GENERAL LINE", in *Vechernaya Moskva*, 5 October 1928.

10

6

44 TWELFTH, in *Sovietskii ekran,* 1928, No. 45, pp. 4–5. Signed by E. and Alexandrov.

45 LE CORBUSIER VISITS S. M. EISENSTEIN, in *Sovietskii ekran,* 1928, No. 46, p. 5. Signed with pseudonym, "R—k".

46 Open Letter, in *Izvestia,* 11· November 1928, p. 5. On the note in the foreign press that E. was "escaping" abroad.

47 "GENERAL LINE", in *Gudok,* 21 November 1928.

48 ONE, TWO, THREE—PANICKERS ARE WE, in *Kino,* Leningrad, 27 November 1928. Signed by E. and Alexandrov.

49 "GENERAL LINE", in *Izvestia,* 6 December 1928. Signed by E. and Alexandrov.

50 MY FIRST FILM, in *Sovietskii ekran,* 1928, No. 50, p. 10. On the film interlude ("Glumov's Diary") made for the Proletcult production of Ostrovsky's *Enough Simplicity in Every Wise Man.* Translated in *Cinema in Revolution,* ed. Luda and Jean Schnitzer, David Robinson (London 1973).

1929

51 OUTSIDE THE FRAME. Afterword to Nikolai Kaufman's *Japanese Cinema,* 1929, pp. 72–92. Translation (as "The Cinematograph Principle and Japanese Culture") in *Transition* (Paris), June 1930; reprinted in *Experimental Cinema,* No. 3, 1932; in *Film Form,* pp. 28–44; in *Film: an Anthology* (New York 1959).

52 FOREWORD, to the Russian translation of Guido Seeber's *Der Trickfilm,* 1929, pp. 3–8. Translation (as "The New Language of Cinematography") in *Close Up,* in May 1929; reprinted in *Film Essays,* pp. 32–34.

53 "GENERAL LINE", in *Komsomolskaya pravda,* 3 February 1929. Signed by E. and Alexandrov.

54 AN EXPERIMENT UNDERSTOOD BY MILLIONS, in *Sovietskii ekran,* 1929, No. 6, pp. 6–7. Signed by E. and Alexandrov. Reprinted in *Izbranniye stat'i* (1956).

55 FATHER MATVEI, in *Sovietskii ekran,* 1929, No. 7. A reminiscence from the filming of *General Line.*

56 ENTHUSIASTIC WORKDAYS, in *Rabochaya Moskva,* 22 February 1929. On the approaching release of *General Line*; signed by E. and Alexandrov.

57 WITHOUT ACTORS, in *Ogonyok*, 1929, No. 10, pp. 10–11. Signed by E. and Alexandrov. Translation in *Cinema* (New York), June 1930.

58 GTK—VUZ, in *Kino*, 12 March 1929. A proposal to reorganize the film technicum on a higher educational level.

59 THREE YEARS, in *Literaturnaya gazeta*, 1 July 1929. On the making of *General Line*; signed by E. and Alexandrov.

60 ABOUT THE FILM-SCHOOL, in *Rabis*, 1929, No. 32, pp. 6–7.

61 PERSPECTIVES, in *Iskusstvo*, 1929, No. 1–2, pp. 116–122. First translated from a condensed German text (prepared by E. for *Der Querschnitt*, January 1930) in *The Left* (Davenport), Autumn 1931; complete essay translated in *Film Essays*, pp. 35–47.

62 THE FILMIC FOURTH DIMENSION, in *Kino*, 27 August 1929. Translations in *Close Up*, March 1930, and *Film Form*, pp. 64–71.

63 THE SOUND FILM HERE, in *Rabis*, 1929, No. 38, p. 4.

On 19 August 1929 E., Alexandrov and Tisse leave the Soviet Union for a work-visit to Europe and America.

64 ON THE FORM OF THE SCENARIO, in *Bulletin kinokontori Torgpredstva SSSR v Germanii*, Berlin, 1929, No. 1–2, pp. 29–32, and in *Literaturnaya gazeta*, 9 December 1929.

65 DER FILM DER ZUKUNFT, in *Vossische Zeitung*, Berlin, 15 September 1929. Another section of "Perspectives", revised to announce project for filming *Capital*. Translated excerpt in New York *Herald Tribune*, 22 December 1929.

66 DER KAMPF UM DIE ERDE (Berlin 1929). Translation, by Erwin Honig, of the *Old and New* scenario, by E. and Alexandrov. Translation in *Film Writing Forms*, ed. by Lewis Jacobs (New York 1934); E.'s preface ("Drehbuch? Nein: Kinonovelle!"), partially translated in New York *Times*, 30 March 1930, is a German translation of No. 64.

67 Letter to the Editors of *Film Kurier*, 17 October 1929. A denial that he had directed scenes for Dubson's *Giftgas*.

1930

68 [Soviet Cinema], in *Voices of October* (New York 1930), pp. 225–239. Written in 1928, for incorporation into Joseph Freeman's essay on Soviet cinema in this volume. Reprinted in *Film Essays*, pp. 20–31.

69 GENDARMES IN THE SORBONNE, in *Kino*, 10 March 1930. Signed with pseudonym, "R.O.Rik".

70 LES PRINCIPES DU NOUVEAU CINEMA RUSSE, in *La Revue du Cinéma* (Paris), April 1930. Transcription of E.'s lecture at the Sorbonne University, 17 February 1930.

71 [Methods of Montage], published as "The Fourth Dimension in the Kino: II", *Close Up*, April 1930, pp. 253–268. Written in London (dated Autumn 1929), to supplement the essay translated in *Close Up*, March 1930. Reprinted in *Film Form*, pp. 72–83.

72 OUR FILMS MUST SOUND AND SPEAK, in *Za kommunisticheskoye prosveshcheniye*, 18 September 1930.

73 Letter to Léon Moussinac (from Hollywood), published in *Cinémonde* (Paris), 9 October 1930.

1931

74 THE DYNAMIC SQUARE, in *Close Up*, March, June 1931. Based on the Hollywood speech made by E. during a discussion on the wide film, 17 September 1930; written in Mexico. Reprinted, in shortened version, in *Hound and Horn*, April 1931; reprinted in full in *Film Essays*, pp. 48–65.

75 THE PRINCIPLES OF FILM FORM, in *Close Up*, September 1931, pp. 167–181. Translation by Ivor Montagu from a German MS. (dated Zürich, 2 November 1929); also in *Experimental Cinema*, No. 4, 1932; expanded translation (as "A Dialectic Approach to Film Form") from an untitled German MS. (dated Moscow, April 1929) in *Film Form*, pp. 45–62.

76 Letter to GIK (from Guadalajara), published in *Kino*, 1 September 1931.

77 AMERICAN TRAGEDY, in *Proletarskoye kino*, 1931, No. 9, p. 59. Signed with pseudonym, "R.O.Rik".

78 Letter to the Editors of *The Nation*, published 9 Decem-

ber 1931. A reply to Edmund Wilson's article of 4 November 1931, "Eisenstein in Hollywood".

On 9 May 1932 E. and Tisse return to Moscow.

1932

79 INVESTMENT IN THE BUSINESS OF SOCIALISM, in *Za bol-shevistskii film* (the Mosfilm newspaper), 16 May 1932.

80 THE MOST AMUSING, in *Sovietskoye iskusstvo*, 9 August 1932. On the staging of comedy.

81 OVERTAKE AND SURPASS, in *Proletarskoye kino*, 1932, No. 15–16, pp. 20–32. Translation (as "The Cinema in America: impressions of Hollywood, its life and values") in *International Literature*, July 1933.

82 OCTOBER AND ART, in *Soviet Culture Review*, 1932, No. 7–9. Russian text (as "Through Revolution to Art—Through Art to Revolution") in *Sovietskoye kino*, 1933, No. 1–2, pp. 34–36; and in *Izbranniye stat'i*. English translation reprinted in *International Literature*, October 1933; in the *Daily Worker* (New York), 29 January 1934; and in Marie Seton, *Sergei M. Eisenstein* (London 1952), pp. 479–481.

83 MUCH OBLIGED!, in *Proletarskoye kino*, 1932, No. 17–18, p. 19–29. Translation (as "Detective Work in the GIK", "Cinematography *with* Tears" and "An American Tragedy") in *Close Up*, December 1932, March and June 1933; E. added material from another article to the first translation; original text translated (as "A Course in Treatment") in *Film Form*, pp. 84–107.

84 IN THE FIRST RANK, in *Kino*, 6 September 1932. A salute to the anti-war congress in Amsterdam.

85 DIE ERSTE KOLONNE MARSCHIERT . . ., in *Kino*, 18 September 1932. On the film industry's thematic plan.

86 TO A FOUNDER OF CULTURE, in *Kino*, 24 September 1932. Greetings on the 40th anniversary of Gorky's literary career.

87 ON DETECTIVE WORK, in *Kino*, 18 October 1932. Translation incorporated into "Detective Work in the GIK", *Close Up*, December 1932.

ber 1933. A reply to a questionnaire on the All-Union Thematic Conference on Cinema.

1934

103 FOR HIGH IDEALS, FOR FILM CULTURE!, in *Kino,* 22 January 1934. A report to the 17th Party Congress on the plan for *Moscow,* and on the work of GIK.

104 I OWE ALL TO THE PARTY, in *Rabis,* 1934, No. 1, p. 22.

105 THE AMERICAN WORKERS' FILM AND PHOTO LEAGUE, in *Kino,* 10 February 1934. Signed jointly with Pera Atasheva and Edward Tisse.

106 QUE VIVA MEXICO!, in *Experimental Cinema,* New York, No. 5, 1934, pp. 5–13, 52. The outline for the Mexican film written in 1931 by E. and Alexandrov. Reprinted in Eisenstein, *Que Viva Mexico!* (London 1951).

107 ON FASCISM, GERMAN FILM ART AND REAL LIFE, An Open Letter to the German Minister of Propaganda, Dr Goebbels, in *Literaturnaya gazeta,* 22 March 1934. A reply to the propaganda minister's address to German film producers in February 1934. Translations in *International Theatre,* October 1934; *Film Art,* London, Winter 1934; and in the New York *Times,* 30 December 1934.

108 "E!" ON THE CLARITY OF FILM LANGUAGE, in *Sovietskoye kino,* 1934, No. 5, pp. 25–31. Translation (as "Film Language") in *Film Form,* pp. 108–121.

109 INCOMPARABLE, in *Literaturnaya gazeta,* 18 June 1934. On the *Chelyuskin* exploit.

110 SIKO, in *Kino,* 28 June 1934. Obituary of the director Siko Palavandishvili.

111 METRO, MOSCOW, LITERATURE, in *Pravda,* 17 August 1934.

112 END OF THE MANSARD ROOF, in *Izvestia,* 19 August 1934. On problems of the scenario, addressed to the First Congress of Soviet Writers; reprinted in *Izbranniye stat'i.*

113 WITH THE WEAPON OF CINEMA, in *Komsomolskaya pravda,* 7 November 1934. On the role of film in defence.

114 AT LAST!, in *Literaturnaya gazeta*, 18 November 1934. On the three stages of the Soviet cinema's development, and on *Chapayev* as a synthesis of the three. Translation (as "The New Soviet Cinema; entering the fourth period") in *New Theatre*, New York, January 1935.

115 FINISH OFF THE ENEMY, in *Komsomolskaya pravda*, 4 December 1934. On Kirov's assassination.

116 THE MIDDLE OF THREE (1924–1929), in *Sovietskoye kino*, 1934, No. 11–12, pp. 54–83. Translation (as "Through Theatre to Cinema") in *Theatre Arts Monthly*, New York, September 1936, and in *Film Form*, pp. 3–17.

117 KOMSOMOLS IN CINEMA, in *Kommunist*, Odessa, 5 December 1934. On the work of the Odessa studio.

118 PAUL ROBESON, in *Pravda*, 23 December 1934.

1935

119 GTK—GIK—VGIK, PAST—PRESENT—FUTURE, in *Sovietskoye kino*, 1935, No. 1, pp. 54–60. On the 15th birthday of the Cinema Institute. Reprinted (as edited by E. in 1947) in *Izbranniye stat'i*. Translation in *Film Essays*, pp. 66–76.

120 THE MOST IMPORTANT OF THE ARTS, in *Izvestia*, 6 January 1935. On the 15th anniversary of the Soviet film industry; revised by E. as "Le plus important", for *Quinze ans de cinématographie soviétique* (1935), pp. 53–58; expanded version printed in *Izbranniye stat'i*.

121 IN THE DAYS OF THE FIFTEENTH . . . , in *Za kommunisticheskoye prosveshcheniye*, 15 January 1935.

122 IN THE SIXTEENTH YEAR, in *Komsomolskaya pravda*, 11 January 1935.

123 THE TRUTH OF OUR EPOCH, in *Pravda*, 12 January 1935. E.'s speech at the Bolshoi Theatre ceremony of the 15th anniversary.

124 CONCLUDING SPEECH AT THE FIRST ALL-UNION MEETING OF CREATIVE WORKERS, in *Kino*, 17 January 1935; also in *Literaturnaya gazeta*, 15 January 1935. Translated excerpts in Seton, *Eisenstein*, pp. 331–335.

125 [Opening address], in *Za bolshoye kinoiskusstvo* (1935), pp. 22–49, 160–165. Translation (as edited by E.) in *Life and Letters To-day* (London), September–December 1935; in *New Theatre and Film* (New York), April, May, June 1936; and in *Film Form*.

126 WE KNOW WHAT WE MUST DO, in *Kino*, 15 January 1935.

127 BEZHIN MEADOW, in *Komsomolskaya pravda*, 5 February 1935. On a new film project.

128 PEASANTS, in *Izvestia*, 11 February 1935. Review of Ermler's new film.

129 CINEMA—A MIGHTY WEAPON, in *Radioprogramma*, 18 February 1935.

130 THE THEATRE OF MEI LAN-FANG, in *Komsomolskaya pravda*, 11 March 1935; expanded by E., as "The Enchanter of the Pear Garden", for the brochure published by VOKS on the occasion of Mei Lan-fang's performances in the Soviet Union (1935). Translation in *Theatre Arts Monthly* (New York), October 1935; a condensed translation in *International Literature*, No. 5, 1935.

131 LETTER TO PIONEERS, in *Znamya Tryokhgorki*, 8 April 1935.

132 THE APRIL DECREE OF THE PARTY—A BASE FOR CREATIVE GROWTH, in *Kino*, 22 April 1935.

133 FROM THE SCREEN INTO LIFE, in *Komsomolskaya pravda*, 27 June 1935. The history of the making of *Potemkin*, as told by E. at the 30th anniversary of the mutiny.

134 OURS, in *Kino*, 5 September 1935. An obituary of Henri Barbusse.

135 I CHALLENGE TO SOCIALIST COMPETITION, in *Za bolshevistskii film*, 9 September 1935.

136 WE CAN, in *Za bolshevistskii film*, 9 September 1935. A reply to those workers at Mosfilm who protested against working conditions there. Reprinted in *Izbranniye stat'i*.

137 A SENSIBLE MEASURE, in *Kino*, 17 November 1935. On the choice of new talents for Mosfilm.

138 WE'LL KEEP OUR PROMISE, in *Kino*, 23 November 1935.

139 THE YEAR IN ART, in *Sovietskoye iskusstvo*, 29 December 1935. A reply to a questionnaire on which art

experiences had made the strongest impression during the past year; E.'s response provoked some angry comments in *Kino* and at Mosfilm.

1936

140 IN 1936, in *Izvestia*, 1 January 1936. Reply to questionnaire.

141 [Foreword], to Vladimir Nilsen's *The Cinema as a Graphic Art* (when translated in London, 1936); reprinted in *Theatre Arts Monthly* (New York), May 1938.

142 IN PLACE OF A SPEECH, in *Kino*, 11 March 1936. On the questions of formalism and naturalism in the arts raised by recent articles in *Pravda*.

143 THIS WILL BE A FILM ABOUT HEROIC CHILDREN, in *Za kollektivizatziyu*, 18 March 1936.

144 "BEZHIN MEADOW", in *Krestyanskaya gazeta*, 31 March 1936.

145 PROGRAMME FOR TEACHING THE THEORY AND PRACTICE OF DIRECTION, in *Iskusstvo kino*, 1936, No. 4, pp. 51–58. Translation in *Life and Letters To-day* (London), June, July 1936; and in *Lessons with Eisenstein* (London 1962).

146 ABOUT MYSELF—ALOUD, in *Kino*, 6 May 1936. An analysis of his work in connection with the current discussion on formalism and naturalism in the arts.

147 A SCENARIO OF GENIUS FOR THE FUTURE, in *Kino*, 17 June 1936. On the proposed constitution for the USSR.

148 THE GREATEST CREATIVE HONESTY, in *Kino*, 22 June 1936. On the death of Gorky. Translation in *Notes of a Film Director*, pp. 138–140.

149 Letter to the Editors of *Kino*, 17 August 1936.

150 PUNISH THE MURDERER, in *Sovietskoye iskusstvo*, 23 August 1936.

151 PAUL ROBESON, in *Rabochaya Moskva*, 20 December 1936. On Robeson's Moscow concerts.

1937

152 Letter to the Editors of *Izvestia*, 8 February 1937. Contradicting rumour in foreign press about E.'s arrest.

153 THE MISTAKES OF "BEZHIN MEADOW", in *Sovietskoye iskusstvo*, 17 April 1937; reprinted in the brochure, *About the* Bezhin Lug *Film* (1937); and in *Izbranniye stat'i*. Translation in *International Literature*, No. 8, 1937; reprinted in Seton, *Eisenstein*, pp. 372–377.

154 WHY DID "BEZHIN MEADOW" FAIL?, in *Vechernaya Moskva*, 25 April 1937. E.'s speech at the Mosfilm discussion on the film.

155 THE EPIC IN SOVIET FILM, in *International Literature*, No. 10–11, 1937. An introduction to Vsevolod Vishnevsky's scenario, *We, the Russian People*, as translated from *Roman-gazeta* (1938); E.'s Russian text published in *Izbranniye stat'i*; reprinted in *Voprosi kinodramaturgii* III (1959).

156 RUSS, in *Znamya*, 1937, No. 12. The scenario (later produced as *Alexander Nevsky*) by E. and Pyotr Pavlenko.

157 IMAGE OF ENORMOUS HISTORICAL TRUTH AND REALITY, in *Za bolshevistskii film*, 27 December 1937. On *Lenin in October*.

1938

158 LAND OF THE SOVIETS, in *Kino*, 17 February 1938. On the new film by Schub and Tisse.

159 THE FILM OF ALEXANDER NEVSKY, in *Krasnyi Oktyabr*, Syzran, 28 June 1938. Article on the filming in Pereyaslavl-Zalesski, signed by E., and D. Vasiliev.

160 Letter to the Editors of *Teatr*, 1938, No. 7, pp. 156–158. On the necessity for establishing a people's theatre in the Park of Culture and Rest.

161 ALEXANDER NEVSKY AND THE DEFEAT OF THE GERMANS, in *Izvestia*, 12 July 1938. The historical events at the base of the film.

162 WHAT FILM-DIRECTORS ARE MAKING, in *Proletarskaya pravda*, Kalinin, 26 August 1938. Reply to questionnaire.

163 PATRIOTISM IS OUR THEME, in *Kino*, 11 November 1938. Reprinted in *Izbranniye stat'i*. Translation in *International Literature*, No. 2, 1939, and in the *Daily Worker* (New York), 1 April 1939.

164 WE ARE READY FOR ANY TASK, in *Za bolshevistskii film,* 11 November 1938. On the crew filming *Alexander Nevsky.*

165 ALEXANDER NEVSKY, in *Gudok,* 14 November 1938.

166 A FILM ON THE GREAT PATRIOTISM OF THE RUSSIAN PEOPLE, in *Krasnaya gazeta,* Leningrad, 29 November 1938.

167 NOTES OF A DIRECTOR, in *Ogonyok,* 1938, No. 22, pp. 20–21. Characteristics of Alexander Nevsky and an account of the film about him.

168 WE AND THEY, in *Kino,* 5 December 1938. On meetings with Griffith, Chaplin, Flaherty.

169 HIS LIFE WAS A VICTORY, in *Sovietskoye iskusstvo,* 16 December 1938. On the death of Chkalov.

170 ENTHUSIASM IS THE BASIS OF CREATIVE WORK, in a collection, *Young Masters of Art* (1938), pp. 56–57. Reprinted in *Izbranniye stat'i.*

171 ALEXANDER NEVSKY (1938), pp. 76. The scenario (third and final version) by E. and Pyotr Pavlenko; reprinted in *Historical Scenarios* (1946), in *Selected Scenarios of Soviet Cinema* (1950), vol. IV; (1951), vol. III; in Pavlenko, *Film Scenarios* (1952); in Pavlenko, *Plays and film Scenarios* (1954). Translated in *Eisenstein: Three Films* (London and New York 1974).

1939

172 MONTAGE IN 1938 in *Iskusstvo kino,* 1939, No. 1, pp. 37–49. Reprinted in Lev Kuleshov's *Fundamentals of Film Direction* (1941), and in *Izbranniye stat'i.* Translation in *Life and Letters To-day,* June–November 1939; and as Chap. I ("Word and Image") of *The Film Sense*; and in *Notes of a Film Director.*

173 BOOM YEAR FOR SOVIET CINEMA, in *Rabochii krai,* Ivanovo, 1 January 1939.

174 CORRECT PRINCIPLE, in *Kino,* 5 January 1939.

175 TO THE GLORY OF THE COUNTRY, in *Sovietskoye iskusstvo,* 4 February 1939. On creative responsibilities.

176 WITH HONOUR WE RECEIVE THE HIGH AWARD, in *Za bolshevistskii film,* 8 February 1939. On the Order of Lenin awarded to Mosfilm.

177 WE SERVE THE PEOPLE, in *Izvestia*, 11 February 1939. On the recent awards to film-makers. Reprinted in *Izbranniye stat'i*.

178 BEFORE MAKING A FILM ON FRUNZE, in *Kino*, 23 February 1939. On the planned film, *Perekop*, and on meetings with Frunze at Proletcult.

179 PROUD JOY, in *Za bolshevistskii film*, 23 March 1939. On Mosfilm's honours.

180 LENIN IN OUR HEARTS, in *Izvestia*, 6 April 1939. On *Lenin in 1918*.

181 HELLO, CHARLIE!, in *Kino*, 17 April 1939. On Chaplin's fiftieth birthday. Reprinted in *Izbranniye stat'i*. Translation in *Notes of a Film Director*, pp. 197–198.

182 SPEECH AT THE MEETING OF INTELLECTUALS FROM MOSCOW'S STUDIOS, in *Kino*, 23 April 1939. An edited stenographic report.

183 THE SOVIET SCREEN (1939), pp. 39. A pamphlet (in English) issued for the Soviet pavilion's exhibit at the New York World's Fair.

184 FOREWORD to *Soviet Films 1938–1939* (1939). E.'s foreword (in English) is dated April 1939.

185 GRANDEUR OF SOVIET AVIATION, in *Vechernaya Moskva*, 1 May 1939.

186 25 AND 15, in *Kino*, 23 May 1939. On the 25th anniversary of Tisse's film career, and on his 15 years of work with E. Reprinted in *Izbranniye stat'i*. Translation in *Notes of a Film Director*, pp. 145–149.

187 ON STRUCTURE, in *Iskusstvo kino*, 1939, No. 6, pp. 7–20. Previously published, in shortened version, in *Anthology on Film Direction* (1939), and reprinted in *Izbranniye stat'i*. Translation (as "The Structure of the Film") in *Film Form*, pp. 150–178; in shortened version in *Notes of a Film Director*, pp. 53–62.

188 FILM ABOUT THE FERGHANA CANAL, in *Pravda*, 13 August 1939, and in *Iskusstvo kino*, 1939, No. 9, pp. 6–7.

189 FERGHANA CANAL, in *Iskusstvo kino*, 1939, No. 9, pp. 8–20. A shooting-script based on a treatment by Pyotr Pavlenko and E. (dated August 1–2–3, 1939); reprinted in *Voprosi kinodramaturgii* III (1959). Translated excerpt in *The Film Sense*, pp. 256–268.

190 A REGION BECOMES UNRECOGNIZABLE, in *Pravda*, 2 September 1939. On the builders' enthusiasm at the Ferghana Canal.

191 ALEXANDER NEVSKY, in the collection, *The Soviet Historical Film* (1939), pp. 14–25. Reprinted (as enlarged by E.) in *Izbranniye stat'i*. Translation in *Notes of a Film Director*, pp. 32–43.

1940

192 PRIDE, in *Iskusstvo kino*, 1940, No. 1–2, pp. 17–25. Translation in *International Literature*, April–May 1940, in the *Anglo–Soviet Journal*, April 1941, and in *Film Form* (as "Achievement"), pp. 179–194.

193 BIRTH OF A MASTER, in *Iskusstvo kino*, 1940, No. 1–2, pp. 94–95. On E.'s introduction to Dovzhenko and his work. Reprinted (as expanded by E. in 1946) in *Izbranniye stat'i*. Translation in *Notes of a Film Director*, pp. 140–145.

194 RAGING ARTISTS, in *Sovietskoye foto*, 1940, No. 1.

195 THE MOTHERLAND EMBRACES ITS WORTHY SONS, in *Literaturnaya gazeta*, 30 January 1940. Greetings to the returned ice-breaker *Sedov*.

196 THE SOVIET HISTORICAL FILM, in *Pravda*, 8 February 1940. Reprinted in *Izbranniye stat'i*; expanded as "The Problem of the Soviet Historical Film", and published in *Theses of the Addresses* . . . (1940), pp. 3–15. The full text of E.'s speech (delivered 8 January 1940) published in *Iz istorii kino*, No. 4 (1961), pp. 7–27.

197 TWENTY, in the collection, *20 Years of Soviet Cinematography* (1940), pp. 18–31. Reprinted in *Izbranniye stat'i*.

198 WE ARE TWENTY YEARS OLD, foreword (dated 15 February 1940) to the anniversary album, *Soviet Film Art 1919–1939* (1940), pp. 5–7. Reprinted in *Izbranniye stat'i*.

199 NOT COLOURED, BUT OF COLOUR, in *Kino*, 29 May 1940. Reprinted in *Izbranniye stat'i*. Translation in *Notes of a Film Director*, pp. 114–119.

200 AGAIN ON STRUCTURE, in *Iskusstvo kino*, 1940, No. 6, pp. 27–32. Translation in *Film Essays*, pp. 92–108.

201 VERTICAL MONTAGE (First Essay), in *Iskusstvo kino*, 1940, No. 9, pp. 16–25. Translation as Chap. II ("Synchronization of Senses") of *The Film Sense*.

202 THE EMBODIMENT OF A MYTH, in *Teatr*, 1940, No. 10, pp. 13–38. The principles of E.'s staging of *Die Walküre* at the Bolshoi Theatre. Condensed translation in *Film Essays*, pp. 184–191.

203 THE EMBODIMENT OF A MYTH, in the brochure, *Walküre* (1940). Another treatment of the same subject.

204 CREATIVE ENCOUNTER WITH WAGNER, in *Ogonyok*, 1940, No. 29, pp. 18. Translation in *Sunday Worker* (New York), 20 April 1940.

205 GREAT HAPPINESS, in *Trudovaya gazeta*, Riga, 24 August 1940.

206 BEFORE THE PREMIER OF WALKURE, in *Vechernaya Moskva*, 21 September 1940.

207 GREETINGS TO ARMENIA ON THE VICTORY OF SOCIALISM!, in *Kommunist*, Yerevan, 26 November 1940.

208 WHAT THE STUDIOS ARE WORKING ON, in *Izvestia*, 27 November 1940. A reply to a questionnaire; E. answers for Mosfilm.

209 FOREWORD to Lev Kuleshov's *Fundamentals of Film Direction* (1941), first published in *Sovietskii ekran*, 1940, No. 23, p. 12.

210 VERTICAL MONTAGE (Second Essay), in *Iskusstvo kino*, 1940, No. 12, pp. 27–35. Translation as Chap. III ("Colour and Meaning") of *The Film Sense*.

211 Letter to the Editors of *International Literature*, November–December 1940. On *The Birth of a Nation*. Russian text published in Russian edition, No. 5, 1941.

1941

212 VERTICAL MONTAGE (Third Essay), in *Iskusstvo kino*, 1941, No. 1, pp. 29–38. Translation as Chap. IV ("Form and Content: Practice") of *The Film Sense*.

213 FOR FRUITFUL WORK, in *Za bolshevistskii film*, 1 January 1941.

214 OUR CREATIVE TASKS, in *Za bolshevistskii film*, 12 February 1941.

215 ON THE "SECRETS" OF FILM TECHNIQUE, in *Illustrirovannaya gazeta*, 2 March 1941.

216 MEMORABLE DAYS, in *Izvestia*, 18 March 1941.

217 FORWARD!, in *Za bolshevistiskii film*, 21 March 1941. Announcement of the film about Ivan Grozny.

218 JUSTIFICATION FOR CONFIDENCE, in *Kino*, 21 March 1941.

219 FILM ABOUT IVAN GROZNY, in *Izvestia*, 30 April 1941. On the historical role of Ivan IV.

220 HEIRS AND BUILDERS OF WORLD CULTURE, in *Pravda*, 30 April 1941. On the responsibilities of Soviet filmmakers.

221 THREE DIRECTORS. 1. A man and his film [Mikhail Romm]; 2. An original master [Friedrich Ermler]; 3. Artist-bolshevik [Alexander Dovzhenko]; in *Iskusstvo kino*, 1941, No. 5, pp. 32–37.

221a TEN YEARS AGO, in *Literatura i iskusstvo*, May 1 (?) 1941.

222 IVAN GROZNY, in *Vechernaya Moskva*, June 1941. A news item including portions of E.'s speech at a party-production conference at Mosfilm.

223 LET US MAKE EVEN STRONGER THE MILITARY MIGHT OF OUR COUNTRY, in *Za bolshevistskii film*, 3 June 1941. On the State Loan for the third five-year plan.

224 COMMENTS ON YOUNG CINEMATOGRAPHERS, in *Pravda*, 16 June 1941. Reprinted in *Izbranniye stat'i*.

225 "THE DICTATOR", CHARLIE CHAPLIN'S FILM, in *Kino*, 27 June 1941. Reproduced, in different variants, in several newspapers during June and July 1941; reprinted in *Izbranniye stat'i*. Translation in *Notes of a Film Director*, pp. 199–202.

226 A JUST MATTER, in *Kino*, 27 June 1941.

227 ORGANISATION AND DISCIPLINE, in *Za bolshevistskii film*, 1 July 1941. Mosfilm's adaptation to war-time conditions.

228 FASCIST BEASTLINESS ON THE SCREEN, in *Krasnyi voin*, 11 July 1941.

229 DESTROY, SMASH THE VILE INVADERS, in *Krasnyi flot*, 18 July 1941.

230 HITLER SQUEEZED IN THE PINCERS, in *Kino*, 18 July

1941. On the agreement between the USSR and England to unite their efforts against Germany.

231 CINEMA AGAINST FASCISM, in *Pravda*, 8 October 1941. On foreign anti-fascist films.

232 FASCISM MUST AND SHALL BE DESTROYED, in the collection (in English), *In Defence of Civilization Against Fascist Barbarism* (1941).

233 Speech, in brochure, *To Brother Jews of All the World* (1941), pp. 25–26. Transcription of a filmed speech.

1942

234 FOREWORD to *The Film Sense* (New York 1942). Translation reprinted in *Soviet Russia Today*, August 1942.

235 TEN YEARS AGO, in *Literatura i iskusstvo*, 1 May 1942. Memories of the last pre-Hitler May Day in Berlin.

236 IVAN GROZNY, in *Literatura i iskusstvo*, 4 July 1942. Translation in *VOKS Bulletin*, 1942, No. 7–8.

237 FRIENDS OVER THE OCEAN, in *Literatura i iskusstvo*, 15 August 1942. In preparation for a conference on American and British cinema.

238 AMERICAN FILMS REFLECT FIGHTING QUALITIES OF AMERICAN PEOPLE, in *Information Bulletin*, Embassy of the USSR (Washington), 1942 (Special Supplement). Partial text of a speech delivered at the Conference on American and British Cinema, Moscow, 21–22 August 1942.

239 "AN AMERICAN TRAGEDY", Reel 10, and "SUTTER'S GOLD", Reel 4, in *The Film Sense* (New York 1942), pp. 236–250. Excerpts from two scripts, written in Hollywood, 1930, by E., Alexandrov and Ivor Montagu.

240 ROUGH OUTLINE OF THE MEXICAN PICTURE, as drafted for Upton Sinclair, in *The Film Sense* (New York 1942), pp. 251–254.

1944

241 DICKENS, GRIFFITH AND WE, in the collection, *Amerikanskaya kinematografiya: D. U. Griffit* (1944), pp. 39–88. Reprinted (as revised by E. in 1946 for his proposed *Three Masters*) in *Izbranniye stat'i*. Translated in *Film Form*, pp. 195–255.

242 THE PERFORMANCE STIRS AND TOUCHES, in *Kazakhstan-*

skaya pravda, Alma-Ata, 6 August 1944. On an Alma-Ata production of Puccini's *Madama Butterfly*.

243 IVAN GROZNY (1944), pp. 189. The script, in treatment form. Translation in *Life and Letters*, November, December 1945; January–July 1946; 'a variant translation published 1963, New York and London.

1945

244 OUR WORK ON THE FILM, in *Izvestia*, 4 February 1945. On *Ivan Grozny*, Part I. Translation in *Film Chronicle*, February 1945.

245 IN A REGISSEUR'S LABORATORY, in *Film Chronicle*, February 1945. Revised translation in *Film Form*, pp. 261–265. Russian text published in *Iskusstvo kino*, No. 2, 1957.

246 THE GREATEST OF STATESMEN, in *Ogonyok*, 1945, No. 9–10, p. 14. On the image of Ivan IV in *Ivan Grozny*, Part I.

247 THE LIBERATION OF FRANCE, in *Sovietskoye iskusstvo*, 19 April 1945. On the new film compilation by Yutkevich. Reprinted in *Izbranniye stat'i*. Translated excerpt in *Films Beget Films* (London 1964), p. 70.

248 REBIRTH, in *Literaturnaya gazeta*, 23 June 1945. On Leningrad's reconstruction. Reprinted in *Izbranniye stat'i*.

249 IN CLOSE UP, in *Iskusstvo kino*, 1945, No. 1, pp. 6–8. Translation in *Film Essays*, pp. 150–154.

250 CHARLIE THE KID, in the collection, *Charles Spencer Chaplin* (1945), pp. 137–158. Reprinted (as expanded by E. in 1946 for his proposed *Three Masters*) in *Izbranniye stat'i*. Translation in *Sight and Sound*, Spring, Summer 1946; reprinted in *Film Essays*, pp. 108–139; another translation in *Notes of a Film Director*, pp. 167–197.

1946

251 PRKFV, an introduction to *Sergei Prokofiev: His Musical Life*, by Israel Nestyev (New York 1946); an expanded Russian text is published in *Izbranniye stat'i*. Translation (of the expanded version) in *Notes of a Film Director*, pp. 149–167.

252 ABOUT THE FILM "IVAN GROZNY", in *Kultura i zhizn*, 20 October 1946. An analysis of the mistakes in *Ivan Grozny*, Part II. Translation in Seton, *Eisenstein*, pp. 460–463.

253 HOW I BECAME A DIRECTOR, in the collection, *Kak ya stal rezhisserom* (1946), pp. 276–292. His experiences as a theatre-goer that led to his work in theatre and film. Reprinted in *Izbranniye stat'i*. Translation in *Notes of a Film Director*, pp. 9–18.

1947

254 PURVEYORS OF SPIRITUAL POISON, in *Kultura i zhizn*, 31 July 1947. Translation in *Sight and Sound*, Autumn 1947.

255 TO THE SOVIET MILITIAMAN, in *Na boyevom postu*, 12 November 1947..

1948

256 ABOUT STEREOSCOPIC CINEMA, in *Iskusstvo kino*, 1948, No. 2, pp. 5–7. Reprinted in *Izbranniye stat'i*. Translation in *Penguin Film Review*, No. 8 (London 1949) and in *Notes of a Film Director*, pp. 129–137.

On 11 February 1948 Sergei Mikhailovich Eisenstein died at the age of 50.

257 SPECTATOR-CREATOR, in *Ogonyok*, 1948, No. 26 [from a manuscript dated 7 November 1947]. Reprinted in *Izbranniye stat'i*.

257a [Letter to Georges Sadoul, 10 March 1947] In *Ciné-Club* (Paris) No. 5, March 1948.

1949

258 THIRTY YEARS OF SOVIET CINEMA AND THE TRADITION OF RUSSIAN CULTURE, in *Iskusstvo kino*, 1949, No. 5, pp. 7–11 [written in 1947 for the 30th anniversary of the October Revolution]. Translation in *The Anglo-Soviet Journal*, Summer 1950; reprinted (slightly abridged) in *Masses and Mainstream*, November 1950, as "The Soviet Cinema".

1950

259 BIRTH OF A FILM, in *Iskusstvo kino,* 1950, No. 4, pp. 13–16 [written in 1945 for an unpublished collection of essays on *Potemkin*]; reprinted in *Izbranniye stat'i.* Translation (as "The Twelve Apostles") in *VOKS Bulletin,* 1950, No. 63; in *The Cinema 1952* (London 1952), pp. 158–173; other translations in *The Hudson Review* (New York), Summer 1951; and in *Notes of a Film Director,* pp. 18–31.

260 IVAN GROZNY, in the collection, *Selected Scenarios of Soviet Cinema* (1950), vol. IV, pp. 483–524. Part One, as filmed; reprinted in *Selected Scenarios . . .* (1951), vol. IV.

1951

261 SIQUEIROS, a speech delivered at a 1931 exhibition of the paintings of David Siqueiros, in *Siqueiros . . .* (Mexico 1951).

1952

262 EVER FORWARD!, in *Iskusstvo kino,* 1952, No. 1, pp. 107–109. Written in 1947 as an "afterword" to a proposed collection of E.'s essays. Reprinted in *Izbranniye stat'i.* Translation in *Notes of a Film Director,* pp. 203–208.

263 AFTERWORD to the Libretto of *Que Viva Mexico!* [written in 1947], translated in Seton, *Eisenstein,* pp. 504–512. Russian text published in *Iskusstvo kino,* 1957, No. 5, pp. 113–117.

264 [Letters to various correspondents], published in Seton, *Sergei M. Eisenstein* (London 1952).

265 UNITED (IDEAS ON THE HISTORY OF SOVIET CINEMA), in *Iskusstvo kino,* 1952, No. 11, pp. 10–14. Written in November 1947, for the 30th anniversary of the October Revolution. Reprinted in *Izbranniye stat'i.*

1954

266 PROBLEMS OF COMPOSITION, in the collection, *Voprosi kinodramaturgii* I (1954), pp. 116–140. Stenographic record of a lecture given to the direction class at VGIK, 25 December 1946. Reprinted in *Izbranniye stat'i,* in

On Film Scenarios (1956), and in Nizhny's *Lessons with Eisenstein*. Translation in *Film Essays*, pp. 155–183.

1955

267 [Three manuscripts relating to a book planned by E.: *Pushkin and Cinema*], in *Iskusstvo kino*, 1955, No. 4, pp. 75–96: (1) Foreword, dated Kokand, 13 October 1939; (2) Examples for the Study of Montage Style (a lecture given at VGIK, 13 October 1937); (3) Pushkin, Montageur (a chapter from the unfinished book). Translation of the Foreword (as "Lessons from Literature") in *Film Essays*, pp. 77–84, this translation previously published in *The Anglo-Soviet Journal* (London), Summer 1963.

1956

268 MONTAGE LISTS OF THE FILM, "BATTLESHIP POTEMKIN", in the collection, *Voprosi kino iskusstva* (1956), pp. 213–231, with facsimiles; prepared for publication by G. Chakhiryan. Translated in Eisenstein, *Three Films* (London and New York 1974).

[Previously unpublished manuscripts], in *Izbranniye stat'i* (1956), edited by R. Yurenev.

269 FOREWORD to a proposed collection of E.'s essays, dated Moscow-Kratovo, August 1946. Translations in *Film Form and The Film Sense* (combined Meridian edition, 1957), pp. ix–xi, and in *Notes of a Film Director*, pp. 5–8.

270 PEOPLE ON A FILM, fragment of a proposed book (in 1947) about the people who worked on *Ivan Grozny*; this fragment is about Lydia Lomova, dresser, and Goryunov, make-up man.

271 BOLSHEVIKS LAUGH (Thoughts about Soviet Comedy), written in 1937, for a proposed extensive work on comedy. Translation in *Notes of a Film Director*, pp. 106–112.

272 WOLVES AND SHEEP (Director and Actor), written in 1935, in reply to criticism that some directors crush the

actor's will. Translation in *Notes of a Film Director*, pp. 112–114.

273 COLOUR FILM, the last unfinished essay by E., written in the form of an open letter to Lev Kuleshov, for use in a proposed second edition of Kuleshov's *Fundamentals of Film Direction*. Translation in *Notes of a Film Director*, pp. 119–128.

274 TRUE WAYS OF INVENTION, on sources of Alexander Nevsky, written 14 October 1946. Translation in *Notes of a Film Director*, p. 43–52.

1957

275 HOW I LEARNED TO DRAW, in *Kultura i zhizn*, 1957, No. 6. Fragment of E.'s memoirs. Translation in English edition (*Culture and Life*), reprinted in S. Eisenstein, *Drawings* (1961), pp. 15–19.

276 ["OCTOBER"], in *Iskusstvo kino*, 1957, No. 10, pp. 104–129. Outlines for the script (dated 26 February 1927) and shooting-script for unrealized reels (dated 12 October 1927), introduced by co-author, G. Alexandrov.

276a LECTURES ON DIRECTION, edited by Vladimir Nizhny from stenographic notes, VGIK, 1957. Revised and enlarged in 1958, as *Lessons with Eisenstein*. English translation, London 1962.

1958

277 NOTES ON V. V. MAYAKOVSKY, in *Iskusstvo kino*, 1958, No. 1, pp. 73–75. Manuscript dated 5 April 1940. Translation in *The Anglo-Soviet Journal*, London, Summer 1958.

278 [Notes and drawings for unrealized films, including *Ferghana Canal* and *A Poet's Love* (*Pushkin*)], in I. Weisfeld, "Birth of an Idea", *Iskusstvo kino*, 1958, No. 1, pp. 86–94.

279 AUTOBIOGRAPHICAL NOTES, in *Kultura i zhizn*, 1958, No. 5, pp. 40–43. Written in 1939 for the 20th anniversary of Soviet cinema. Translation in English edition (*Culture and Life*).

280 [Shooting-script] (dated 17 December 1930) for the Epilogue of *Que Viva Mexico!*, and letter to Salka

Viertel, 27 January 1932], in *Sight and Sound*, Autumn 1958, pp. 305–307. (E.'s original German text of the letter printed in *Sergei Eisenstein, Künstler der Revolution*, Berlin 1960, pp. 196–201.)

1959

281 [Scene from Pushkin's *Boris Godunov*, for the planned film on Pushkin], in *Iskusstvo kino*, 1959, No. 3, pp. 111–130. E.'s drawings and notes for a shooting-script, reproduced in facsimile* introduced by L. Pogozheva.

* Omitted from the facsimile is the original heading in English (complete with pun), dated 4 March 1940:

> If Godounoff
> and if not—a good
> exercise for the use of
> colour, word and sound.

Translated in *Visual Scripting*, ed. John Halas (London and New York 1976).

282 MY DRAWINGS, in the collection, *Mosfilm: Articles*, etc, No. 1 (1959), pp. 207–212. On the sketches for *Ivan Grozny*, dated Alma-Ata, October 1943. Reprinted (as "A Few Words about My Drawings") in S. Eisenstein, *Drawings* (1961). Translation in S. Eisenstein, *Drawings* (1961), pp. 194–196.

282a [Letters to Esfir Schub] In Schub, *Krupnym planom* (Moscow 1959; enlarged edition 1972).

1960

283 MISTER LINCOLN BY MISTER FORD, in *Iskusstvo kino*, 1960, No. 4, pp. 135–140. An essay (dated 1945) on John Ford and *Young Mr Lincoln*, written for a proposed volume on John Ford, in the series, "Materials on world cinema history" (volumes published on Griffith and Chaplin). Translation in *Film Essays*, pp. 139–149.

284 COLOUR—CLEAN, SHARP, RESONANT, in *Literaturnaya gazeta*, 9 July 1960. Translated (as "One Path to Colour") in *Sight and Sound*, Spring 1961.

285 PAGES OF A LIFE, in *Znamya*, 1960, No. 10 (pp. 147–176), No. 11 (pp. 146–190). Extracts from E.'s memoirs, written in 1946. Translated selections in *Soviet Litera-*

ture, 1961, No. 2, 3; two sections ("People, Events, Life ..." and "Intellectual Cinema") revised and reprinted in *Atlas* (New York), May 1961.

286 BATTLESHIP "POTEMKIN", in *Sovietskii ekran*, 1960, No. 21, pp. 18–19. An extract from E.'s memoirs.

1961

287 QUESTIONS OF THE HISTORICAL FILM, in the collection, *Iz istorii kino*, No. 4 (1961), pp. 7–27. Stenographic record of a speech delivered 8 January 1940.

288 TO LIVE THUS WOULD BE UNTHINKABLE, in *With Their Own Weapons* (1961), pp. 279–286.

289 FROM THE CORRESPONDENCE OF S. PROKOFIEV AND S. EISENSTEIN, in *Sovietskaya muzika*, 1961, No. 4, pp. 105–113. Letters, 1939–1946. Translated in *Cinema Journal* (Evanston) 13, Fall 1973.

290 ABOUT ART AND MYSELF, in *Nedelya*, 29 April 1961. Extract (subtitled "Inexhaustible topic") from E.'s memoirs. Translation in *Soviet Weekly*, London, 31 August 1961.

291 "POTEMKIN" IN AMERICA, in *Soviet Weekly*, 7 September 1961. From E.'s memoirs.

292 COLOUR AND MUSIC, The Colour Genealogy of "Moscow 800", in the collection, *Mosfilm: Articles*, etc. (1961), pp. 239–245. Printed from a manuscript dated 30 September and 29 November 1946, incorporating notes for portions of E.'s memoirs, especially for the section translated as "One Path to Colour".

293 [*A Poet's Love*], in Ilya Weisfeld, *The Craft of Film-Writing* (1961), pp. 214–224. A treatment for this colour-film project on Pushkin's life.

1962

294 AUTOBIOGRAPHICAL NOTES, in *Iskusstvo kino*, 1962, No. 1, pp. 127–146. Further autobiographical fragments; prepared for publication by Yuri Krasovsky.

295 [Documents on the preparation of "Ivan Grozny"], in *Voprosi kino-dramaturgii* IV (1962), pp. 343–390. Notebook entries dated from 21 September 1941 to 8

May 1943; prepared for publication by Naum Kleiman.

296 NATURE IS NOT INDIFFERENT, in *Iskusstvo kino*, 1962, No. 11, pp. 99–122. Fragments of a theoretical essay written in 1945; prepared for publication by Leonid Kozlov.

1963

297 Two fragments ("El Greco y el cine" and "Yermolova") from unpublished book, *Montage*; in *Voprosi kinoiskusstva*, No. 7, prepared for publication by Leonid Kozlov.

298 Second Letter to GIK from Mexico (1931). In VGIK newspaper, *Put k ekranu*, 21 January 1963.

298a [Two letters to Sylvia Beach, 1933] in *Mercure de France*, August–September, pp. 123–126.

1964

299 *Selected Works in Six Volumes*, vols. I, II and III. Volume I contains *Memoirs* (1946); Volume II includes *Montage*; Volume III includes *Nature Is Not Indifferent*.

300 *What Lenin Gave Me*, in *Iskusstvo kino*, No. 4, pp. 2–8. A 1932 manuscript (an unpublished response to a questionnaire from *Kino*), prepared for publication by Naum Kleiman.

301 Notes on Mayakovsky, in *Mayakovsky and Soviet Literature*, ed. Z. S. Paperny. Rough notes for a lecture in Alma-Ata (April 1942), prepared for publication by A. Fevralski. Translated in *Artforum*, January 1973.

302 [Letters to Léon Moussinac] in Moussinac, *Serge Eisenstein* (Paris). Translated in Moussinac, *Sergei Eisenstein* (New York 1970).

1965

303 [Filming diary of *October*] in article by Yuri Krasovsky, "How the *October* film was made," in *Iz istorii kino*, No. 6.

304 Fragment of essay "Judith," 1947. In *Literaturnaya Rossiya*, 14 May 1965. On Judith Glizer.

305 PEACE AND THE ATOM BOMB, in *Iskusstvo kino*, No. 12, 1965. Written in autumn 1945.

1966

306 Volume IV of *Selected Works in Six Volumes*, pp. 789, compiled by Pera Atasheva and Naum Kleiman. Contains the unfinished draft of *Direction, Art of Mise-en-scène*.

307 ARSENAL, in Leonid Kozlov's article, "Eisenstein and Dovzhenko." In *Voprosi kinoiskusstva*, No. 9.

308 Letter to Yuri Nikolayevich Tynyanov (April 1944). In *Yuri Tynyanov* (series, *Lives of Remarkable Men*), pp. 176–181.

1968

309 Volume V of *Selected Works*, pp. 599, compiled by Atasheva and Krasovsky. Critical and art history essays, 1926–1947.

310 GENERAL LINE (first variant of scenario, 1926). In *Iz istorii kino*, No. 7, pp. 159–182.

311 VISIT TO A MILLIONAIRE (1939), in *Literaturnaya Rossiya*, 7 November 1968.

312 [Literature in Film], including a 1934 essay on imagery in literature; a lecture at GTK, 21 September 1928 on Zola; and passages from VGIK lectures in the '30s and '40s. In *Voprosi literatury*, No. 1.

1969

313 THE AUTHOR AND HIS THEME (AFTER TWENTY YEARS), dated 21 November 1944. Translated in *The Battleship Potemkin*, 1978, ed. Herbert Marshall.

314 *Year 1905*, script written with Nina Agadzhanova–Shutko (1925).

315 CONSTANZA (WHERE THE BATTLESHIP POTEMKIN REACHED PORT), 1926.

The above three texts were first published in *Battleship Potemkin*, ed. by N. Kleiman and K. Levina for the series, *Chefs-d'oeuvre of Soviet Cinema*.

1970

316 [Obituary for V. E. Meyerhold] (1931), quoted in Koz-lov's essay in *Voprosi kinoiskusstva*, No. 12, pp. 117–119. While in Mexico Eisenstein heard a rumor of Mey-erhold's death.

317 [Correspondence with Upton Sinclair and others], in *The Making and Unmaking of* Que Viva Mexico!, ed. by Harry Geduld and Ronald Gottesman (Bloomington 1970).

1971

Volume VI of *Selected Works*, pp. 559, compiled by Andronikova, Kleiman and Krasovsky. Scripts and doc-uments relating to E's realized films (including *Que Viva Mexico!*). First publication of the following:

318 STRIKE, 1924 (shooting script for Reels 1 and 2; scenario outlines for Reels 3 to 8).

319 OCTOBER, 1927 (final script for Part I; early variant for Part II, unrealized). Translation in *Three Films* (London and New York, 1974).

320 GENERAL LINE, 1928 (third shortened variant).

321 BEZHIN MEADOW, 1936 (shooting script of second var-iant, written with Isaac Babel).

322 [Further documents on the preparation of *Ivan Grozny*].

323 [Theater and cinema] stenogram of lecture at GIK, 22 September 1934, in *Iz istorii kino*, No. 8; prepared for publication by R. Yurenev.

324 Letter to Serafima Birman, 17 May 1944, in Birman, *Destinies of Talented Encounters*; reprinted in *Eisenstein in the Memories of His Contemporaries*, 1973.

325 NOTES ON THE PROJECT FOR "LOVE OF A POET" (1940), in Galina Manevich, "A Color Biography of Pushkin," *Voprosi literatury*, No. 10.

326 "ADVENTURE AT A RESORT," 1933, in *Tvorchestvo*, No. 11; prepared for publication by Oleg Khadyk.

1972

327 [Letters to L. Monosson (1931-1932)], in almanac *Pro-metei*, No. 9, published by R. Yurenev as "S. M. Ei-senstein, letters from Mexico."

328 "BEYOND THE STARS" (1940), published in vol. 2 of the Bulgarian edition of *Selected Works*.

1973

329 [Notes for a Film of *Capital*], in *Iskusstvo kino*, No. 1, prepared for publication by Naum Kleiman. Translation in *October* (New York) 2, Summer 1976.

330 [Letters to Maxim Strauch and Ilya Trauberg], in *Eisenstein in the Memories of His Contemporaries*, ed. R. Yurenev. Translated in *October* 14, Fall 1980.

1974

331 On the composition of the short fictional scenario, stenogram of VGIK lecture of 11 and 18 September 1941, prepared for publication by Naum Kleiman. In *Voprosi kinodramaturgi*, No. 6 (*Kharakter v kino*, ed. Ilya Weisfeld, pp. 215–253).

332 MONTAGE OF FILM ATTRACTIONS, dated October 1924, prepared for Alexander Belenson but totally revised by him in *Kino-segodnya* (1925). Published in French edition of *Selected Works: Au-delà des étoiles*, vol. 1; translated in *Eisenstein at Work* (New York 1982).

333 [Letters to Victoria Ocampo], in *Sur* (Buenos Aires), June 1974.

1975

334 "FROM THE AUTHOR" (1946) in *Iskusstvo kino*, No. 12. The full text of the preface prepared for the unpublished Panigel edition of E's writings.

1976

335 [Letters to Nikolai and Nina Cherkasov, 1942], in *Nikolai Cherkasov*, contribution by Nina Cherkasova, "From *Alexander Nevsky* to *Ivan Grozny*."

336 [Letter to Sergei Yutkevich, 18 January 1922], in Mikhail Dolinsky, *Svyaz vremen*.

1977

337 M M M (1932–1933), in *Iz istorii kino*, No. 10. Text

prepared for publication by Vladimir Zabrodin; annotated by M. Andronikova. Translation of Prologue in *Eisenstein at Work*.

338 EL PROMETEO DE LA PINTURA MEXICANA, in *América Latina* (USSR), No. 2, 1977, pp. 190–196. Translated in *¡Orozco! 1883–1949* (Oxford 1980); see also translation in this edition of *Film Essays*.

339 [Letter to Wilhelm Reich, 28 June 1934], in *Sociological Research*, Moscow, No. 1. Published by Leonid Ionin with letter from Reich to E.

1978

340 Two fragments—on color and on montage—not yet published in Russian texts. In an Ukrainian collection of E's writings, *Estetika kinomistetstva*, Kiev.

341 [Letter to Sergei Skvortsov, March 1946], in VGIK newspaper, *Put k ekranu*, 13 March 1978.

1979

342 THE GLASS HOUSE (1926-1930), in *Iskusstvo kino*, 3, 1979. History of project, notes, drawings; prepared for publication by Naum Kleiman. Partial translation in *Eisenstein at Work* (1982).

343 EXPRESSIVE MOVEMENT, written in 1923 with Sergei Tretyakov for a training pamphlet. Translated in *Millenium Film Journal* (New York), 3, 1979.

344 A projected production of Sergei Prokofiev's opera, *War and Peace* (1942–1943), in *Sovietskaya muzyka*, 1979, No. 9, pp. 83-91. Translated in *Eisenstein at Work* (1982).

1980

345 ON DETECTIVE STORIES (1943–1944), in collection *Priklyuchencheskii film: puti i poiski*, published by VNIIK, 1980, pp. 132-160. Fragment from unpublished *Method*, prepared for publication by N. Kleiman.

346 PSYCHOLOGY OF ART (program for a course of lectures, 1940, 1947), in collection, *Psychology of the process of artistic creation*, pp. 173–203. Prepared for publication by N. Kleiman and T. Drozhina.

In *Cinématisme, Peinture et cinéma*, ed. François Albéra (Brussels 1980) the following texts were published for the first time:

347 PROMETHEUS, a variant (written in English and Russian) of the Orozco essay.

348 A FEW WORDS ON PLASTIC AND AUDIO-VISUAL COMPOSITION (1945), possibly written for *Nature Is Not Indifferent*, but transferred to the manuscript of *Method*.

349 THE DICHOTOMY OF UNITY [and] EVEN-ODD (1945), written for *Nature Is Not Indifferent* and transferred to *Method*.

350 RODIN AND RILKE, written in July 1945, to be incorporated into *Nature Is Not Indifferent*.

1981

351 *Léon Moussinac Izbrannoye* (Moscow 1981), including a partial Russian translation of the Moussinac-Eisenstein correspondence (1928-1947).

1982

Eisenstein at Work, ed. Jay Leyda and Zina Voynow (New York 1982) includes the following documents:

352 "GLUMOV'S DIARY," fragment of shooting script (1923).

353 Sound Plan for *Old and New* (letter to E. Meisel, 17 August 1929).

354 Notes and sets for *Sutter's Gold* (1930).

355 Notes and sketches for *An American Tragedy*, with fragments of shooting script, 26 September 1930.

356 BEZHIN MEADOW, fragment of shooting script, 1936.

357 "EXPERIENCE IN SOUND" (on *Bezhin Meadow*), 15 January 1936.

358 "TAMERLANE'S TOWER" (for *Ferghana Canal*), shooting script and designs.

359 *Die Walküre* (and *Ring*), designs.

360 Outline and fragments of shooting script for a Pushkin film (*The Love of a Poet*).

361 Documents and sketches for *Ivan Grozny*, Parts I, II, III.

362 Curriculum vitæ prepared in 1938.

363 Letters (some in facsimile) to various correspondents.

Additions to writings and translations made with the assistance of Anthology Film Archives, New York, and Eisenstein Committee, Moscow.

COLLECTIONS OF EISENSTEIN'S WRITINGS IN ENGLISH

The Film Sense (1942)
contains Nos. 234, 172, 201, 210, 212, 2, 239, 240, 189.

Film Form (1949)
contains Nos. 116, 42, 51, 75, 62, 71, 83, 108, 125, 187, 192, 241, 40, 245.
[When these two collections were combined in a paperback edition by Meridian Books in 1957, No. 269 was translated as an introduction.]

Notes of a Film Director (1958)
contains Nos. 269, 253, 259, 191, 108, 172, 83, 271, 270, 199, 273, 148, 193, 186, 250, 181, 225, 262.

Film Essays (1968)
contains Nos. 14, 8, 68, 52, 61, 74, 119, 267, 202, 200, 250, 283, 249, 266.
[Grigori Kozintsev's introduction was written for his Eisenstein chapter in *The Deep Screen*. The 1982 edition also contains 338.]

APPENDIX B

The following essay, comparing the work and personalities of Diego Rivera and José Clemente Orozco, was written but left unfinished in 1935. The editor has attempted a conflation of two manuscripts: the earlier draft (No. 347, in the preceding list), partly in English, is more spontaneous and personal. There are also extensive notes, dated 25 Oct. 1935, that match this "final" version. The immediate stimulus for the essay was a large group of photographs (by Tina Modotti) of Orozco's Mexican frescoes, brought to Eisenstein from Alma Reed, followed by a publication, The Orozco Frescoes at Dartmouth.

THE PROMETHEUS OF MEXICAN PAINTING

Diego is a good, old friend. Across an arc from snowy Moscow, my home, to silent Coyoacan, his home—crowded with huge and prehistoric deities in wood, stone or terra cotta—Aztec and Mayan.

But I have never met the man about whom I am now writing—
OROZCO.

Our paths crossed three times—in Los Angeles, New York, and Mexico City—and three times we missed the opportunity for the handshake that we have hoped for for so long. Even though geography has not helped us, we managed to find a meeting point. Somewhere in the Elysian fields of ecstasy, we met.

There is an old, convenient method for classifying personalities, especially when two are to be compared: either the Apollonian or the Dionysian. This is so old and convenient that it has gone out of style. Nevertheless, let us adopt it for our pair, Orozco/Diego—Diego/Orozco.

This makes the strangest shape that the eternal wanderers, Apollo and Dionysos, could stumble upon here, in their ceaseless metempsychosis through creative personalities. Really! Imagine swift, slender Apollo recognizing himself in the Pantagruel shape of Gargantua-Diego bursting out of his trousers, wiping his lips after dining à la Grand Gousier on all the greatest walls of Mexico with all the Mexican peoples unrolled on them.

Dionysos, however, would recognize himself at once in the tense, killing, mad glance from behind those thick spectacles recorded by Weston, as thick as the porthole glass of Captain Nemo's *Nautilus*. A Promethean look, and it is not by chance that one of his great frescoes pictures Prometheus.*

Though both difficult *and* ridiculous, this trivial antithesis of Apollo and Dionysos has materialized in its own paradoxical way, in the delirious murals of these two artists.

Brought up within and bursting from the same social explosion, in theme and spirit alike, considered from inside their work is a macrocosm of their two characters, so definite, so opposite, so irreconcilable.

They both plead the same cause.

But next to a Falstaffian Martin Luther shrieks a fiery Savonarola.

As the men—so their work.

Their intensity is distinct. Quantitative in Diego. Qualitative in Orozco.

Square kilometers in area for the one, and so much explosive energy for the other.

Like a magnified self-portrait of the inner Diego—in his gluttony, his voracity of space, sex, food, and form.

The static quality of Diego. Mrs. Bloom of *Ulysses* dashed to the ground in the fresco "Luncheon of the Aesthetes." This is a glove thrown down by Diego to those who are not body and soul with the best there is in Mexico.

Squeezed. Narrowed. Pressed. Concentrated in an outburst of one tremendous, unnatural, clenched, crashing fist—appears Orozco in the Preparatoria walls.

Or he shrinks behind the wall in the endless deserts of the Soldadera's tragic route—seen as through a window opened on a never-to-be-reached horizon.

A scream on a surface *through* form and *through* style. In his "Trench"—three men on a barricade. Only one is balanced

* In Pomona College, Claremont, California.—J.L.

on the surface. One flies toward the spectator. Another, following his fist, thrusts himself into the depths beyond the barricade which they are defending. The fist, huge in its proportions, projects from the wall above the heads of those who draw near to look.

The Soldadera walks out across a plain that is twisted by the fierceness of the agave plants. These cutting edges hurt one's eyes as do the pages of Los de Abajo ["The Underdogs," a novel by Azuela, illustrated by Orozco]. Walls are not painted in this way. Illustrations are not made like this.

This is not the kind of thing to be painted on walls. On the first floor of the Preparatoria, while enlarging Posada's satirical print—maidens seeking suitors—who was it who forgot to clear away this chaotic composition, painted in broad strokes as if it were a poster to be seen and then destroyed in a day? It was the same person who, a few steps away, fixed on the wall the story of St. Francis kissing the leper.* You have stumbled into an anatomic catalogue of diseases and deformities.

I saw many a blanching spectator, less in love than I with the beauty that reaches atrocity and the atrocity that can burst into sublime beauty. I saw many a trembling spectator groping for the *cover* of this catalogue, to *close* it, to escape the fascinating appeal of these pages of horror depicted with all the wounds, the flesh torn by thorns, and the living corruption.

This is the man who plays with the projecting low angles of walls, bringing them together in images of generous hands and poorboxes. Coins, given by the poor, fall into the greasy hands of a priest.

These are not the subjects nor the ways that Orozco should paint on walls. These are not displays of bodies and outlines of machines. The surface explodes. The bodies and columns plunge headlong. An agglomeration of surfaces. Revolutionary force. Cyclone.

Orozco goes on to Dartmouth. There it was the most terrible. Superhuman passions. And amongst these social outcries and fierce caricatures, a handsome young boy, with that ease which only Americans have, sits peacefully reading in that room

---

* Orozco's title for this fresco is "The Friar and the Indio."—J.L.

overflowing with a social tumult of color. Orozco does not compromise. He does not go down to the Stock Exchange in San Francisco like his Apollonian colleague. This must be Mrs. Moody, the tennis champion that Charlie Chaplin and I admired at the Los Angeles tournament, now staring at us from the staircase of the San Francisco Stock Exchange. Does she represent California—or Maternity. Earth. Again Mrs. Bloom?

*　　*　　*

Have you ever noticed Diego's frescoes in the Upper Gallery of the Educación patio?

Repeated curves of the backs of peasant, soldier, corn and sack, and soldier, corn and sack again?

Where is the optical precedent for this perception?

Is it not in the abundant treelike nopal cactus—the fleshy pancakes of which project themselves in an infinite variety of curves, from circles to straight lines, depending on the angle where they are caught by the spectator's eye, gathered in masses or ranged along . . . walls.

I would dedicate the nopal to Diego.

Myriads of needles flash from it—like the many-walled satires of Diego. His luncheon of the millionaires, of the aesthetes, his burning Indios.

Arriving at an apogee in the tragic buried portrait of Zapata in Chapingo's unforgettable chapel.

But Diego can bloom as well—just as the sharp stings of the nopal, with pink, yellow, blue, and white buds, equal the sweet Sandunga or the flower fiesta of Xochimilco.

Tourists who shudder before his enormous distorted sleeping and waking Earths can repose their nerves as their hearts are quieted in the descent from Mexico City's altitude, down to Cuernavaca—enjoying the linear and coloristic mildness of the "painted" atrocities of the Spanish conquest helpfully embraced by missionary fathers and cheerfully woven in the carpet of the wall . . .

Pitiless to himself, pitiless in what he touches, a hell boiling inside, the man Orozco cannot know such islands of relief.

The iron grill of Cuahtemoc, the pagan martyr, seems ever glowing under him.

The merciless long thorns of the maguey.

Impossible to melt himself into a surface—a triangular wound unable to heal itself—unbending, merciless—I would choose the maguey to characterize Orozco.

Its weapons and its juice—the maddening ritualistic poison of the ancient *pulque*—this is the blood that burns in his veins. The grin of Quetzalcoatl would be his smile.

Not the smile of conciliating roundness playing over the joyous circles of ironic Mayan masks—Diego's smile!

* * *

The portraits that Andrea del Sarto painted of the most varied persons all resemble one person—Andrea himself.

As the painter always flings his emotions upon the walls, why not aspects of himself?

How many self-portraits of Diego smile from the staircase and the gallery walls of the Educación!

These self-portraits may also be symbolic. Inhuman. Superhuman.

The blue covers of Joyce's masterpiece,* the worldwide persecuted *chef-d'oeuvre Ulysses*, become the frame for another portrait of Diego. Symbolic this time—but not by his brush. This time by a pen, perhaps surpassing him in vigor . . .

Once more take an hour's stroll through the galleries of Educación. Suddenly Diego's frescoes melt together, growing identical, incessantly flowing—no commas, no stops—resembling that last chapter of *Ulysses*, the inner monologue of Mrs. Leopold Bloom.

Diego flows across these walls in one gorgeous multicolored stream, not destroying like lava, but like mysterious Nature in periods of springtime and fertilization, vitality overflowing from one shape into another, ever reemerging in an infinite diversity of forms and creations.

Mrs. Bloom is more than a singer and the occasional wife of an advertising agent. More—Mrs. Bloom is the Mother of

---

* From the enthusiastic early draft: "*Ulysses*—Joyce's masterpiece—the greatest work in world literature, overshadowing Rabelais, Balzac, Dante . . ."—J.L.

Things. Mother Earth. And her perpetual fertility—she is the mightiest personification of this fundamental principle among the symbols of world literature.

I would set up Diego alongside Mother Earth and Mother of Things, with his arched exodus of animals in human shape—human beings reduced to the exploitation of animals.

The womb could be the symbol of the continuing creativeness of this man.

See how in Chapingo his symbolism of Revolution rises from the symbolism of birth: from the red, bloody wrappings of the dead Zapata grow the strong plants of a future freedom, through the triptych of the fighters' faith (procreation of the seed) up toward the enormous figures of Earth asleep and Earth awakened.

In symbols of cosmic fertility the hugeness of Diego's creative power asserts itself.

*   *   *

In the well-meaning libraries, Orozco's cries from the street seem to echo behind the lenses of his glasses, and sharpen his social vision like a telescope. Here the surroundings are a barrier against the noise of the street where the class struggles take place. The bookish spirit of sleeping conscience passes without questioning among this poetry of myth and nightmare, caught in the frames of the bookshelves. This young boy scares me. He seems in an aquarium, where whatever hidden horrors and snakes there are, he is safe behind glass.

Here Orozco's work is also encased in glass. Spectators contemplate and enjoy its social horrors as *Grand Guignol*. Horror is neutralized.

Orozco's frescoes ought to be waging war out there—destroying Old Worlds and directed toward the creating of New Worlds.

Now is the time to replace the beard of mythical Quetzalcoatl with that of the combative Marx.

The banner over the unknown soldier falls allegorically and remotely, softening the horror of the Aztec sacrifice. No longer the direct, the present. No longer the shock. The combat. The roaring explosion!

227

The eyes that look at Orozco's works push them onto a plane which the painter himself transcends. They do for him what Diego does for himself. Orozco becomes a painter without an audience. Orozco ought to be with us. Overthrowing Cosmos. Disturbing Olympian balance. Revolutionizing. Bursting in all-entangling flashes of flame opposing the placid sun—that shines on both good and evil.

*   *   *

A necklace of gold . . .

What is the good of seeing everything as a symbol?

This is merely a new figure in comparing Diego and Orozco.

A golden necklace, applied *en relief* in gold leaf, around Mrs. Moody's neck—

and Orozco's icy, gray, metallic garrote with the ghastly cry of the strangled victim.

Around Mrs. Moody's neck, a golden circlet—like the mystical Sun of the Shintoists.

As detached and dazzling as the sun.

Warming both the good and the evil.

As you see I eulogize my friends in great breadth and
    depth.

But hidden within these hymns is a certain criticism . . .

Is what Orozco does with a wall's surface allowable from the viewpoint of fresco aesthetics?

Doesn't this bring a cry of "Guilty!" from such porfirists of art history as Muter and Lubke?*

Don Porfirio [Diaz], Don Venustiano [Carranza] were also shocked when the fist of a Mexican insurgent broke through the fortified walls of their tyranny . . .

Should we blame the *Mexican*?

Such Olympian circumspection spread doubts over enthusiasm: and yet there must be enthusiasm for creative expansion.

Absolutely the same blood-brotherly enthusiasm as that of the soldier shooting perpendicularly from the wall [in "The Trench"]!

* Richard Muther? Wilhelm Lübke?—J.L.

We love that in which we recognize ourselves . . .
As for myself I love both emotionally through myself—this concerns the single road of knowledge.
It is between these two poles that I shuttle back and forth.
Let me try a quick outline of the polarity of these two great masters.
I offer an original response by finding the same polarity at the core of myself and of my cinema—of my moving frescoes (for we also work on walls!).
Potemkin bursts through the screen into the auditorium.
The General Line pulls onto the plane of contemplative space both the vertical

and
the horizontal—

such is the definition given me by Fernand Leger (see *Le Monde*).
This is what gives me the possibility of seeing their work *in this way*.

This is what forces me to see them *in this way*.
Perhaps it's a vision, a prevision.
Is a synthesis possible on a wall's space?

Can it contain the furious tension that pulls across its surface like a bow about to let fly its arrow, like a balloon about to burst—can all this be put on a wall?—and still be a wall?

*   *   *

Near the large official patio of the Preparatoria where tourists are accustomed to stroll, there is a smaller patio.*
Impossible *not* to see Diego's frescoes in the Secretariat.
But it is only with great tolerance that you are shown Orozco's frescoes.
And it is only by being stubborn that you can persuade the guides to lead you to the little patio behind the School.

---

* This section of Eisenstein's notes is concerned with Siqueiros, whose described "Burial of a Worker" (eventually destroyed) governed part of the Prologue to *Que Viva Mexico!*—J.L.

To the sound of whispers, the malicious sniffing of aged professors—aesthetes who acquired their concepts of art from those who taught them . . .

It is here, amidst these scratched and mutilated walls and fading colors, that one perceives, nearly lost beneath the wall's surface, luminous next to bald white plaster, unfinished and empty,—

a coffin of intense aquamarine.
We know this treatment of coffins from the engravings of
  Posada.
Our screen knows something similar.

The mourning brown faces of workers burying a comrade, this coffin stretches through the surface in a tragic crack in the silent conflict between pain and anger . . .

The conflict on the wall is a paroxysm of despair, wanting to burst into sobs—

—and frozen in a synthesis of the wall.
The fresco is unfinished.
Other frescoes have not followed it.
A prison-door was slammed shut behind the author . . .
Siqueiros.
(and the embryo of this fresco's synthesis has no
  continuation).
The lid of the blue coffin is closed again.

A prison-cell lends itself badly to fresco. Little gray paintings—sobs crucified on the easel—their format limited by cot and stool. Their color comes from the close-stool. Gray-brown paintings in the semi-obscurity of incarceration—the fatal rhythm of detention followed the procession behind the blue coffin.

Prison molded David Alfaro [Siqueiros] into a painter.

Synthesis is a dangerous thing . . . It sometimes descends from the wall, to use the picturesque amidst the melée as a substitute for painting a penetration into the melée of reality.

Gray paintings in which the deep somber eyes of Indios endlessly question; similar to the gray shadows of memory, they inhabit the great empty room that is perched high on a rock raised over Taxco (there's a dizzying balcony without a guard-rail) where Siqueiros now works, preparing an exhibition for New York, that New York of dealers and wealthy patrons.

In the blinding sunlight, choking the red of the flowers that they call *sangre del toro*—Taxco seems not to exist.

Attentive shutters protect the gray-blue eyes that are used to the semi-darkness of the prison-cell. Hiding the movements of the brush that used to be a gun, and at any moment may become one again.

Farther down, countless churches, countless chapels reflect the heat from roofs of Spanish tiles . . .

And the two opposing lines continue to burn on the walls of the world—even beyond the borders of Mexico . . .

[unfinished]

Remarks by Eisenstein at the opening of a Siqueiros exhibition, February 1932 [No. 261]:

Siqueiros is the best proof that a really great painter has first of all a great social conception and an ideological conviction. The greater the conviction the greater the painter.

Siqueiros is not the faithful calligraphic recorder of a popularized mass concept of a great idea as is Diego Rivera. Nor is he the ecstatic shout of an individual inflamed by the lava of mass enthusiasm as we find in José Clemente Orozco. Siqueiros is a wonderful synthesis of mass conception and an individually perceived representation of it.

Between the emotional outburst and the disciplined intellect Siqueiros leads the stroke of his brush with the implacability of a jackhammer in the line to the final goal he always has before him.

Index

235